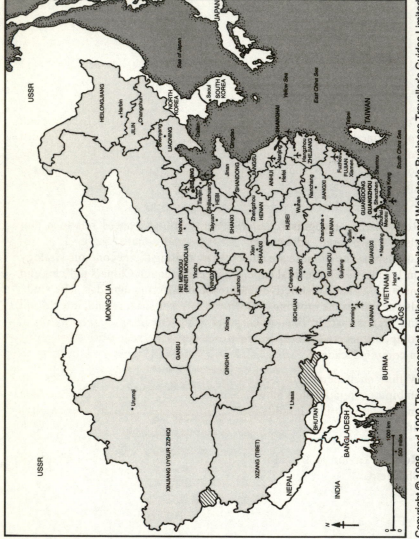
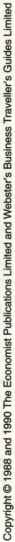

Copyright © 1988 and 1990 The Economist Publications Limited and Webster's Business Traveller's Guides Limited

Greater China and Japan

Contemporary relations between Greater China and Japan have been conditioned both by differing responses to the impact of Western colonialism during the mid-nineteenth century and the legacy of the cold war. There are mutual suspicions: the Chinese fear of a Japanese military revival and the Japanese concern over increasing Chinese economic competition and territorial ambitions.

Rober Taylor recognises the mistrust in Sino-Japanese relations, but also sees shared advantages in this traditionally adversarial relationship. The Chinese are currently modelling their economic strategy on Japan's developmental experience, even though China's policies and institutions have distinctive features and differing agendas. The study also examines the growing momentum towards sub-regional integration and argues that, in East Asia, as in other emerging economic blocs, competition between corporate entities may supersede national rivalries in coming decades.

Within such perspectives, *Greater China and Japan* explores the ambiguous relationship between these two major powers of East Asia and the implications it holds for the future of the region into the twenty-first century.

Robert Taylor is Director of Chinese Studies at the University of Sheffield.

Sheffield Centre for Japanese Studies/Routledge Series

Series editor: Glenn D. Hook, Professor of Japanese Studies, University of Sheffield

This series, published by Routledge in association with the Centre for Japanese Studies at the University of Sheffield, will make available both original research on a wide range of subjects dealing with Japan and will provide introductory overviews of key topics in Japanese studies.

The Internationalization of Japan
Edited by Glenn D. Hook and Michael Weiner

Race and Migration in Imperial Japan
Michael Weiner

The Steel Industry in Japan
A Comparison with Britain
Harukiyo Hasegawa

Race, Resistance and the Ainu of Japan
Richard Siddle

Greater China and Japan

Prospects for an economic partnership
in East Asia

Robert Taylor

London and New York

First published 1996
by Routledge
11 New Fetter Lane, London EC4P 4EE

Simultaneously published in the USA and Canada
by Routledge
29 West 35th Street, New York, NY 10001

Routledge is an International Thomson Publishing Company

Typeset in Times by
Ponting–Green Publishing Services, Chesham, Bucks

Printed and bound in Great Britain by
Clays Ltd, St. Ives PLC

British Library Cataloguing in Publication Data
A catalogue record for this book is available from the
British Library.

Library of Congress Cataloging in Publication Data
Taylor, Robert, 1941–
    Great China and Japan : prospects for an economic partner-
ship in East Asia / Robert Taylor.
        p.   cm.
    1. China – Foreign economic relations – Japan.   2. Japan –
foreign economic relations – China.   3. China – Economic
policy – 1976– . 4. China – Military policy.   5. East Asia –
economic integration.
    I. Title.
HF1604.Z4J3674   1996
337.51052–dc20
                                                    95–42961
                                                         CIP

ISBN 0–415–12446–8 (hbk)

ISBN 0–415–12447–6 (pbk)

To my parents

Contents

Tables

1 Introduction: China and Japan in Asia

The historical setting

Contemporary relations between China and Japan have been conditioned by the responses of the two nations both to the military, economic and cultural impact of the West since the mid-nineteenth century and to the great-power rivalries of the cold war years. China and Japan each responded differently to the Western challenge. Historically, Japan was more predisposed than China to meet that challenge effectively. It had a tradition of cultural borrowing and took over the Chinese written language and Confucian social status system, even though with modifications, while the socioeconomic changes that occurred in Japan immediately prior to the Western impact were similar to those which had been present in early modern Europe and which had facilitated the industrial revolution.

Thus the Japanese were more receptive to adopting the technology and firepower necessary to resist the Western powers on their own terms; infringements of sovereignty like the loss of tariff autonomy were short-lived and the achievement of a high rate of literacy through universal education, as well as conscription, forged national unity, as did a modern, though authoritarian, political system, with the Emperor as the focus of loyalty. So successful were such modernisation policies that by the early years of the twentieth century Japan had become a major industrial power and, lacking raw material resources, had embarked on a series of colonial conquests in China, rivalling the Western powers. Ultimately, defeat in the Pacific War ended Japan's aggression in China, leaving a legacy of bitterness which still informs China's ambivalent attitude towards economic cooperation with the Japanese.

In spite of wartime devastation, pre-war infrastructure provided the foundations for Japan's post-war recovery and ascent to economic superpower status.

China, in contrast, seen by its Imperial rulers as secure and sufficient unto itself, the culturally superior 'Middle Kingdom', failed initially to comprehend the dire threat to sovereignty posed by the Western powers in the mid-nineteenth century. China's last Imperial rulers, the Qing, belatedly attempted to graft Western technology and economic institutions onto existing Confucian social and political institutions and values. But the old status system gave lowly position to the now needed merchant and entrepreneur. This failure to understand the link between Western economic and military supremacy on the one side and socio-political institutions on the other prevented the reforms necessary to forestall infringements of Chinese territorial integrity; unequal treaties were imposed and enclaves opened to foreign trade. The Western powers and Japan were able to divide China into their respective spheres of influence; onslaught from without coincided with internal rebellion, another traditional sign of dynastic decline. The fall of the Qing and the advent of the Republic did little to produce a credible political system; the resulting authority crisis led to a vacuum at the centre of government and provincial particularism. The Guomindang, founded by Sun Yat-sen and later led by Chiang Kai-shek, achieved a semblance of unity in China during the decade from 1927 to 1937 but, faced with full-scale Japanese invasion, it ultimately lost power as the Chinese Communist Party (CCP) exploited peasant nationalism and posed as the only true patriotic resistance to Japanese aggression. The CCP, under Mao Zedong, acceded to power in 1949 after victory in civil war against the Guomindang, and achieved the political unity of China for the first time in over a century.

The cold war placed China and Japan in opposing camps both politically and economically: China was allied to the Soviet Union and operated a system of central planning under a command economy; Japan was allied to the United States and retained a form of market economy, albeit in the context of a close relationship between business and government, a tradition dating back to the Meiji Restoration which began the process of Japan's modernisation through major state investment in economic enterprise.

Such was the setting in which Sino-Japanese relations were resumed on an informal basis in the post-war years. It says much for the pragmatism of both the Chinese and the Japanese leaders that, even at the height of the cold war in the 1950s and 1960s, the absence of formal diplomatic ties, precluded by cold war alliances, did not prevent increasing economic interaction at an unofficial level between the two countries. Nevertheless, Chinese foreign policy was strongly nationalist and in the years immediately after their accession to power in 1949 the

CCP leaders sought to eliminate all vestiges of earlier Japanese colonialism and assert themselves as representatives of an independent sovereign nation founded on socialist principles. A member of the international Communist movement, China wished to woo Japan away from the United States alliance and, stressing the subordination of economics to politics in foreign relations, attempted to use trade as a lever to obtain Japanese government recognition. But because of Japan's alliance with the United States, in the 1950s and 1960s Sino-Japanese commerce could be conducted only through the face-saving device of unofficial informal trade on the barter principle. Initially, two-way trade was minimal, amounting to barely US$60 million in 1950 and involving, for example, exchanges of Chinese coal and soy beans for Japanese textile machinery and galvanised iron plates. The United States' strategic embargo on trade with Communist countries was largely responsible for the low level of activity, and in the late 1950s trade was virtually curtailed altogether because of increasingly stringent Chinese political conditions. China's Premier, Zhou Enlai, reopened trade in minor food and medical products in 1959 but simultaneously tried to exert political leverage, holding out the bait of further commerce.

But, with the onset of the Sino-Soviet dispute in the 1960s, the Chinese leaders had to be even more flexible and increasingly looked elsewhere for economic partnership; given continuing antipathy to the United States, they turned to Japan and Western Europe for the capital goods necessary to further China's economic development. They were thus prepared to make further concessions, no doubt with a long-term view to obtaining industrial equipment no longer being supplied by the Eastern bloc. For the Japanese part, as exports played a growing role in their economic growth, China seemed a natural market for Japanese products. But Sino-Japanese trade was still private and unofficial, with a monopoly created for the so-called friendly firms which operated through the mediation of Japanese Communist front organisations. Unfortunately, these companies were small operators unable to satisfy China's need for industrial plant, heavy machinery and fertilisers. By the early 1960s trade was being placed on a firmer footing; purchases were being paid for in cash and the Chinese dealt directly with Japanese manufacturers. In 1962 the semi-governmental Liao–Takasaki Agreement, named after the two signatories, was concluded. The friendly companies, however, continued to play a role. The range of permissible goods was extended in 1967 with the institution of Memorandum Trade, which superseded the 1962 accord and was renegotiated each year. Nevertheless, by the end of the 1960s the Chinese were putting further pressure on Japan by refusing to do business with firms assisting the economy of the Republic of China (Taiwan) or helping the American war effort in Vietnam.

During the 1960s Japanese companies, especially steel concerns, began to envisage a potentially lucrative Chinese market and started to lobby sympathetic factional leaders in Japan's ruling Liberal Democratic Party (LDP). In addition, some conservative politicians began actively to promote the idea of diplomatic relations with the Chinese People's Republic. Not surprisingly, Japan's Ministry of International Trade and Industry (MITI), by virtue of its function, stood for increased trade with China.

These pressures led to an increase in the value of Sino-Japanese trade which reached a total of US$822 million in 1970, making Japan China's primary trading partner, accounting for 20 per cent of its world total.[1]

Meanwhile there were major changes in international power relationships. Following the Sino-American rapprochement, the Japanese restored diplomatic relations with China in 1972, severing official connections with the Chinese Nationalists on Taiwan. There were now fewer barriers to Sino-Japanese trade. Significantly, the Japanese imported Chinese crude oil for the first time in 1973. In addition, mindful of the future trade potential, the Japanese decided to allow the Chinese greater access to Export Import Bank funding for industrial plant contracts.[2]

In their business practice the Japanese are known for taking a long-term view, being prepared to sacrifice short-term profit for future growth. Another feature of Japanese success is sustained reconnaissance. In the 1970s the Japanese began to mount a well-coordinated intelligence campaign to gain ascendancy in the China market. They could build on the knowledge gained and connections made in pre-war China, albeit in the context of Japanese militarism. Japan's culture bears the imprint of borrowing from China, and Chinese studies have long been included in the curricula of Japanese schools. In the 1970s trading companies rapidly established representative offices in Beijing, staffed by experienced Chinese-speaking employees. Few Western companies could match the linguistic and cultural competence of their Japanese counterparts. Finally, the Japanese were quick to emphasise the complementarity of the two economies: China's natural resources allied to Japan's technology.

Throughout the 1970s international relations developments further facilitated the burgeoning Sino-Japanese relationship. The Peace and Friendship Treaty of 1978 ended the state of war between the two powers and was accompanied by commercial agreements; meanwhile moves towards detente between the two superpowers and the death of

Mao Zedong, China's veteran leader, in 1976 helped to pave the way for the initiation of China's economic open door policy in 1978.

The Third Plenum of the Eleventh Central Committee was a landmark in the history of post-war China. It was there that China's paramount leader, Deng Xiaoping, put his seal on China's open door policy, in a sense a continuation of the 'Four Modernisations' enunciated by China's late Premier Zhou Enlai in the 1970s. Essentially Deng and his supporters had concluded that there were limits to economic development through the central planning inherent in a Soviet-style command economy and via policies of self-reliance. From then on foreign trade would no longer be a mere adjunct to the domestic economy, and imports would become an integral part of China's strategy for growth. China's raw materials and manufactures would pay for crucially needed capital goods imports. In this scenario, Japan would be the natural, though not the only, trading partner; Chinese raw materials were to be an economic complement to Japan's high-tech products. Such economic complementarity could be a driving force behind both trade and investment, even though as a general principle the Chinese resolved not to depend too heavily on any one country as a market or source of supply. Japan would be at least a major if not the only partner in China's modernisation programme.

China's foreign policy: economic development as national security

It will be seen from the foregoing that views of Japan loom large in Chinese foreign policy thinking. China and Japan are the major powers of East Asia, and Chinese government sources are replete with arguments that Sino-Japanese political and economic cooperation is the key not only to mutual prosperity but to the peace and development of the region as a whole. Such sentiments are shared by both sides, though with reservations; while welcoming more economic exchanges with Japan, both in specific Chinese and overall Asian contexts, a Chinese Foreign Ministry source claimed to echo the fears of Asian countries regarding Japan's growing military strength.[3] In similar vein, Japan's Prime Minister Yomiichi Murayama, quoting the official view, claimed that a stable relationship between the two countries was crucial for Asian peace and security and Japan would accordingly give priority to its relations with China.[4] Nevertheless some Japanese observers look askance at China's growing military power, regarding it as a possible threat to Japan's security in the medium term.

Thus while the Sino-Japanese relationship is a crucial element in

Chinese diplomatic thinking, it must now be placed within the overall framework of China's foreign policy, as focused in the context of the Asian regional configuration of power. There is no doubt that in their economic open door policy Deng Xiaoping and his likely successors have staked their political legitimacy not on the ideology of Marxism-Leninism *per se* but on their own capacity to improve the living standards of the Chinese people. Successful economic development equals political stability. To achieve this they claim to need a stable predictable environment at home and abroad, especially in Asia.

In the post-cold war context, then, Chinese foreign policy perspectives are increasingly being structured by the demands of economic development and the shifting balance of power in Asia, even though developments in July and August 1995, especially worsening relations with the United States, indicated that issues relating to sovereignty, as defined by the Chinese, remain paramount. Although in implementation often more flexible than the public rhetoric of Chinese leaders would have suggested, until the early 1970s China's foreign relations were informed by the ideological certainties of Marxism-Leninism and frequently expressed in terms of commitment to world revolution, including support for armed insurgency in East Asia. Since the institution of the open door policy in 1978, however, and especially since the beginning of the 1990s, Chinese foreign policy has been omni-directional and issue-orientated, with a stress on multilateral diplomacy designed to establish and improve relations with both developed and developing countries and emphasising practicality rather than dogma. Renewed emphasis has been given to the Five Principles of Peaceful Coexistence, first enunciated by the Chinese in the wake of the Bandung conference of non-aligned countries held in Indonesia in 1955, and now seen by China's leaders as major guidelines in the conduct of diplomacy with countries of different political systems, especially in Asia. Thus the Chinese claim that a new order should be built on these five principles: (1) mutual respect for sovereignty and territorial integrity; (2) mutual non-aggression; (3) non-interference in each other's internal affairs; (4) equality and mutual benefit; and (5) peaceful coexistence.

China's foreign relations, whether with the developed nations of the West or the fast-developing countries of the Asia-Pacific, are increasingly directed by an economic imperative: the need to acquire expertise and experience in such areas as technology transfer, vocational training and the reform of industrial management. Such relations are governed by the five principles. In summary, China's foreign policy in the 1990s and beyond will be largely, though not exclusively, determined by the country's economic development needs.

From East–West confrontation to North–South divide

In spite of the ending of the cold war and growing economic inter-dependence among nations, international relations are not without contention. In the Chinese leadership's view, East–West detente has not produced equity between North and South, that is the developed and developing nations respectively, and wealth disparities are ever increasing. Despite disagreements in the Chinese leadership concerning foreign policy during the years since 1949, a commonly held view has been support for the aspirations of developing countries. In the context of the 1990s enhancing solidarity and cooperation with developing countries is said to be a cornerstone of China's foreign policy. Such nations still suffer from adverse terms of trade *vis-à-vis* developed countries. There are, of course, increasing wealth differentials, al-though, because of a growing economic division of labour within Asia, the Chinese leaders use more flexible categories of analysis than implied in the former 'Third World' classification. Yet at the same time they urge solidarity and optimistically appraise the region, contrasting its relative stability with a turbulent Europe. In identifying with Asian interests the Chinese seek economic cooperation with all countries, regardless of political complexion. Similarly, the Chinese reject Western criticism concerning human rights; like the Japanese, who more rapidly returned to economic cooperation with China after the Tiananmen incidents than did Western countries, the Chinese see such rights in terms of national prosperity rather than individual well-being.[5]

Perceived threats to China's security

In 1995 articles in Chinese international relations journals, with an official imprimatur, were surveying changes in the Asian power configuration, and it is on these assessments that China's defence policy and strategy are necessarily based. Unlike the cold war scenario, the new strategic balance is said by Chinese sources to be pluralistic, based on the mutual constraint of a number of powers in the region. The United States, wary of involvement in local Asian conflicts, has been placing greater reliance on Japan to take responsibility commensurate with its economic power. Nevertheless, a growing concern of United States policy is trade conflict with Japan and, fearing excessive Japanese influence in the region, American leaders have sought fuller participation in bodies like the Association of South East Asian Nations (ASEAN) on Asian security issues. Another major power in the region, Russia, has ostensibly been seeking a peaceful environment for the economic development of its Far East and aims to further cooperation in Northeast Asia as a whole through closer relations with the United States, China, and the Republic of Korea. At the time of writing, at least, the nuclear threat from North Korea has been resolved, and here China has considerable economic leverage; this could well increase if the post-Kim Il Sung leadership decides to proceed with a Chinese-style modernisation programme and open door policy.

In the Chinese view it will be impossible, given this pluralism or multipolarity, for one or even a group of countries to control the entire region, because the multipower coexistence of China, Japan, the United States and Russia as well as ASEAN serves to create an overall balance of power.[6]

There is no doubt, however, that in Chinese perceptions Japan is a, if not the, major player in the region. Chinese leadership attitudes are ambivalent; Japan is clearly an economic partner but also a competitor in a number of spheres, including the military. In June 1994, for example, a Chinese naval journal implied that Japan's naval forces were a potential threat to China and must be closely monitored. Japan's naval strategy was said to have evolved from defence of neighbouring waters in the 1960s and 1970s to active defence of distant waters from the early 1980s. The change in orientation was attributed not only to Japan's desire to protect its status as an economic superpower but also to its alleged militaristic tendencies. Other evidence cited was the dispatch of Japanese forces abroad for United Nations peacekeeping operations, made possible by Japanese Diet legislation, and provision of minesweepers for action in the Persian Gulf area. Thus, in spite of protestations of Sino-Japanese friendship and economic cooperation, China's military at least harbour suspicions of Japanese motives in Asia.[7]

Other Chinese sources have discussed the rationale for Japan's defence and foreign policies. For instance, Japan supports China's economic growth, but does not wish its own interests to be threatened. Leverage said to be available to Japan includes the shortening of loan credit periods and restrictions on the use of economic assistance. Japan is said to fear closer Sino-American relations which could be designed to contain its influence. Japan, however, cannot afford not to cultivate China's friendship. Japanese foreign policy has now been extended from economic to political and security spheres, and bilateral relations have taken second place to regional cooperation. In this sense the Japanese see China's support as crucial for the maintenance of stability in Northeast Asia and the western Pacific, and the Chinese may well hold the key vote if the Japanese are to achieve their ambition of gaining a seat on the United Nations Security Council. In short, Japan is engaged in a balancing act, seeking to assert its independence of the United States and pursue an independent foreign policy. A balance in the triangular relationship between Japan, the United States and China must be maintained, if Japanese national interests are to be served.[8]

A number of security and general regional questions are contentious, each bearing some relation to the perceived Japanese threat to China. Insensitive comments, however motivated, have inflamed Chinese feelings: witness the Japanese Environment Agency Chief, Shin Sakurai, who stated that Japan had not intended to fight a war of aggression in China during the 1930s and 1940s, even though Japanese officialdom later expressed contrition for such remarks which also brought protests from South Korea.

More fundamental, however, are questions of national sovereignty. At the establishment of diplomatic relations in 1972 the Japanese acknowledged that there was only one China and that Taiwan was part of it. Japan could then only undertake unofficial contacts with Taiwan but in September 1994 the Japanese government was accused of allowing official representatives from Taiwan to visit the country on the occasion of the Asian games. There is little, however, that the Chinese can do in retaliation, although the benefits to Japan of economic cooperation with China are frequently stressed by Chinese leaders.

For some years the two sides have been engaged in a minor territorial dispute over the Diaoyutai Islands, located northeast of Taiwan, and called the Senkaku Islands by the Japanese. Interest focuses on the believed presence of oil deposits beneath the islands and, in February 1992, in another assertion of sovereignty, the Chinese passed a law, strongly backed by the military, which empowered the Chinese navy to use force against any incursion on the islands or surrounding waters.[9]

An even more complex issue which indirectly involves Japan is that of the Nansha (Spratly) and Xisha (Paracel) Islands in the South China Sea. The Spratly Islands are claimed by China, the Philippines, Vietnam, Malaysia, Taiwan and Brunei, and are believed to be above large oil and gas reserves. While a 1992 declaration by the protagonists pledged peaceful development of the resources, the Chinese have since fortified the islands and, like the Vietnamese, have leased oil-drilling rights to an American company. Currently, however, the real value of the islands is strategic; 70 per cent of Japan's oil imports and other important shipping traffic pass through the nearby sealanes. With planes based in their province of Hainan together with 94 submarines, 19 destroyers, 37 frigates and 260,000 sailors, the Chinese have the potential to dominate the islands, the sealanes and the oil. In the past the Americans guarded the route; the Japanese might have less desire to rely on China. Should the Chinese obstruct the shipping routes, however, the Japanese threat could become a self-fulfilling prophecy.[10]

China's defence policy

Nearly all nations formulate a defence policy and maintain armed forces, regardless of any immediate ostensible threat. As already discussed, China's open door policy is seen as one guarantee of national defence, an issue which must be evaluated in comprehensive terms; the modernisation of the armed forces is only possible when based on high-tech industrial development. In seeking a safe Asian environment, the primary objective of the Chinese leaders is to defend China's territorial integrity through developing friendly relations with neighbouring states: in other words, the creation and extension of buffer zones. Accordingly, the Chinese signed with Russia a limited border agreement and documents on bilateral economic cooperation in 1992, and these were significantly accompanied by a joint statement abjuring both first use of nuclear weapons and the targeting of strategic missiles at each other. On its southern borders, China has entered into border negotiations and bilateral economic cooperation with states like Burma.

Chinese military strategists see no immediate danger to national security, perceiving the country's vast territory, huge population and growing economic strength as deterrents. Any increases in military spending are therefore purely defensive, whether in the field of conventional forces or that of nuclear weaponry. Thus official Chinese sources are at pains to point out the low level of military expenditure in China: in per capita terms this is US$6 as contrasted with a figure of $1,100 for the United States and $300 for Japan. Needless to say, however, given the vagaries of the exchange rate for the *renminbi*, a non-convertible currency, such figures must be treated with some caution.[11] Similar peaceful intentions are claimed by the Chinese in connection with their nuclear programme. Cited are their accession to the Treaty on the Non-Proliferation of Nuclear Weapons, restraint in conducting nuclear tests, of which they have conducted fewer than any other nuclear power, and commitment not to use nuclear weapons against non-nuclear states or nuclear-free zones.

In response to criticism of their continuing underground nuclear testing Chinese leaders have countered that the existing moratorium agreed by the United States, France, Russia and Great Britain has merely frozen in place the advantages those countries have in possessing advanced nuclear arsenals. Clearly, the Chinese wish to complete their test programme before the new global test ban treaty comes into effect, probably in 1996.[12] Nevertheless it is notoriously difficult to distinguish between defensive and offensive military capability, whatever the Chinese protestations. In fact, in the context of their country's changing role in international affairs, Chinese officials have tacitly justified an ambitious military modernisation programme. One source suggests that even a limited conventional war with a major power could pose a tactical nuclear threat, in anticipation of which eventuality China must prepare a distinctively mobile nuclear deterrent in conjunction with the conventional one.[13] Moreover, as China plays a greater role in international trade and becomes more integrated into the world economy, the country will be increasingly vulnerable to blockade with sealanes assuming greater significance for national security. Thus the development of naval power, as yet considered by Chinese analysts a weak link in national defence, is being given greater priority, especially in view of such issues as the Spratly Islands.

Not surprisingly, Japanese and United States analysts detect territorial ambitions in China's military modernisation programme. Difficulty of analysis is, of course, compounded by Chinese official secrecy concerning military expenditure but the armed forces have been receiving substantial budget increases since the 1989 Tiananmen incidents. The official 1993 budget figure was $7.3 billion, far behind Japan, Taiwan and South Korea. Most experts, however, have estimated the actual budget, much of which derives from the economic activities in which the military have been encouraged to engage, at between $27 and $53 billion. If upper estimates were accepted, China would be placed second only to the United States in military spending.[14] China has about 4 million personnel under arms but, in spite of a large weapons inventory, much military equipment is not the most up-to-date. Perhaps the greatest potential threat presented by China to the region is the upgrading of its naval capacity. Chinese naval strategists have targeted the transformation of the navy from a coastal defence force into an offshore fleet capable of defending national territorial interests as the short-term central task of naval construction. Objectives include the building or purchase of a nuclear-powered aircraft carrier and the development of laser weapons systems.[15] In addition, the Chinese are trying to build a more compact missile for their nuclear arsenal which would be more mobile, harder to detect and easier to use in submarines; hitherto heads have been mainly fitted to large ground-based ballistic missiles, ostensible targets being Russia and India with which China still has ongoing border disputes.[16] China's strategic reach will also be extended when it takes over a naval base in Hong Kong in 1997. In addition, to enhance naval capability beyond coastal waters, three large naval bases are to be built along China's eastern seaboard by 1998 in order to provide key logistical support to a new-style Chinese fleet capable of ocean-going operations, the new facilities to be located in Liaoning Province in the northeast, a site near Shanghai and another at Zhanjiang in the southern Guangdong Province. These facilities are designed as a logistical support system capable of sustaining aircraft carriers in the future; a strong mobile fleet will act as a deterrent force as naval operations are extended from coastal protection duties to ocean patrols.[17]

There is, however, always the danger that any military modernisation programme may be perceived not as defensive but provocative. If China and Japan are potential rivals for paramountcy in East Asia, then Japan is strategically the more vulnerable of the two since it possesses few natural resources, much of its energy is still imported, and trade trends suggest that it may come to rely heavily on China for some categories of food. In addition, in military terms, to defend Japan is a formidable task, requiring control over surrounding sea and air space.[18] Nevertheless, from the viewpoint of conventional forces, Japan has one of the best-equipped armies in Asia and a defence budget for the 1991–5 period totalling US$180 billion. Thus while such forces cannot match their Chinese counterparts in numbers, with Japanese self-defence personnel numbering only 273,000, their armoury is impressive, including 1,200 tanks, 350 aircraft, 160 warships, of which 59 are destroyers and 15 submarines. The Japanese are superior in overall quality of firepower and up-to-date weaponry. Japan, however, does not have a nuclear arsenal.[19]

Moreover, given that East and Southeast Asia were traditionally Chinese spheres of influence, albeit through gradual cultural assimilation rather than direct military intervention, the nations of the region are now wary of manifestations of Chinese power, even though this might act as a counterweight to Japan's economic might.

In fact, it is in the arena of East Asian economic integration that competition or cooperation between the two powers will be most amply demonstrated in coming years.

Prospects for economic integration in East Asia

It has become a commonplace among Western academic commentators to speak of the twenty-first century as that of the Asia-Pacific but Chinese and Japanese ruling circles, while generally positive in view, express reservations, particularly concerning the optimum pace and extent of regional economic integration.[20] Chinese and Japanese views will now be considered in turn.

It has been a cardinal principle of Chinese foreign economic policy to diversify markets as well as sources of supply and investment, and it is envisaged that the United States, the European Union (EU) and Japan will continue to play major roles in the transformation of China. However, in the official Chinese view there are powerful arguments for gradual moves towards the creation of an Asia-Pacific economic community in the long term, with the immediate prospect of capital and production factor mobility.

A compelling argument for closer economic ties within the region is the growth of regional blocs throughout the world, with attendant suspicions of exclusivity and protectionism voiced by outsiders, the EU being but one example. Chinese official writers note this trend towards 'regionalisation', arguing that relations between blocs are replacing relations between individual countries in the economic sphere, even though intensity of interaction varies. One of the main features of such blocs is economic complementarity and this is particularly true of East and Southeast Asia. Moreover, the Asia-Pacific region as a whole has abundant natural resources: 70 per cent of the world's coal and 40 per cent of its oil, for example. The region also includes countries at different stages of development, so raw materials and cheap labour may be combined in synergy with capital and technology.[21] China could thus benefit from cooperation with the region as a whole. More importantly, during the last thirty years the economic growth of the Asia-Pacific region has been impressive by any standards: statistics show an average rate of 6.8 per cent during the period from 1980 to 1992, a level far higher than that for the advanced industrialised countries in other regions.[22] Chinese sources argue that contributing factors have been the economic miracle of Japan which by 1990 had a Gross National Product (GNP) 62.8 per cent of that of the United States – or in per capita terms 25 per cent higher – and the emergence of the so-called four smaller dragons, Singapore, South Korea, Hong Kong and Taiwan, which in many respects have emulated Japan, their export-led growth being derived from production sectors latterly vacated by Japanese manufacturers because of rising domestic costs.[23] China is to a large extent following this path. Recent Chinese sources are full of discussions of the virtues of such economic strategies as import substitution and export-led development. There is continuing commitment to the open door policy which the leadership claims will remain unchanged for a hundred years. A decision to follow aspects of the export-led strategy, thus emulating the 'four dragons', has been reflected in measures to attract foreign investment from Asia and elsewhere, such as a reduction in foreign exchange controls, greater tax concessions to overseas investors and the establishment of free ports. But following the creation of the European single market and its projected enlargement, as well as the coming of the North American Free Trade Area (NAFTA), the Asia-Pacific countries, including China, will not be able to sustain, let alone substantially increase, their exports to the United States (currently one of China's major trading partners) and Western Europe. Consequently China's leaders have encouraged and received investment from a number of countries. While, in addition to major investors like Hong Kong, Taiwan and Japan, joint ventures financed by European and American companies have become prominent, in future investment by the latter could increasingly be diverted back to EU countries and the United States. There are strong indications that the further development of the Asia-Pacific will be generated through cross-investment within the region, and investment in China itself is beginning to reflect this trend.

Significantly, the basis for greater Asia-Pacific economic integration is being laid through bilateral relations and multilateral political mechanisms. A major example of the latter is the Ministerial Conference on Asia-Pacific Economic Cooperation (APEC), with representation from the main countries of the area. China and Japan are members; the former joined the organisation in 1991, while Taiwan and Hong Kong joined as economic regions. APEC is clearly destined to play a leading role in coordinating economic relations. Although already internal trade among Asian countries has reached half of their total trade volume, with dependence on European Union and North American markets reduced, varying levels of economic development in the Asia-Pacific region as a whole suggest the need for further cooperation and coordination. In this direction much is being achieved. Advanced countries like Japan and the 'four dragons' export capital and technology to other Asia-Pacific countries to assist their industrial renovation and restructuring. Thus in the 1990s a division of labour is emerging in the region.

From the foregoing it may be seen that China's leaders accept the desirability of intensifying economic cooperation within the region. But Chinese sources stop short of endorsing the principle of economic integration, including an exclusive trading bloc, for the foreseeable future. This stance was made clear by China's Foreign Minister Qian Qichen at a news conference in 1992.[24]

In this vein Chinese official statements have pointed to the huge imbalance in economic growth among APEC members. While complementarity is desirable, such disparities do make the integration process more difficult. In addition, much needs to be done before free trade, a necessary prerequisite, can be achieved in the region, even though moves are afoot in preparation for eliminating tariff and non-tariff barriers by the end of the century. In short, while the Chinese leaders value APEC as an important form of economic cooperation in the short term at least – and indeed their trade with the roughly coterminous ASEAN was in 1993 worth ten times its value a decade earlier – the organisation's main importance is believed to be as a consultative forum. These views, however, are in a sense a rationalisation; the Chinese leadership considers it in its interests to support global free trade and does not wish to see the world divided into competing economic spheres, with APEC becoming an exclusive bloc like the European Union. If the Chinese seek regional spheres of influence in Asia, they also have boundless trading ambitions, with economic growth judged the key to joining the club of the developed countries by the early decades of the twenty-first century. Economic interdependence and the globalisation of business are described in Chinese officially inspired academic journals as irreversible trends, and playing a major role in this scenario are the multinationals, which China itself is gradually establishing as the spearhead of its overseas investment.[25]

In short, the Chinese believe that it is in their nation's interest publicly to support international free trade, and they do not wish to be bound by the exclusivity of an integrated regional economic bloc.

In recent decades Japan has been playing an important part in the economies of Southeast Asian countries, arousing fears among Chinese and other regional commentators of the revival of the exploitative Co-Prosperity sphere designed by the Japanese colonialists in the interwar and Pacific War periods. In the immediate post-war period Japan, as a result of the terms of the United States Occupation, was isolated from the rest of Asia and heavily dependent economically and diplomatically upon America, which gradually introduced the Japanese to world markets. By the 1960s the Japanese were paying war reparations to Asia and this paved the way for increased trade and investment. Japan was also so successful on European and United States markets that protectionist barriers threatened, in the wake of the European single market and American trade deficits. In addition, as domestic wage levels have risen in Japan, manufacturing investment by Japanese companies in Asia has become increasingly attractive. Uncompetitive Japanese industries have also been moving offshore. Moreover, given the end of the cold war and of superpower confrontation, as well as

Japanese economic prowess, successive Japanese governments have sought for their country greater independence from the United States.

Consequently, greater Japanese dependence on Asian economies has been reflected in aid, investment and trade figures. By 1993, 60 per cent of Japan's development aid went to Asia, major recipients being Indonesia, China and Thailand. Significantly, also, in 1992 Japanese investment in Asia amounted to $60 billion as compared to $19.5 billion in 1985. Such Japanese aid and investment have played a key role in moving Asian economies to higher stages of economic development; a new division of labour has been created, with Japan's increasingly high-tech economy the regional leader. Thus other Asian countries are exporting fewer raw materials but more consumer and producer goods. In this context it is also instructive to compare Japan's Asian trade with its US trade. Japan's exports to Asia rose by 14 per cent between 1991 and 1992, while exports to the United States increased by only 7 per cent. In 1992 Japanese exports to Asia accounted for 38.8 per cent of the nation's total exports, while exports to the United States represented only 28.8 per cent. Japan's imports from Asia rose by 6 per cent in the same year, while those from the United States fell by 3 per cent. In 1992 Japan's imports from Asia accounted for 45 per cent of its total imports, while those from the United States amounted to only 22.4 per cent. Thus, collectively, Asia has become Japan's largest trading partner, overtaking the United States. As of the early 1990s seven nations and regions, China, Taiwan, Hong Kong, South Korea, Singapore, Thailand and Malaysia, figured on Japan's top ten list of export markets.

But while Japan is undoubtedly the pre-eminent economic power in Asia and its leaders seek to use such institutions as APEC to counter the protectionism of the European Union and NAFTA, the Japanese do not have complete freedom of initiative. In fact, Japanese governments do not believe it either possible or desirable to rely exclusively upon links with Asian countries, let alone regional integration. Japan cannot entirely dispense with its Western markets; the United States, for instance, takes one-third of Japanese exports. Japan also has a stake in Western Europe and America through a wide range of manufacturing and service investments.

Japanese moves in Asia are increasingly influenced by the foreign policy of the United States which, by geographical location and increasingly by political inclination, is an Asia-Pacific power. The Clinton administration has shifted the United States strategic focus from the Atlantic to the Pacific as a means of revitalising the national economy, with the long-term goal of linking APEC with NAFTA.

Given that Japan cannot absorb all the exports of Asian countries, which rely partially on the American market, and because it also needs sales in the United States, its room for manoeuvre is limited. In theory, Japan does have a number of options. The first is to adhere to free trade and eschew Asian economic cooperation. The second is the confrontational mode, using Asia as a counterweight to the European Union and NAFTA. The third is a compromise between these two positions. As Japan needs the United States economically and politically if it is to become a member of the United Nations Security Council, the third is the most likely scenario: both cooperation and competition with the United States. This means maintaining global free trade, keeping the security alliance with America and subscribing to a degree of Asian regional cooperation in the foreseeable future.[26]

The limitations which the Chinese and Japanese conceptions place on regional integration derive in part from perceptions of their respective national interests. It will, however, have become apparent from the foregoing that a number of economic changes need to take place, and institutional mechanisms need to be devised, before a regional bloc on the lines of, say, the European Union, can become a reality. The first barrier to unity is the North–South divide or uneven economic development within the area as a whole, between both regions and nations. Hong Kong and Singapore enjoy greater per capita income than, for instance, Cambodia.

There are huge disparities within individual countries, the contrast between China's southeastern seaboard and the western hinterland being a case in point. Moreover, in the immediate term the Asia-Pacific will not be able to sustain its development without investment and trade links with countries outside the region. Even allowing for the role of Japan as a market and a source of technology transfer, East and Southeast Asia remain dependent on trade surpluses with the United States for their economic growth. In fact, bilateral trade between the United States and the Asia-Pacific has grown very rapidly and is expected to double by the end of the century. One-fifth of America's total investment abroad is in the region.[27] Finally, whether or not the idea of an Asia-Pacific economic bloc ultimately materialises will depend on the resolution of conflicts born of different social, political and economic systems. But in spite of disparities which encompass, for instance, totalitarian political parties, military regimes and democracies as well as command and market economies, not to mention varying levels of development, a strong case remains for some form of integration.

Sub-regional economic integration

Attention will be focused on two zones: south China, where regional trade and investment flows are intensifying to such an extent that integration is becoming a reality, and Northeast Asia or the Tumen Zone, where potential undoubtedly exists for such development in the early years of the twenty-first century.

The South China Economic Zone encompasses the southeastern coastal provinces of China, Hong Kong, Macao and Taiwan. It implies a Greater China concept, that is cooperation involving the above Chinese states and territories, as well as the Southeast Asian countries like Singapore and overseas Chinese entrepreneurs.

Keys to the concept are economic complementarity and division of labour. The Chinese mainland can provide a cheap labour force, abundant natural resources and huge product sales for Hong Kong, Taiwan and Macao; the three latter in turn can offer China funds as well as advanced technical and marketing expertise to gain access to international markets. To the extent that all the parties involved are dependent on Western sales, economic cooperation may offer an alternative, thus enabling them to avoid the full blast of any protectionism in the European Union or NAFTA.

Chinese officialdom is keen to point out that the mainland offers lucrative opportunities to investors from Taiwan, Hong Kong and Macao. Land, labour, water and electricity are cheaper on the mainland, thus conferring product price competitiveness on world markets. In addition, foreign investors manufacturing in China are increasingly being permitted to sell goods on the domestic market where overseas style products are in great demand for their fashion and design qualities.

Attention will now be briefly focused on the advantages of mainland trade and investment for each of the three territories in turn. For Taiwan's investors the mainland confers a number of unrivalled benefits, as compared to Southeast Asia. Over and above common linguistic and cultural factors are geographical proximity, facilitating use of Hong Kong's transshipment facilities, and the colony's personnel exchange and information services. Low wages and land prices on the mainland itself are also an attraction; uncompetitive Taiwanese investors may be relocated to the mainland, thus aiding the island's economic restructuring.

Like Taiwan, Hong Kong's economy is increasingly being integrated with that of the mainland. The port has become the largest source of foreign capital, with Hong Kong's manufacturers moving many of their plants to southern China. Moreover, thousands of Chinese firms now have investments in Hong Kong. Additionally, because the government of the Republic of China (ROC) on Taiwan still forbids direct economic activity between the island and the mainland (although restrictions are now being eased), Hong Kong serves as an entrepôt for trade and investment.

The last of the three territories to be discussed is Macao, the Portuguese colony adjacent to Zhuhai, one of the first Special Economic Zones to be created in China. While possessing funds and business marketing networks, Macao lacks the land and labour resources which Zhuhai has in abundance. Thus the scope for Macao-Zhuhai cooperation is considerable, with Zhuhai benefiting from Macao's ties to international markets and sources of capital.

The other major player in the South China Zone is Japan. Statistics show that Japan's investment in the southern provinces is much lower than that of either Hong Kong or Taiwan. Nevertheless the extent of Japanese capital input is much greater than would appear at first sight, since many Hong Kong manufacturing concerns investing in, say, the province of Guangdong, are in fact subsidiaries of Japanese companies. Additionally, Japanese trade with and investment in Taiwan aided the island's economic takeoff in the 1960s and 1970s and continue to assist industrial restructuring. Japan's role in the sub-region seems set to grow.

To indicate these trends towards economic integration, it is worth emphasising that in 1991 over 50 per cent of the outside capital absorbed by the mainland came from Hong Kong, Macao and Taiwan, and of Chinese exports 42 per cent was destined for the three territories, even though the caveat must be entered that a considerable proportion of goods sold to the British colony are subsequently re-exported to the United States and Europe.[28]

Two reservations must nevertheless be added to optimistic appraisals by the various partners. Firstly, differing social systems and levels of development may impede closer economic integration which would require cooperation across entire industries and in sectors of high technology in order to further greater interdependence. Secondly, East Asia is still at least partially dependent on the trade and technology of Western countries.

The Northeast Asian Zone is not yet a reality but Chinese policy makers regard it as having great potential. Within its proposed confines are the three northeastern provinces of China, Japan, North Korea, South Korea and the Far Eastern region of Russia. Ideally, the finance and technology of Japan and South Korea are to be allied to the natural and human resources of China and the other relatively underdeveloped areas. Surveys and feasibility studies are being conducted under a United Nations programme.

Apart from the physical logistical problems which the above surveys are addressing, the key to the establishment of the zone lies initially in relationships between the relevant powers. One propitious sign is the improvement in Sino-Russian relations. Even in the days of the Sino-Soviet dispute there was considerable cross-border trade but since the end of the cold war economic agreements have been signed, including provision for extensive trade at a national level.

The Russo-Japanese relationship, however, is made more contentious and complicated still by the issue of the northern islands, some of which were promised to the Soviet Union by the Yalta Agreement of 1945. The dispute did not, however, prevent economic agreements on the exploitation of Siberian gas and forestry resources in the 1970s. Such cooperation could now be extended, even though Japan has since diversified sources of energy supply. Significantly, though, the Japanese have softened their approach to Russia, deleting the word 'threat' from diplomatic and defence commitments affecting Russia.

To complete the circle China's relations with the Korean states will now be examined. Establishment of diplomatic relations between China and South Korea in 1992 gave further impetus to already growing trade and investment links. The Chinese have since been at pains to reaffirm friendship with North Korea; the latter's leaders in any case have little room for manoeuvre since 60 per cent of the country's oil and 75 per cent of its imports are from China. North Korean participation in sub-regional economic cooperation will nevertheless depend on its achievement of political stability in the wake of the succession to Kim Il Sung.[29]

In summary, many of the resource endowments and economic complementarities necessary for the establishment of the Northeast Asian Economic Zone are already in place but further progress is largely attendant upon infrastructural development.

This introduction has focused on the various aspects of the contemporary Sino-Japanese relationship which have been conditioned by the responses of the two countries to the West and the legacy of the cold war. While China and Japan share cultural affinities, they are divided by historical animosities and mutual mistrust.

Nevertheless, the power configuration in East Asia and trends towards regional integration in a world of economic interdependence suggest that the two parties are likely both to compete and cooperate in the context of East Asia in coming decades.

It has been implied above that the Sino-Japanese relationship has a number of dimensions and these will be explored in following chapters. In their commitment to market socialism the Chinese leaders seek to emulate aspects of the Japanese model of development, where the state plays a crucial role in economic enterprise. Suitability of such a model is the subject of Chapter 2. Chapter 3 is concerned with the various forms of Japanese investment on the Chinese mainland by industrial sector and location, and assesses the contribution of such capital input to China's modernisation programme. Chapter 4 examines trade flows in the light of China's foreign trade as a whole and suggests future trends. The Greater China concept is the topic of Chapter 5, which focuses on sub-regional integration in South China and the Northeast Asian Zone, demonstrating that the Sino-Japanese relationship has implications for East Asia as a whole. The Conclusion is designed to bring together the above themes and projects the evolution of Sino-Japanese relations in the twenty-first century.

Attention is now turned to the influence of the Japanese model of development on China's current economic strategy.

2 The Japanese model of development and China's economic strategy

The Japanese model

Institutions

In little more than a century since 1868 when the new Meiji government leaders determined to turn Japan into an advanced industrial power, it has risen to economic superpower status and become one of the few successful modernisers in the non-Western world. In the post-war years Japan's example has been emulated by a number of Asian states and territories like the Republic of China (Taiwan), South Korea, Singapore and Hong Kong, which are now joining the ranks of the developed countries. Significantly, these Asian states have, like China and Japan, been influenced by Confucianism, an authoritarian sociopolitical tradition which has been instrumental in creating consensus of purpose for clearly defined national objectives. While an intensely personal creed involving, for instance, ritual in the worship of ancestors, Confucianism is a morality rather than a religion, and its sanction lies in the here and now rather than in the world to come, concerned as it is with the correct ordering of human relationships. While the authoritarian political systems of East Asia have the outward forms of Western-style representative government, they are nevertheless not governed by democratic values and norms. Every government, however, is to a greater or lesser extent accountable to the people it governs, and while inhabitants of such countries do not have full power to influence their rulers, they do expect the provision of material goods and services in return for sociopolitical loyalty. Thus the legitimacy of East Asian governments rests fundamentally on ever improving standards of living. In this context, Confucianism has proved ideally practical and flexible; it has provided social cohesion in support of national objectives. Chinese Communism, in spite of its stated goals, has never succeeded in eradicating Confucianism, and in fact has absorbed a number of its tenets, especially in relation to political control and human perfectibility. Importantly, in late 1994 a number of Chinese official sources praised Confucianism, arguing for its adaptation to further the goals of China's modernisation programme.[1]

There is no doubt that this type of Confucian social cohesion has played a major role in the economic development of China and Japan. Ironically, the Confucian social status system accords a lowly position to the merchant and the entrepreneur, and at first sight this would appear antipathetic to economic growth. For centuries East Asia has had an abundance of commerce but the route to political power and influence has very often been through government administration rather than economic activity or the acquisition of wealth as such. Thus, traditionally, to appear legitimate, economic activity has had to be seen as the wider interest, say under the auspices of government rather than an independent centre of power in its own right.

In the case of Japan, economic success during the last century has often been attributed to the relationship between government and business. Such apparent unity of purpose, often remarked upon in the context of post-1945 Japan, was originally inspired both by the Confucian ethic and a commonly perceived threat of foreign encroachment during the 1860s. In fact, the leaders of the 1868 Meiji Restoration were able to build on a long tradition of government intervention in economic affairs. The previous military administration operated a clearly defined status system restricting both occupational mobility and consumption patterns but, as this structure began to break down in the wake of socioeconomic change occasioned by 200 years of internal peace, a money economy began to emerge and economic controls started to shift to markets, prices and production. Not only did the military government administer major financial and commodity markets, it controlled major resources like mines and forests. In addition, any new important economic enterprise required government approval. Goods of national importance came under the jurisdiction of official marketing boards from production to purchase. A number of these boards evolved into private companies after 1868. This legacy, together with the granting of pensions to the old warrior class (or samurai), for later investment in industrial enterprises, forged the link between the Meiji government and business, a heritage which has come to be seen as a key factor in Japan's post-war economic miracle.[2] Thus, in Meiji Japan the state, because of an initial scarcity of investment capital, played a great role in economic enterprise, even though in later decades it sold off industrial concerns to private interests. In summary, during those years government helped to develop economic enterprise and, needless to say, public utilities of national importance remained under state control.

Contemporary Japan has often been regarded as a paragon of free enterprise but the pre-eminence of planning there places it in the ranks of developing countries rather than Western market economies. The close relationship between government and business has persisted during the post-war period, and planning mechanisms have been more in evidence since the end of the American Occupation. The famous system of administrative guidance by the Japanese bureaucracy is the main hallmark of planning and government–business cooperation. In this process the Ministry of International Trade (MITI) and the Economic Planning Agency are key mechanisms, and it is through them that planning and guidance on the part of government and the market have joined together to achieve high growth.

Economic success in Japan has also been facilitated by the very structure of business itself. Japan's distinctive form of business organisation, the keiretsu, or conglomerate, includes within its fold customers, suppliers and banks, and each competes with other conglomerates of similar structure. The keiretsu have also aided the government's planning of industry. Inducements to industry to target, say, new areas of production have been channelled through administrative guidance via organisations like the deliberative bodies composed of representatives from government, industry and academia, which also have provided economic information networks. Of course, Japan's post-war economic planning has had its failures as well as successes. The Japanese have acquired a reputation for backing winners among industrial pioneers but the record shows that not all the industrial targets justified such support; for instance, the aircraft industry for a long time did not develop rapidly. Some industries, like – surprisingly – automobiles, initially received little support, even though they were soon to stimulate exports. Nevertheless, a number of industries did benefit from financial input from government-funded banks; most importantly perhaps, there was solid support for technological development, particularly in the case of medium-sized and small enterprises, with state research institutions being mandated to help apply new scientific findings.

Ultimately, however, it must be concluded that while government financing and research support have been important, the key to the success of Japan's industries has lain in their own investment in modern equipment and, most importantly, in the rivalry within, initially, intensely competitive domestic markets and, later, international markets. It is therefore that unique blend of the plan and the market which could prove most pertinent to China's current economic strategy.

As a conclusion to this discussion of the unique relationship between business and government in post-war Japan, it could, however, be argued that each nation's economy is dynamic. In the wake of the re-evaluation of the yen since the mid-1980s and the recession of the early 1990s, Japan's industrial structure is changing. Component companies of the keiretsu, for example, are seeking business partners outside their group. Public utilities like the National Railways and Nippon Telephone and Telegraph are being privatised. In a sense what is being observed is therefore the Japanese model of development of the past. Moreover, the caveat must always be added that economic systems are conditioned by unique national cultural and political processes which are not replicable in their entirety in a foreign setting. The Chinese have indicated awareness of such limitations; accordingly official comment-ators have also critically surveyed the dynamic changes involved in the various stages through which Japan's and other Asian countries' economic development has passed during the post-war period. It is to those dimensions that attention is now turned.

Stages of development

Japan, like China, came late to the industrial revolution and at the time of the Meiji Restoration in 1868 was still a resource-poor country; in subsequent years, through exploitation of the primary sector by means of land taxes and the adoption of Western technology, Japan became an industrial state powerful enough to challenge the might of the West in war, though in some respects still less economically advanced than Europe and North America. By 1945 the Japanese economy was devastated and the country remained in the pursuer mode, aiming to reach the high GNP and standard of living enjoyed by Western countries. The United States, initially via the Occupation Authorities, helped to reconstruct the Japanese economy by permitting the use of American patents, insulating Japan from international competition, and gradually introducing exporters to world markets. By the end of the Occupation in 1952 recovery was under way, and penetration of world markets had already begun, although it was not until the 1960s and 1970s that exports started to play a significant role in the Japanese economy. Light industrial products like textiles were exported, pro-viding a source of accumulation for the purchase of capital goods as well as machinery and technology for the heavy and chemical indus-tries, thus obviating the need for research and development expenditure at the early stages of economic takeoff. The steel and shipbuilding industries were then developed, in turn increasing exports. As consumer sectors like electrical goods and cars were targeted, the Japanese adopted a policy of import substitution, a key feature of which is the protection of domestic markets and infant industries from the influx of competitive foreign products through the institution of tariff and non-tariff barriers. Meanwhile rising wage levels increased purchasing power but at the same time facilitated a high rate of personal savings, the latter essential in view of the lack of state welfare and pension provision; in turn a huge domestic market was created simultaneously with growing investment in industry. Thus, even though foreign brand products were still notably absent in certain consumer sectors, the keiretsu, or conglomerates, engaged in fierce rivalry for customers, and this stood them in good stead when the time came to compete on international markets in the 1960s and 1970s.

These trading advances were made possible by the use of foreign technology, and the Japanese genius has lain in adapting and applying this in the creation of goods high in quality and well designed, initially for the mass market, the classic example being the popular cars produced for the European and American markets in the 1970s and 1980s. Nevertheless there proved to be limits to this strategy, and by the late 1980s Japan was moving towards the pioneer mode; in fact, as early as the 1970s the Japanese government and industrial enterprises were boosting investment in research and development. In recent decades the government has been providing aid for small and medium-sized enterprises pioneering high-technology sectors like satellite communications, crucial if Japan is to diversify in the wake of trade surpluses and mounting protectionism in the European Community and NAFTA markets.

These are the stages of development through which Japan has passed during the post-war period. A similar path has been followed by South Korea and Taiwan, and to a much lesser extent by Hong Kong and Singapore, even if these, and the latter two territories especially, have not possessed a domestic market on the scale of Japan. In essence, success has been achieved through export-orientated industrialisation policies. In addition, while there have obviously been some differences in the degree and scale of industrialisation among these states, never-theless they have all effected a smooth transition from import substi-tution or protectionism to an export orientation aimed at providing highly competitive industrial goods for foreign markets. Latterly, such economies have been moving into the heavy machinery and chemical sectors and, in the case of Japan especially, high-tech industries.

This phenomenon has been outlined in the 'flying geese' theory, formulated by the Japanese economist, Akamatsu Kaname, whereby less advanced countries move into industries newly vacated by developed countries and pass through a number of stages leading to higher levels of technological sophistication. There is investment input by the leader or leaders of the flight into the other countries in the follower mode; Japan achieved economic takeoff in the 1960s and then helped South Korea, Taiwan and Hong Kong to attain that status in the 1970s. The Japanese were active, for instance, in Taiwan's export processing zones. Since the 1980s the above countries have been investing in China which has latterly been moving through similar stages of development.[3]

Chinese emulation of the Japanese model
Institutions

If their economic strategy is increasingly influenced by the lessons of Japan's development experience, the Chinese leaders are also paying close attention to Japan's planning mechanisms. They do not seek, however, to produce exact replicas of Japan's planning and economic institutions; their aim is a socialist market economy which involves a number of features unique to their country. China's socialism is based on the premise of public ownership and the supremacy of the Communist Party but it nevertheless incorporates capitalist elements in the running of the economy. Thus, as in the case of Japan, a powerful role for the state in economic enterprise is legitimised. Moreover, as China moves from an economy based on Soviet-style central planning to one based on market forces, new planning mechanisms are necessary to guide, though not direct, the increasing private sectors of industry. In this sense the emulation of Japanese planning mechanisms is designed to effect increasingly sophisticated controls, for example in fiscal and monetary areas. A few examples will suffice to indicate the adoption and adaptation of Japanese practice.

A focus of Chinese attention is Japan's MITI. Mr Cai Weici, deputy director of China's Ministry of Machinery Industry, called for emulation of the Japanese Ministry when guiding Chinese companies, especially in a period of rapid growth similar to Japan's economic takeoff in the 1960s. Interest is clearly reciprocated, as the Chinese language has been chosen for the first foreign translation of a seventeen-volume history of MITI and Japan's post-war development. Thus recently introduced macroeconomic control mechanisms have parallels in the Japanese experience. In the early 1990s the Chinese established the Office of Trade and Economics, headed by Zhu Rongji, a Vice-Premier and effectively China's economic overlord, and this is closely modelled on MITI. Similarly, China's State Planning Commission, as its name suggests, has central power over the economy, and is currently being given a role more akin to Japan's Economic Planning Agency, even though the position of the Chinese body has been somewhat diminished in recent years with the institution of market reforms and the encouragement of a private enterprise sector less and less amenable to government direction. In summary, while Japan's market economy like that of any other country is *sui generis*, it is similar to that envisaged by the Chinese; while China's system is socialism with Chinese characteristics, Japan is a capitalist country with Japanese features.

Nevertheless, Japanese experience is not the only influence on China's development. China is a member of the World Bank and the International Monetary Fund, and close consultation with international institutions will increasingly be a feature of Chinese decision making. But Japanese-style practices are given great weight and their application to China in such sectors as monetary and fiscal controls will be covered in later sections of this chapter.

Stages of development

In many respects China's post-war economic development followed a path different to that of Japan until 1978 but since then the strategy of China's leaders has taken into account the stages passed through by other Asian countries. The Chinese seek to learn from that experience in a number of respects. Under the central planning of the Soviet-style command economy adopted in the early 1950s the Chinese received assistance in the form of Soviet loans and blueprints for industrial plant construction, the latter being designed and executed by Russian experts. Foreign trade played but a limited role in China's economy, being considered an adjunct to domestic activity and intended to satisfy requirements for raw materials and industrial plant. Exports were generally only promoted in that context. The watchword was self-reliance, if not self-sufficiency, which was seen as an even greater virtue as Sino-Soviet relations soured. Certainly, trade with Japan increased in the 1960s but it was not until the mid-1970s that the limitations of self-sufficiency were really implicitly admitted. By 1978 it was being agreed that only if China played a role in international economic relations could the country's ambitious modernisation goals be realised.

The open door policy has brought patterns of development similar to those fostered by Japan and other East Asian countries. In certain respects China's post-1978 economic strategy has been similar to that of Japan in the post-war period, pursuing policies of import substitution as well as export orientation. Thus up until the early 1990s foreign-invested enterprises in the Special Economic Zones of China's south-eastern coast were virtually compelled to export; in addition, consumer demand was as far as possible to be satisfied by domestic production and a policy of import substitution was simultaneously pursued through high tariffs on goods purchased from abroad.

Since the early 1980s a more sophisticated system of tariffs and import duties has been imposed. Such measures are, of course, similar to those adopted by other late developing countries like Japan. Thus raw materials crucial for China's industries, commodities in short supply and component parts for machinery now attract lower import duties, while a range of consumer and luxury goods, which can be produced in China, like beer, carpets and cars, face heavier levies. Such import restrictions and strict regulation of investment in various sectors like automobiles are effective, even if temporary, ways of protecting infant industries.

In fact, China's export thrust may well eventually be proved to have been at least partly boosted by a competitive domestic market, as was the case in Japan. The Chinese leaders have since 1978 given personal consumption a key role in the nation's economic development; an improved standard of living is seen as an incentive for management and worker initiative. In this light the decisions taken by China's leaders in 1978 and 1979 represented a watershed in the evolution of the country's post-1949 economic strategy, as they sought to raise the population's purchasing power, increase the supply of consumer goods on the domestic market, and enhance the competitiveness, especially internationally, of Chinese products. Thus the economic reforms initiated in 1979 readjusted the old post-1949 development strategy which had stressed accumulation and neglected consumption, and at the same time abandoned the emphasis on heavy industry.

Significantly, one of the first post-1978 reforms was in the rural sector where the break-up of the collectives and concessions to private use of land released the energies of the peasantry, producing high grain yields which, together with a new system of government quota purchases, increased personal incomes in the countryside. Also stimulated was light industry which in the early 1980s became the major factor behind economic growth. From the early 1980s to the beginning of the 1990s the development of the electrical appliance sector, for example, stimulated growth in the engineering electronics industry, which subsequently became a pillar of the national economy. Thus consumer goods industries multiplied. By the early 1990s, however, heavy industry was once again growing more quickly than light industry, precisely because the consumption structure was changing. Consumer durables had been rapidly popularised, particularly in the cities, and by the early 1990s demand was turning to housing, cars and other higher-priced goods, which in turn require a strong heavy industrial base. Moreover, since 1978 especially, China has had a high rate of investment. For example, some sources suggest that China's savings ratio was between 30 and 40 per cent in 1992, a significant potential source of investment and a strong impetus to the further growth of heavy industry.[4] Chinese official sources are now stressing that heavy and chemical industries should again be given preferential treatment for they remain the foundation of economic development.

In summary, in moving towards heavy industry-dominant growth, China has entered the stage of economic takeoff. The path followed by Japan and other East Asian states suggests that this stage will be characterised by a high rate of economic growth averaging about 10 per cent over ten to twenty years. During this time China should be in a position to develop its own high-tech industry after substantial input of both domestic and foreign direct investment in this sector.

It has been said that the earlier to an industrial revolution, the sooner obsolescent. Conversely, it has frequently been demonstrated that late developing countries can telescope stages through the input of technology developed elsewhere. Japan is an obvious example and China shows signs of being another. On the basis of such assumptions, China could well attain economic superpower status more rapidly than Japan.[5]

The institution of macroeconomic controls
The banking system

The underlying assumption of China's open door policy, initiated in 1978, is that the country's modernisation goals can only be achieved through transition from a command to a market economy and participation in international economic relations. Accordingly, private enterprise outside the state sector as well as foreign investment in industry have been encouraged. As a result of the rapid growth of domestic and foreign private ventures, more and more economic activity has been taking place outside the direct control of central and local government, necessitating the implementation of more sophisticated macroeconomic controls characteristic of Western countries. The role of the State

Planning Commission, formerly the organ of economic direction by the central government, has now been changed to that of indirect supervision, akin to the function of Japan's Economic Planning Agency. Industrial policies, for example, are initially to be drafted by relevant specialist departments of the State Planning Commission but, before submission to the State Council, China's cabinet, must pass through what is called 'scientific assessment and democratic deliberation'. A wider range of institutions and personnel, admittedly still largely under CCP and state aegis, are being involved in consultation; they include representatives from industrial management, academic circles and consumer organisations. Such representation is, of course, indicative of the increasingly pluralist nature of China's market economy; because of more complex economic interactions, there are now more specialist centres of influence independent of government. Because of this diversity, such mechanisms as interest rates, taxation, pricing and tariffs will come to be of even greater significance. In summary, the State Planning Commission, as a key planning institution, formulates policies through a process of wider consultation; it also oversees the implementation of state industrial policy through a variety of macroeconomic controls.

Three such mechanisms, the role of the banks, taxation and pricing, are crucial for the realisation of China's industrial plan for the 1990s and for the transformation of state enterprises into corporations. Each will be discussed in turn.

In a modern market economy it becomes necessary to balance the interests of a number of actors, say producers and consumers, in order to ensure the public good. Levers available include interest rates and control over the money supply, through government intervention via the banking system. Prior to the 1978 reforms, however, Chinese banks did not behave as their Western market economy counterparts. They certainly played a role in the allocation of funds to, and the distribution of profits from, the predominant state-controlled industries but did so through the administration levers of government rather than economic forces as such. In addition to the Bank of China there were other banks with clearly defined jurisdictions, for instance in relation to industrial and agricultural sectors, and there was little concept of competition between them. As in the case of Japan during the Meiji period, and indeed post-war prior to the liberalisation of Japan's financial markets in the 1980s, banking practice in China reflected the predominant role of the state in economic enterprise. But in order to guarantee the success of market forces in the agricultural, industrial and service sectors, China's economy now demands adjustment in the financial sphere. In fact, changes in each sector must proceed in tandem. Since 1979 the banking system has been evolving; originally little more than a means of directing credits to state industrial enterprises according to the central credit plan, it has now become an increasingly important source of funds for industry as well as an instrument for recycling the growing pool of domestic savings. The first real reforms came in 1984 when the People's Bank of China became the Central Bank, with its commercial activities transferred to the newly created Industrial and Commercial Bank of China. Meanwhile the other three state banks were allowed to expand outside their traditional areas of agriculture, construction and trade finance. Moreover, since the mid-1980s the number of non-banking financial institutions allowed to engage in domestic currency lending and direct investment has proliferated. In addition, the government has already injected an element of competition by granting licences to foreign banks, even though their jurisdiction is limited, as they are barred from domestic business. They have, however, made deep inroads into the trade finance market.

By 1994 further measures were being taken to make the banks more responsive to market forces. In August Zhu Rongji, economic overlord and governor of the People's Bank of China, called for the further conversion of the specialised state banks into commercial banks at the central level; at the same time he called for the establishment of banking institutions at the behest of local authorities, in order to guide regional economic development. Simultaneously, macroeconomic control would be furthered on two fronts, through the indirect regulation of interest rates and the tightening of the law in managing all financial institutions.

But there are two major obstacles to the creation of a commercial banking system and thus liberalisation of the financial sector. The first is that the banks remain obliged to lend to state enterprises, which are often heavily 'in the red' and inefficiently run, regardless of commercial criteria. In many cases repayment of loans is long overdue but the authorities dare not enforce bankruptcy laws lest resulting unemployment cause unrest, in the absence of an effective social security net. Consequently, a tight rein has so far had to be kept on competition in the banking sector and a realistic interest rate policy has not been possible.

Secondly, in a vast country like China there has always been the problem of local particularism. This brings into focus the fraught relationship between central and local government. The People's Bank of China has a branch network which is utilised by the central government to drain surplus deposits from the richer provinces for distribution to those provinces where the growth of deposits lags behind credit demand. But branches, allied administratively and often personally to officials in local governments, have often sought to withhold finance from the central government by making changes to the credit plan. Thus the People's Bank of China has been losing control of its provincial branches and has consequently had less room to manoeuvre in adjusting macroeconomic policy. Zhu Rongji is re-establishing control of the regional branches of the People's Bank of China as a necessary preliminary to the effective use of interest rates. In addition, the central government has set up three policy-orientated banks which have taken over the non-commercial activities of the state banks, thus allowing the commercial banks to choose their customers and enforce realistic lending rates.

In summary, the insolvency of many state enterprises contributes greatly to current central government deficits. To the extent that the sizeable state industrial sector accounts for a significant proportion of central government revenue and expenditure, banking system reform and full utilisation of such mechanisms as interest rates is impeded. There is, then, a vicious circle; realistic interest rates are necessary to discipline state enterprises and make them competitive on national and international markets but exercise of such levers is not possible until the public industrial sector's debt is reduced and it plays a lesser, and the burgeoning private sector a greater, role in China's economy.[6]

Taxation

The objective of the Chinese leadership is to release the full potential of the industrial and commercial sectors, both state-run and private, through unleashing market forces, while maintaining overall direction of economic activity via such instruments as taxation.

Taxation is a key instrument of macroeconomic management, and by 1994 China's new system, tentatively developed in 1984, was ripe for reform. In the days of the command economy, prior to 1978, personal income and company taxation, the latter category being the major concern of this study, in the conventional sense did not exist in China. Moreover, in the context of that command economy the Chinese state allocated resources and distributed revenues by administrative fiat without reference to the profit motive. But as moves were made to separate ownership and management in the early 1980s, profit sharing between industrial enterprises and the state was replaced by taxation, and these reforms have remained in force. In a sense the 1984 system had been a compromise designed to meet the needs of the transition to a market economy, and as such still bore vestiges of central planning and state management by administrative fiat.

Such compromise, while in many ways unsatisfactory, did nevertheless end the old monopoly of the centre over revenue and expenditure, a feature of the command economy, and strengthened taxation as a macroeconomic control. It served the needs of economic development during the decade from 1984 to 1994.

But tax revenues declined because central and local governments were unable to agree on a clear division of authority. Individual state enterprises were able to negotiate tax arrangements. Falls in central tax revenues were also an intended consequence of a decision to give more autonomy and responsibility to local government. In the late 1980s the central government introduced a new system whereby each province negotiated a three- to four-year tax-sharing contract with the centre. In return local governments were given greater responsibility in providing, for example, housing and welfare services to their population, requiring more locally retained tax revenues.

However, by the early 1990s the encouragement of market forces had meant that more and more spheres of economic activity were outside the range of central control. Accordingly, based on the decisions taken at the Third Plenary Session of the Fourteenth Congress of the CCP, in effect China's top national decision-making body, the State Council, the executive arm of government, moved to implement major structural reforms of the tax system, complementing the earlier measures of the open-door policy in the fields of finance, investment and foreign exchange. In conception, taxation reform was designed to standardise the tax code, equalise tax burdens, streamline procedures, rationalise the division of authority, adjust the distribution of revenue, ensure sufficiency, and establish a system meeting the needs of a market economy. Broadly speaking, the major objectives of reform were to increase national wealth through market forces and foreign investment while at the same time preventing social instability.

One of the main aims is to achieve a proper balance of revenue and expenditure between central and local government. In the 1980s regional inequalities and disparities of wealth between individuals increased. The absence of an equitable taxation system only exacerbated this tendency. Prior to the 1990s central and local governments in China divided fiscal revenues as fixed sums rather than percentages. Thus revenue-rich provinces like Guangdong, which have received much of the country's foreign investment, grow wealthier but the funds the government draws from them have not increased correspondingly. In addition, the gap between rich and poor among the population at large has been growing. To remedy this, the Chinese central government is now devising a tax system which will ensure a more equitable distribution of resources. The tax structure is to be readjusted, and tax rates and categories rationalised. Most importantly, a proper division of tax authority as well as a more equitable distribution of revenue between the central and local governments are to be effected. In sum, progressive rates for income and company tax are being introduced to reduce excessive disparities in individual wealth; similarly, distribution of revenue is being adjusted to ensure more balanced development among the country's regions. Echoes of China's Communist egalitarian past are discernible here. Yet the spirit of the tax reforms is undoubtedly one of equity rather than equality.

The revenue yielded by the new taxation system is divided between the central and local governments. Different taxes are allocated on the basis of administrative authority. For example, the central government receives fixed revenues like most income taxes, customs duties, general consumption taxes and profits of nationally controlled enterprises; local governments enjoy the income taxes of some local enterprises as well as a number of agricultural and livestock taxes. Some revenues, such as the value added taxes on commodities, are shared, 75 per cent being given to the central government and 25 per cent to the local governments. Finally, the central government uses some of its tax revenues to allocate moneys to the localities. As in most developed countries, expenditures follow the division of responsibilities as between the centre and the regions. The national government incurs expenditure for such concerns as defence, foreign relations, state enterprises and central government organisations, while regional government spending relates to the local education and health systems and price subsidies as well as to the encouragement of local business through technical renovation and new product development.

Traditionally in China there has always been at best a delicate balance, and at worst tension, between central and local authorities. Given the centre's desire to promote market forces, some coastal regions, for instance, have grown richer than the hinterland. Thus the central government is using revenue from richer localities to redistribute wealth to the less endowed regions. Some local governments may resent the concessions they have had to make. In purely economic terms, too, there could be disadvantages: in the 1980s richer local governments were able to invest heavily in infrastructure to promote economic development; this may in future be precluded if the centre makes further demands on local revenue. To effect a smooth transition to the new system, however, the central government will continue to grant subsidies for special purposes to the localities.[7]

The above measures have much in common with Western taxation systems but they also draw heavily on the Japanese allocation system which is now being examined by the Chinese Academy of Social Sciences. One of its major functions is the apportionment of financial authority between central and local governments. In Japan, as in China, main initiatives lie with the centre which has the power to draft, approve and revise local tax laws. The government in Tokyo also largely controls financing. This has meant that while the localities have carried major burdens in implementing national policy within their jurisdiction, the central government initially takes most of the revenue. Thus to ensure equity, financial resources are redistributed through such means as remission of certain centrally collected revenues and subsidies to local governments. That the Chinese leaders are attempting to increase local accountability to the centre is reflected in the tentative steps taken in 1993 to tighten the collection of taxes by such means as preventing regional governments from granting unauthorised exemptions to individuals and enterprises as well as increasing the role of banks in the remission of revenue to the state treasury. For these reasons it is the Japanese system of taxation that is being given most attention in Chinese official sources.[8]

Finally, and most importantly, only a credible, equitable system of taxation can ensure that state enterprises operate according to the dictates of the market, furthering their competitiveness at home and abroad.

Reform of the pricing system

Like equitable taxation, a realistic pricing system for all categories of industrial and consumer goods is seen as indispensable for the proper operation of market forces, based on the laws of supply and demand. In the days of the command economy prices were controlled by the central government and so inflation was disguised, but reliance on market forces requires more sophisticated controls. Chinese sources now stress the need to replace administrative fiat with economic levers. These two regulators are not, however, mutually exclusive, and in all systems governments play a direct part in the regulation of prices to a greater or lesser extent. Since 1978 the Chinese leaders have sought to increase private regulation through the market, though aware that neither capitalism nor socialism can dispense with either the plan or the market. In August 1994, for example, *Renmin Ribao*, the official organ of the CCP, extolled the virtues of regulation by the market: price fluctuations resulting from market competition mirror both resource deficiencies and changes in supply and demand, thus facilitating effective allocation and optimum use of such resources in all industries. As a general principle, therefore, the prices of the overwhelming majority of commodities and labour services should be determined by the market. Nevertheless in a number of cases state intervention is seen as restoring equity. For example, where powerful enterprises are able to fix prices and eliminate competition in a situation of near monopoly, state intervention to adjust market shares is in the public interest. *Ad hoc* measures will be implemented while anti-monopoly laws are formulated. But at the same time there is a small number of commodities and public utilities which are natural monopolies; they may both determine production in a number of industries and fulfil social needs. Agriculture, providing food and raw materials, is subject to seasonal supply and price fluctuations which make central regulation essential. Consequently, it may be undesirable to allow unbridled price competition. Similarly, sectors like mining which satisfy the growing demands of energy and transportation require massive investment yielding returns in the long term. On both counts unregulated prices could have adverse effects nationally, and so the government must retain control over pricing and supply.[9]

It must be added, however, that some analysts have entered the counter-argument that artificially low charges for energy resources like coal have led to wastage, and a free market would allow prices to find their own level.

Once again Chinese official sources view the state's role in economic enterprise in Japan as an object lesson. In Japan there are three price categories: the first, subject to direct control, relates to public utilities like electricity and transport, including, for example, rail and air travel, in addition to the telephone and postal services. These together represent about 18 per cent of consumer prices. The remaining two categories account for about 82 per cent of the total; under the second fall prices of agricultural products and other commodities which seriously affect foreign trade, and these are allowed to move within certain bands. They are thus subject to indirect control, as is the third category which encompasses most industrial and consumer goods, whether subject to monopoly or free competition. But while the prices of Japan's retail commodities move freely, the government controls wholesale prices to guarantee what is called free trade and a stable consumer market. Significantly, 80 per cent of fresh food and consumer good prices are influenced in this way. Chinese sources have also remarked favourably on Japanese laws against monopolies and profit-eering, and credible legislation would no doubt prove a crucial adjunct to the macroeconomic controls now under consideration.[10]

Under the Chinese command economy the state controlled distribution but now that this is being deregulated, nationwide wholesale markets are in the process of creation.[11] This, however, is seen to necessitate supervision by national commodity price departments for which the Japanese system has been cited as a possible model. Nevertheless, while such indirect Japanese-style control over prices is likely to be retained, deregulation is proceeding apace. By early 1993, for example, most agricultural and sideline production was no longer governed by mandatory plans and prices had been decontrolled. The prices of only six products, grain, cotton, tobacco, raw silk, tea and timber, continued to be set by the state, though closely following the dictates of the market. In addition, a number of natural resources in the minerals and energy sectors remained under some form of pricing control. As for industrial products there have been similar trends towards deregulation; the proportion subject to mandatory planning fell from 97 per cent to 11.6 per cent during the years from 1978 to 1993. By 1991 the proportion of consumer goods sold at state-set prices had fallen to 21 per cent and that of capital goods to 36 per cent. In mid-1993 one source was claiming that the proportion of products in general subject to price control had fallen to under 20 per cent. It seems likely that price reform will maintain momentum as deregulated commodity market networks are further developed.[12] As official sources quoted above have stressed, however, such trends towards a free market do not preclude government intervention. In June 1994, for example, fearing social unrest and the rapidly deteriorating terms of trade for those in agriculture, the state approved price increases of 40 per cent for wheat, rice and other grains.[13]

Like the other macroeconomic controls of banking and taxation, a pricing policy which balances competition and regulation is indispensable for the operation of a free market; without it state enterprise sector reforms would be null and void.

The following sections will examine state enterprise reforms which, like the institution of macroeconomic controls, bear the imprint of Japanese experience.[14]

China's industrial policy

The foregoing has placed emphasis on the macroeconomic levers available to Chinese leaders seeking to effect transition from a command to a market economy. Attention is focused in the following sections on the microeconomic level of industrial enterprises but it is first necessary to introduce the setting in which proposed changes in the state sector are scheduled to take place.

That setting is provided by the *Outline for Industrial Policy in the 1990s*, approved by the State Council in March 1994. It discusses a number of basic initiatives, one major priority being the development of basic industries to be financed over the long term through bonds and shares, coming from the state and the private sector respectively. Additionally, as basic industries, predominantly state enterprises, are privatised, foreign capital is also encouraged.

Echoing the targeting of priorities by Japan's MITI in the 1960s, a number of sectors are now designated by the Chinese as pillar industries: electronics, machinery, petrochemicals, automobiles and construction. Thus the electronics industry should concentrate on manufacturing microelectronic components and telecommunications equipment as well as newly emerging information products, involving the most up-to-date technologies; again there are resonances of Japanese policies in the 1970s.

Machinery industries have as their aim the manufacture of basic machine tools. Technical standards are to be raised, thus enhancing market competitiveness. These industries are, of course, the cornerstone of a number of others, and in Japan their development facilitated economic takeoff. China's petrochemical industry will expand production and raise its technical level and processing ability; this is crucial for growth in other sectors. In Japan the manufacture of high-quality cars for a competitive mass market at home provided a springboard for successful exports; the Chinese leadership wants priority given to this sector, with a few companies facing orderly competition domestically and increasing their market share. Foreign imports are initially being restricted but domestic rivalry among Chinese manufacturers will ensure eventual competitiveness on international markets. The next priority is the construction industry which has the tasks of developing infrastructure and creating social capital in areas like urban housing. It may be observed, however, that it is only in latter decades that sectors like housing have been consciously targeted by Japanese planners, even if the country's infrastructure has long been the envy of many others.

A very real parallel with Japan may be seen in the financing of such a programme. The Chinese government has been financing internal deficits by bonds; these, in addition to the utilisation of stocks by private companies, will be the mainstay of funds for pillar industries.

Additionally, such industries will be permitted to borrow overseas loans, in accordance with international practice.

Such priorities are reflected in foreign trade policy, where high-tech products will play an increasing role, in contrast with resource-type products in short supply domestically which must be retained at home. Similarly, new technologies and key equipment will be imported, while purchase abroad of consumer goods which can be produced at home is discouraged. In terms of overall strategy there is a discernible policy of import substitution as well as, increasingly, an export orientation.

Most importantly, these policies as a whole point to a new thorough-going macroeconomic reform, with the major focus on state enterprises which in effect are to be gradually privatised, even if this term must be qualified. Key principles are competition and economies of scale. An example is the automobile industry which nevertheless already has a considerable foreign investment input. In addition, the policy documents speak of the reconstruction not only of enterprises but of industries as a whole; thus a division of labour is to be effected among large, medium-sized and small enterprises where many spare parts and components are required. This is an undoubted echo of Japanese organisation *par excellence*, where there are long-term relationships, cross-investment and technology transfer between customers and suppliers. This is contained within the Japanese keiretsu or conglomerate system, usually centred on a bank which funds restructuring and long-term development. This kind of mutual stockholding is also pertinent to the emergence in China of transnational business conglomerates, in contrast with the old command economy where production tended to be located in and directed towards satisfying the needs of particular regions, even if some industrial enterprises under the central government were nationally focused. Thus as China's distribution systems are reformed, truly nationwide markets will emerge, in preparation for export targeting and manufacture overseas.

In the 1950s and 1960s one of the factors leading to economic takeoff in Japan was industry's ability to apply technology transferred from abroad. Additionally, funding of research and development has long been a *forte* of both government and private industry. The keiretsu model may well prove an effective setting in China for the diffusion of technology. Thus within this framework scientific research and development will be clearly targeted at specific industries, stressing both technology transfer and innovation. While the Japanese government and industry have stressed research and development, critics of the country's education system have called for a greater vocational orientation in schools; elite universities have been criticised for the generalist nature of their curricula. In that sense, in encouraging enterprises to strengthen ties with institutions of higher learning, now increasingly orientated towards the practical application of scientific knowledge, the Chinese may well better Japanese practice at an earlier stage of their country's economic development.

A feature of Chinese industrial policy which more closely reflects the Japanese model, however, is the technological upgrading of small and medium-sized enterprises in towns and villages, especially in the centre and west of the country. As will be shown below in the context of Chinese enterprise reform in the 1980s, Japanese government initiatives have recently been directed towards creating small companies devoted to high-tech innovation.

Finally, while in the 1980s the Chinese leadership gave priority to the southern coastal zones in its export orientation, the focus of economic strategy has now been shifted to particular industries rather than regions, and state investment and loans are now targeted accordingly. But the export orientation remains. Overall, China's targeting of industrial sectors, like its planning mechanisms, is increasingly bearing the imprint of Japanese practice.[15]

The reform of state enterprises
Ownership and management

The Chinese leaders are committed to the creation of a socialist market economy but in fact the term itself increasingly reflects the national reality since more than two-thirds of current economic activity takes place outside the state system. In early 1994, however, China's 71,600 state-owned industrial enterprises, or 19 per cent of the total number of companies, still accounted for just over half of the country's total output value, with the sector's taxes and profits accounting for 66 per cent of the total. Nevertheless a number of state enterprises have been suffering long-term losses, contributing significantly to China's fiscal deficits because the taxes and profits they yield to the state treasury have consistently fallen.[16] Early in the reform period China's official economists were acknowledging that state enterprises, insulated from the need to make profits and with their losses made good by state capital input, were plagued by inefficiency and overmanning. Ever since the Twelfth Central Committee of the CCP adopted The Decision on Economic Reform in October 1984 vitalisation of large and medium-sized state enterprises has been a major objective. In an attempt at greater efficiency, following the 1984 decision, a number of measures were taken to separate government administration from enterprise management. Limited enterprise autonomy and management by contract was introduced, although the principle of public ownership was strictly maintained.

These measures, implemented between 1979 and 1984, intensified limited moves towards autonomy and, based upon factory director responsibility, were designed to ground decision making more firmly on economic and material criteria. Potentially, the political influence of enterprise Communist Party Secretaries would be reduced. The profit motive was introduced but it still had to operate under the administrative intervention of the particular ministries with jurisdiction over the enterprises. In any case at that time taxation and a realistic pricing system guaranteeing the full implementation of market forces were not yet in place. It was against this background that the system of management by contract was introduced in most state enterprises in 1987. Enterprise leaders were now to be given incentives to raise efficiency through the setting of management goals. Thus the ministries now concluded contracts with specific managers who would run the enterprises with specific goals in view; if the targets were achieved, the managers would be permitted to use some percentage of the surplus value for new investment, welfare funds and workforce bonuses. In theory, if the goals were not attained, the managers would receive only their fixed salary, and there was always the danger that their contracts with the state would not be renewed.

Contracts were a departure from the previous system where the profits of enterprises were taken by the state, with enterprise leaders being really only representatives of the lowest branch of the administrative hierarchy, effectively China's civil service. Certainly, profit was now a motivation for enterprise managers. In addition, whereas previously enterprises had been controlled by ministries, with managers and workers being remunerated by fixed wages and salaries which remained for long periods virtually unchanged, business results were now more effectively taken into account.

Nevertheless, it must be stressed again that only now are enterprises operating in a situation approaching market competition; in addition, pricing was directly controlled and distribution regulated. Moreover, it has often been said that China is ruled by personalities rather than institutions, and certainly the formulation of contracts and assessment of the profitability of enterprises were often carried out through face-to-face negotiation between contractors and the government, allowing subjective forces like personal relationships built up over the years to be the decisive factors.

Though not without tangible advantages, the contract system was nevertheless a compromise between ideology, the old commitment to the state's role in the economy, and the need to inject the discipline of the market into ailing state enterprises. The separation of ownership and management and the use of a market mechanism were insufficient to solve the fundamental problems facing state enterprises. But the limited success of the contract system was a mandate for more reform, not less. When the contract system was at its height in the middle and late 1980s, the ratio of production by state enterprises to aggregate national industrial output was in decline, falling from about 75 per cent in 1981 to about 53 per cent a decade later. In other words, state enterprises were becoming less important in the national economy. This is indicated also by growth rates; in 1991, while the production values of private enterprises and foreign-affiliated and other companies grew by 24 per cent and 55.8 per cent respectively, state enterprise output only increased by 8.4 per cent, the same proportion as in 1990, far less than industrial output as a whole (14.2 per cent). Thus while there were productivity gains in state industrial enterprises, capital profit ratios dropped, production costs increased and the number of enterprises in deficit rose. Moreover, as this deficit increased, so did 'chain debt', a consequence of some state enterprises becoming indebted to others which in turn could not pay their own debtors. This resulted from a half free market where pricing was gradually being decontrolled and mandatory planning in the provision of raw materials reduced.

Therefore, from the perspective of the early 1990s, the performance of state enterprises under the contract system presented mixed omens but all pointed to the need for more extensive reform. It is always easier to change institutional arrangements than, for instance, corporate cultures. Contracts may have reformed the old system of remission of profits but in the immediate term they could do little to alter the ways in which bureaucrats and enterprise directors thought and operated. Overly paternalistic relationships between these two groups soon meant that punitive sanctions were not enforced; the basic value of contracts tended to be fixed through face-to-face bargaining, and when a target was not achieved, it was revised downward through negotiation. When there are bureaucratic networks, there is often corruption, particularly in a half-reformed economy in transition from command to market.

In addition, this paternalism, when added to other structural factors, made the contract system fundamentally unsound in its original form. As the contracts were effective for four years, managers acquired a short-term orientation and did not engage in long-term strategic planning, being concerned with immediate profits and neglecting research and development. Moreover, in one respect, managers had an incentive to keep profits within bounds, since contract targets were set on the basis of profits in the preceding term. Again, collusion with bureaucrats could intervene to set targets favourable to managers but not necessarily to enterprise efficiency. The contract system had other weaknesses. There was, in fact, no separation in practice between taxation and the payment to the state of profits, earned after all through use of state-owned assets. Furthermore, the profit actually retained by enterprises was often a low proportion of pre-tax total. It was estimated that, in general, state enterprises were paying over 80 per cent of corporate profit to the state. In short, even under the contract system state-owned enterprises were still not profit-making entities in their own right, independent of the state.

By 1992, alternatives being mooted included the renewal of existing contracts. In addition, to eradicate short termism, there was experimentation with more comprehensive contracts with broader targets embracing investment in research and development, and directed towards extending corporate assets and increasing production capacity.

Already, however, the contract system in its various forms has been overtaken by events, as the Chinese private sector and foreign-invested concerns have begun to enjoy the fruits of success, suggesting arguments in favour of free enterprise. Ultimately, the division of ownership from management can only be truly effective, and conflict between the two sides mitigated, if the sanctions of dismissal and bankruptcy are fully applied. Such measures only become possible, however, if there is production factor mobility, for example of labour and capital. These issues are the subject of following sections, as it is on them that true privatisation and the health of the state enterprises are now perceived by the Chinese leaders to depend.[17]

Social security and labour mobility

In the late 1980s the Chinese began to introduce bankruptcy legislation, the first testing ground being Shenyang in the northeast, where much of the country's state industry is located. Initial attempts to enforce the law as a penalty for failure were nevertheless stymied by the fact that state enterprises traditionally provide not only remuneration but lifetime employment, housing, welfare and other benefits. Thus in the 1990s laws concerning bankruptcy and enforced mergers of state enterprises have proceeded only slowly. Welfare provision, like unemployment benefit at national level, is still in its infancy, and the Chinese central leadership has been alert to the dangers of social disadvantage. Enterprise reform as a whole, then, has awaited the installation of a nationwide social security system. In turn labour mobility only becomes possible when such a safety net is in place.

In November 1993 an official at China's Ministry of Labour stated the objective of having a comprehensive social security system, including unemployment insurance, in place by the turn of the century. The system is currently being perfected; funding is by government and enterprises, whether state, private or foreign-invested. By January 1994 most provinces in China had begun to institute an unemployment benefit system, partly funded by contributions from enterprises, which withhold 0.6 to 1 per cent of their employees' wages as mutual assistance insurance funds. The Beijing Municipal Government, for example, made unemployment insurance compulsory for all enterprises in the city, including concerns under the central government and various kinds of Sino-foreign joint ventures, from 1 July 1994. Thus when an enterprise becomes bankrupt, streamlined, closed by the state or its employees dismissed, the unemployed worker is to receive three to twenty-four months' unemployment benefit and, if necessary, a certain percentage of medical fees will be refunded. An official source stated that in 1993 relief was granted to 900,000 unemployed workers. The aim is now to extend the coverage of social security, including unemployment relief, to all urban workers and to improve efficiency in the disbursement of funds.[18] In addition, in an article in the *Renmin Ribao* of 15 November 1994 Vice-Premier Zou Jiahua was exhorting individuals to purchase their own medical and unemployment insurance to supplement the social security system.[19]

Such measures have facilitated the introduction of a contract system of employment. In 1986 the State Council promulgated the Provisional Regulations on the Implementation of Contracts in State-run Enterprises which established as a matter of state policy that workers recruited for regular employment in state enterprises were to be hired on the basis of individually concluded contracts for a specific period, usually ranging from one to five years.[20] Beginning with the recruitment of new workers in state enterprises in some areas in 1986, the contract system of employment has been operational on a trial basis nationwide since 1987. Latest figures to hand suggest that in the state sector 30 per cent of employees now work under contracts which stipulate duties, obligations and rights on both sides of industry, in order to induce competitiveness through worker motivation. By March 1994, according to Labour Ministry statistics, of the 80 million workers in state enterprises 23.3 million were covered by contracts.[21] The reforms appear to be especially advanced in Shanghai where, as of March 1994,

1.6 million employees in state enterprises, accounting for 97.53 per cent of the total, were working under various categories of labour contracts.[22]

Moreover, by the late 1980s, there was evidence that state enterprise managers were using their greater discretionary powers to hire temporary workers. One source estimated that this category accounted for approximately 13 million people or 13.5 per cent of the total labour force in state enterprises in 1988 as opposed to 8.8 million or 10.1 per cent of the total in 1984.[23] What may be emerging is a dualistic division of the Chinese labour force with resulting differentiation in privileges and status.[24] Crucially, perhaps, a workforce without permanent tenure but entitled to unemployment benefit serves as a kind of safety valve in times of economic downturn; it also aids labour mobility.

Like unemployment benefit provision, labour contracts and the emergence of a temporary workforce, employment agencies and recruitment fairs are also fostering labour mobility. As of 1993, 9,700 job introduction agencies, 2,200 re-employment training centres and 200,000 labour service companies for redundant personnel had been established under state auspices over the preceding six years.[25] A notable feature is the careers fair, an example being that held in Beijing in September 1992, the first where state enterprises, in this case numbering 180, were represented.

In fact, labour flexibility is increasingly being achieved through an active competitive personnel exchange market, with extensive job transfers effected by means ranging from the above-mentioned government-sponsored agencies to private employment systems, careers fairs and media advertising.[26]

Other measures have fostered labour mobility and personal preference in employment. Under the command economy university graduates and other qualified personnel were allocated to employment, especially in the state sector, through central direction and regardless of personal choice. By the early 1990s there were moves towards abolition of this system, and in any case private concerns and foreign-invested ventures were developing their own channels of recruitment, using state-run employment agencies and careers fairs. There had also been a tradition of the children of workers replacing their parents on retirement, thereby reinforcing the features of community in enterprises; but in 1986 the Provisional Regulations Governing the Hiring of Workers was introduced to open state enterprise recruitment to all qualified workers. Quality control and competitiveness demand recruitment of the best, and this is reflected in the contract system; if they are to survive, state enterprises must become business profit centres, judged on results, not communities offering permanent tenure of employment.

A theme throughout this study has been the citing of parallels between current Chinese government policies and Japanese experience as well as instances where elements of Japan's post-war economic development have been seen as a guide for China. There are, however, instances where China rather than Japan may be considered the pioneer. In post-war Japan many welfare functions, normally the province of the state in industrial countries, have been taken care of by individual companies, albeit private rather than state-operated as in China, and unemployment insurance, health schemes and pensions have only developed in recent decades at the national level. Similarly, as in China, enterprises have given lifetime employment to the permanent workforce and so labour mobility to that extent has been restricted. The pressures of recession in Japan, however, are indicating the rigidities inherent in permanent tenure and rendering it obsolete; industrial restructuring and priority given to venture capital in high-tech industries demand innovation, retraining and labour mobility. These trends have also affected recruitment in Japan. Until recently recruitment of workers and managers to large Japanese companies was a 'closed shop': employee entry was through alumni networks and personal connections rather than public competition. In terms of development strategy China's position is often compared to Japan's in the 1960s. But in perfecting a comprehensive system of state welfare, admittedly as yet in embryo, and in fostering labour mobility by implementing contract employment rather than the old 'iron rice bowl' or permanent tenure, all in a context where the state sector is declining in importance relative to private industry, the Chinese may have stolen a march on their Japanese counterparts.

From management by contract to privatisation

In retrospect, the management by contract system may be seen as a stage, though a crucial one, on the road to the privatisation of state enterprises, even though the latter term must be used advisedly. By introducing the ideas of accountability and performance, management by contract has helped to foster the mobility of one production factor, labour. But, in order to achieve what is, in essence, privatisation, even if under the rubric of market socialism, it is essential that other production factor markets for capital and stocks be established. This will make possible stock issues for the large-scale corporations discussed below and the stage-by-stage privatisation of small and medium-sized enterprises. The preconditions for such factor mobility are already being laid; the banks are to play a more ostensibly commercial role and stock markets are already in operation at the exchanges of Shanghai and Shenzhen, even if many transactions relate to private companies and Sino-foreign joint ventures. Other factor markets being developed include those for information and technology exchange.

Moves towards privatisation were given further stimulus at the Fourteenth CCP Congress held in late 1992 at which the party leader, Jiang Zemin, put the seal of approval on reforms to date and hailed the state enterprises as the central link in building a socialist market economy. The strategy now was corporativisation, the goal being to make each state enterprise a legal person, operating on its own and assuming sole responsibility for its profits and losses; such reform is given added momentum by the prospect of China joining the World Trade Organisation, the successor of GATT. China's producers will then be forced to compete with foreign goods at home and abroad, without the benefit of extensive tariff protection. In practice, corporativisation would mean a partnership between state and private interests; while the government would retain ownership of major enterprises the assets of others would be sold as shares on the securities markets of Shanghai and Shenzhen. In a period of transition over the next five years managers of former state enterprises will be required to run their operations without direct state assistance; instead of outright fiscal transfers from central government, investment will be furnished through stocks and bank loans. Concomitantly, government and enterprise functions are being separated. In order that bureaucratic interference be eliminated, provincial government bureaux hitherto responsible for controlling industry at the local level are to be split off into corporations and enterprise groups. In the southern province of Guangdong, for example, some such bureaux have already been turned into state-owned corporations, while in the central government some administrative departments of the Ministry of Commerce are to be similarly reorganised.

Turning bureaux into corporations is designed to save costs by reducing the number of bureaucrats, many of whom are now expected to find jobs in corporations or enterprise groups, where they will be more accountable for performance, in theory being subject to market discipline.[27]

It will be noted that official Chinese sources have referred to 'corporativisation' of state enterprises, even though 'privatisation' may result in the long term. But for ideological reasons relating to their own legitimacy the Chinese leaders dare not openly abandon public ownership. Thus contradiction between public ownership and the market has delayed reform because there is consequently vagueness as to who owns the state enterprises and their assets; property rights are, after all, both a legal concept and a social contract determining relations between two parties. Thus corporativisation and the transformation of 3,800 state enterprises into joint stock companies are seen as possible solutions, since investment will come from both government and private sources. Introduction of a stock system results in the independence of enterprise ownership rights from administrative authorities. Accordingly, shares have now been issued; of those available for purchase, many have been bought by workers in a particular enterprise, although a few have been sold to the general public. The experiment is likely to be extended nationwide.[28]

These reforms are still at an experimental stage and it is too early to speak of a standard pattern of stockholding which would take account of state interests. One scheme being mooted, however, would create four distinct kinds of shareholders, and ensure state participation so that the companies could still be called state owned. Shares would be held by a state investment fund under the auspices of the departments and bureaux at present responsible for the relevant industries. In addition, suppliers and various associated companies would have a stake; a number of shares would also be sold to enterprise employees and other investors.[29]

In this transition to corporations and private companies obstruction from entrenched bureaucratic interests cannot be ruled out. A government research team dispatched to the provinces in late 1993 to review the impact of the new measures found that local industrial bureaux were reluctant to surrender control of factories under their jurisdiction. It also remains to be seen whether enterprises in which the central government continues to hold major shares will be able to avoid bureaucratic interference. As argued earlier, bureaucratic and enterprise cultures are slow to change.[30]

The state enterprises discussed above are defined as those under the jurisdiction of central government ministries and their local bureaux. There are, however, a number of collectively owned enterprises which come under the sole auspices of local government. These rural enterprises, sometimes referred to as town and village enterprises, have their antecedents in the old production brigade-level industrial concerns set up during the Great Leap Forward from 1958 to 1961 when the CCP sought to raise living standards in the countryside through introducing elements of a modern economy. These concerns were reorganised in 1978 and again in 1984 when the old system of agricultural communes was dismantled; they then came under the aegis of local governments. The rural enterprises have been engaged mainly in the manufacture of machinery, building materials and textiles. Importantly, they also engage in sub-contracting arrangements with urban industrial enterprises.

An important function of such enterprises has been providing a source of rural employment. In 1979 a system of limited private enterprise in agriculture was instituted, with peasant households allocated plots of land under contract. Greater freedom was given to produce and diversify crops when state grain quotas had been satisfied, with remuneration now linked clearly to output. There were thus greater incentives to raise productivity of both staple foods and cash crops. As a result of agricultural rationalisation, since the 1980s there has been surplus labour in the countryside; over 125 million rural workers have been absorbed into town and village enterprises, and it is estimated that a quarter of the rural population of the southern provinces is employed in rural industry, with resulting improvements in living standards.[31]

In many respects the collectively owned enterprises are little different from private ventures but they are to some extent dependent on local government for funding and the acquisition of raw materials outside the state plan. In addition, they are important sources of revenue for both the state and local governments. For this reason any attempts to turn town and village enterprises into fully private entities is likely to meet bureaucratic resistance similar to that evidenced in the case of urban industrial state enterprises.

The main trend, then, among both state and collective enterprises in the cities and the countryside is towards corporativisation and privatisation. Central government initiatives in this direction are redolent of the industrial policies of Japan's Meiji leaders in the late nineteenth century, when a number of major industries, initially state-financed, were handed over to private industrialists. While the parallel is not exact, Chinese official journals bear eloquent witness to the importance of the Japanese model in the overall restructuring of Chinese industry. In late 1994 an article extolled the merits of privatisation, which, by releasing initiative and innovation and creating an *esprit de corps*, enhances market competitiveness. Some utilities, however, were said to need extensive investment which only the state could afford; these should remain in public ownership.[32]

There was also said to be the intermediate category, public corporations, which retain their own independent decision-making powers, even though benefiting from state investment input.[33]

Here are echoes of the Japanese system, especially the keiretsu or conglomerates which consist of a main company, a customer, surrounded by a number of small and medium-sized suppliers. These inter-company relationships facilitate innovation and productivity growth through dissemination of technology and cross-investment. The smaller companies are in competition within the group and seek to retain their position; they simultaneously try to find markets elsewhere, however. Car manufacturers like Toyota are the best examples of keiretsu organisation. This is the path that the Chinese enterprise groups, reorganised from the local industrial bureaux, may be destined to follow.[34]

As private enterprises, the former state and collective enterprises will be faced with new challenges in addressing the rigours of the market. These will require strategic decision making on the part of managers and the acquisition of new innovative skills for the workforce. The final section on enterprise reform addresses such issues.

Business strategy and management systems

The main purpose of the macroeconomic and enterprise reforms discussed above is to facilitate the introduction of the business strategy and management systems characteristic of Japanese and Western companies operating in competitive markets. Fundamentally, this is a question of changing ingrained anti-commercial attitudes among Chinese managers and workers. Prior to the reforms of the 1980s the decision-making powers of Chinese enterprise leaders were severely circumscribed: production targets, allocation of raw materials, distribution of goods, and disbursement of profits were taken care of administratively by the state ministries, and in effect directors and managers were civil servants at the lower rung of the administrative hierarchy. Enterprises could not go bankrupt, and the state covered deficits. Thus if managers wished to embark on new lines of business, necessary new plant and equipment investment was undertaken according to central government planning as state capital construction projects, the right of approval resting with higher administrative organs. Prior to reform, such lack of manager initiative was one of the major sources of weakness. In addition, state enterprises operated in a closed seller's market which penalised managerial risk taking; products were also targeted at particular regions where the factories were located rather than nationally. Thus there was little, if any, inter-company competition; prices were generally fixed and any market imbalances were adjusted by administrative fiat through a vertical hierarchy of state-controlled distribution. In summary, decision making was separated from those in charge of production.

But whereas state enterprises were formerly the major sectors of production, they are now being rapidly overtaken by private ventures, and moves towards privatisation and production factor mobility have been encouraged to foster greater efficiency and competitiveness. The values and norms of the private sector are the model for adjustment to an unpredictable market environment. This in turn demands the creation of such new corporate functions as research and development, plant and equipment investment, and marketing. Thus, as in the case of successful Japanese companies, the focus is now long term, with emphasis on growth targets like market share or the manufacture of new product lines, as opposed to the 'short termism' of the old market economy, especially immediately after the institution of the management by contract system. Chinese sources quoted above stated that long-term commercial success arising from privatisation would rest on two preconditions: investment and qualified personnel.

It is well known that in the initial stages of economic takeoff the Japanese relied heavily on applying to industry technology developed elsewhere. Importation of technology is a crucial element of China's official policy but the country's own achievements in a number of scientific fields is already considerable and, in relative terms, may well be more advanced than those of Japan at an equivalent stage of development. It is official Chinese policy for high-tech research to be closely linked to industrial production: Chinese universities and research institutes have already been involved in a number of initiatives under the Torch Project, launched in 1988 to commercialise new technologies and transform traditional industries. Such emphasis was also reflected in the officially approved plan of China's Academy of Sciences to transfer 70 per cent of its staff to research directed to the needs of industrial production.[35] In addition, following Japan's path, the technological transformation of both urban and rural small and medium-sized enterprises through plant as well as knowledge-intensive input will proceed on two fronts: through the support of government investment and via close cooperation between companies and research institutes.[36] A feature of such cooperation between government, industry and academia is the conversion of foreign advanced technology; colour television sets, using knowledge from abroad, and considered the cream of China-made products, are a case in point. Such success stories are nevertheless only possible through Chinese industry's application and adaptation of that technology.

It is the role of China's education system to provide the requisite qualified labour force. An increasing vocational orientation is reflected both in university enrolment policies, with recruitment of a number of entrants having practical experience even if no formal qualifications, and in a broader curriculum at secondary level.[37]

Crucial to market success is motivation of both management and workforce. In the past training has focused on hardware features like engineering and technical skills; this was perhaps adequate in a seller's market where concern was mainly with quantitative targets but when quality, fashion and design became features of marketability, then software, knowledge and the human element are uppermost. A key element here is marketing and Japan's corporations have become famous for planning continuous growth, forecasting changes in the domestic and world economies and promoting technical progress to satisfy evolving market demand. Similarly, in the more ostensibly human resource area, the greatest need is for highly motivated, internationally aware managers, as value change through education and training will be decisive. A spirit of entrepreneurship and market sense cannot be taught but may be fostered by greater stress on overall personal development both through formal education and, more effectively, in the workplace itself. It is in workplace organisation that the Japanese have excelled, and concentration is now directed to ways in which the Chinese may benefit from that experience.

Good industrial relations and effective work organisation are the key to production excellence. Another legacy of the command economy and the seller's market has been the lack of cooperation among the different sectors and departments in state enterprises. This is due to specificity of employment in state-owned enterprises, there being a rigid division of labour among middle managers and virtually no horizontal movement among jobs. This is also true of the workforce on the shop floor, a situation which tends to inhibit *esprit de corps*. This is clearly in evidence with regard to quality control. If, for example, defects are found during inspection at the end of an assembly line for washing machines, the causes of the faults and the responsibilities of the relevant sectors may be so diverse that the major factor is difficult to pinpoint. It may be due to design, inferior components or improper assembly operations or all three, and such patterns cannot be solved by individual sectors and their personnel acting alone.

In contrast, the Japanese have excelled at quality control, each section of production being conceived of as a supplier as it passes a finished product to its customer at the next stage. Furthermore, Japanese strengths have lain in consultation and job rotation, both of which contribute to cooperation between different sectors of the workforce. Whereas leadership in Chinese state enterprises has traditionally been of the top-down variety with little regard to the opinions of workers,

Japanese managers maintain liaison with the shop floor, as shown through such devices as quality control circles. This is also facilitated by job rotation; in their first few years with a company managers are successively seconded to a number of departments, where they gain all-round knowledge and develop personal relationships. Emphasis is also placed on retraining which enhances flexibility. But Chinese managers have in the past been ignorant of the activities of other departments, being ensconced in their own specialisms, whether in, say, purchasing, inspection or production. Thus while successful Japanese companies are characterised by cooperation and competition for excellence among their various departments, Chinese enterprises are vertically managed and lack horizontal integration. To date, of course, state enterprises have not been disciplined by a fiercely competitive domestic market but, as this emerges, Japanese practice could become a model in industrial relations as in other areas.[38]

Summary

In this chapter it has been suggested that the economic development of modern Japan, especially post-war, holds important lessons for China, and the Chinese leaders themselves have stressed its relevance. While the economic systems of China and Japan in many respects contrast, nevertheless they have the common feature of major state intervention in industrial enterprise. Institutions underpinning the close relationship between business and government in post-war Japan, like MITI and the Economic Planning Agency, now find their parallels in the Trade and Economic Office headed by Zhu Rongji, and the State Planning Commission, while China's newly unveiled industrial plan bears resemblance to equivalent Japanese documents in its targeting of specific economic sectors through government investment and technology as well as its implied protection of infant industries. A key to China's economic progress is the reform of the inefficient and over-manned state enterprises, even though they are accounting for proportionally less and less of China's industrial output. Production factor mobility, especially of labour and capital markets, social security provision and contracts for workers and managers are aiding restructuring. The goal is to make China's goods competitive on markets at home and abroad, as protection is removed on China's accession to the World Trade Organisation. The method of achieving that end is privatisation, initially through the creation of joint stock companies. When faced with the rigours of the market, China's state enterprise managers must undertake the strategic decisions which were formerly taken by officials in government ministries under the old command economy. Response to the market also involves greater flexibility in production to develop new products in accordance with current quality, design and fashion specifications. A buyer's market accordingly also necessitates greater coordination in work organisation. Consultation between management and workforce in the various sectors of production could release initiative, resulting in higher morale and motivation. In addition, in line with their industrial policy, the Chinese leaders are promoting closer links between universities, research institutions and industrial enterprises, with additional emphasis on vocational education at all levels. A concomitant, retraining on the job, another Japanese strength, could also prove decisive.

Models of development are nevertheless by definition dynamic and China's economic growth will not necessarily prove a replica of Japan's. In any case China's policy makers do not intend to emulate the Japanese model, as outlined above, in its entirety. They accept, for example, the need to diverge from Japanese practices, given the vast economic contrasts between the two countries. Moreover, China's development is taking place in a world very different from the immediate post-war setting in which Japanese recovery and growth were achieved. One example of divergence from the Japanese model lies in China's greater openness to foreign investment; in contrast, Japan's laws have been and still are much more restrictive. In addition, there is already evidence that the Chinese may fuse a number of stages of development and move, for instance, towards an export orientation more quickly than did Japan.

Nevertheless, Japan's institutions and experience remain a focus of reference for China's leaders. A shared Confucian heritage and Japan's leap to economic superpower status in just over a century make the Japanese model compelling, even if emulation will necessarily be selective. Finally, economic complementarity and the Japanese need to diversify markets as well as sources of supply, in the wake of growing calls for protectionism in the European Union and NAFTA, make China a natural investment and trading partner. It is to these issues that attention is now turned.

3 Japanese investment in China

National motives

The Chinese leaders' strategy in seeking Japanese investment input reflects both their country's industrial plans and their conception of its evolving role in the economic development of East Asia, a role which itself brings into focus what may well become one of the major issues of the twenty-first century, namely Sino-Japanese rivalry or partnership in the region as a whole. There is strong potential for partnership or even a special relationship between the two countries, in spite of historical animosities and the oft-discussed Chinese suspicion of a possible growth of Japanese military power in Asia. There is apparent economic complementarity, implying a vertical division of labour: China's abundant natural resources and cheap labour force contrast with Japan's capital and technology, even though most of China's exports now consist of manufactures necessitating the input of natural resources. In a political sense, too, there are affinities: both have governments imbued with authoritarian traditions; these provide services for the populace who do not rate highly their ability to influence the policies of national authorities. Freedom and prosperity are seen in terms of the nation rather than the individual. But all governments are to a degree accountable to those they lead, and the Chinese leaders increasingly conceive of their own legitimacy, their country's social harmony and the stability of the Asian region as a whole as lying in economic development.[1] Views on human rights and civil liberties tend to coincide with those of Japanese government leaders; criticisms voiced in Japan concerning human rights in the wake of the 1989 Tiananmen incident were much less strident than those of Western leaders. There is thus a sense in which the Japanese establishment shares the official Chinese definition of human rights in terms of economic rather than political freedoms; it is perhaps significant that

Japanese democracy works differently from that in the Western countries and that the long supremacy of the Japanese ruling party, the Liberal Democratic Party (LDP), from 1955 until the end of the 1980s rested heavily on economic growth and the ability to satisfy rising expectations. There is little reason to believe that the current administration will prove any less dependent on economic indicators. Likewise Zhu Rongji, China's economic overlord, has stressed economic growth, implicitly accepting the wider cultural influences that foreign investment and private enterprise bring, but has shown no enthusiasm for political reform.[2] If Japan's political parties may be described as coalitions representing diverse interests, it could be argued that as China's economic system becomes more pluralist, then there will be competing claims for political influence leading to wider representation at national level, a situation not dissimilar to that of Japan.

Nevertheless, attitudes to the Sino-Japanese relationship are ambivalent and on both sides motives for economic cooperation are mixed. In the 1960s and 1970s the Japanese, dependent on the United States nuclear umbrella, were used to having a so-called free ride on defence. But subsequently, as successive governments began to articulate a more independent role in the region and especially since the end of the cold war in the 1990s, a comprehensive security policy has been designed, involving diversification of sources of raw materials, energy and markets, thereby making East Asian countries dependent upon Japanese trade and investment. In the wake, too, of recession, at least partially derived from a downturn in Western markets and yen appreciation, the best option would appear to be intensified cooperation with economically dynamic Asian countries like China. Thus, especially at government but also at business levels, Japanese motives for increased investment in China are to a great extent a reflection of Japan's changing economic structure. As discussed below, Japanese government loans strengthen China's infrastructure, and industrial investors take advantage of cheap labour and tax incentives, particularly in the Special Economic Zones. Investment in China by Japanese industrialists has been fuelled by rising production costs at home in the wake of the yen appreciation; production bases abroad are being expanded so as to regain the competitive edge. In the 1980s, however, the Japanese companies were often accused of withholding advanced technology lest China be built up as their competitor in world markets. But latterly this policy has been changing, perhaps a tacit recognition that, because of advanced communication systems, the dissemination of technology knows no boundaries, while rivalry between corporations and regions is superseding that among nations. The arguments for further economic cooperation seem overwhelming, as reflected in Japanese government policy.[3]

The Chinese leaders for their part believe that Japanese investment input is indispensable for economic takeoff, itself a guarantee of national security and ultimately leadership in East Asia. Japan is the major desired partner by virtue of cultural affinity, geographical proximity and advanced technology. Their public stance is to stress a coalescence of social and international views; Jiang Zemin emphasised in April 1992 that of all 'Western' countries Japan shared a political language with China, and furthermore it was crucial for Japan to cooperate economically with China to sustain and extend its influence worldwide. Trade and scientific cooperation were thus conducive to the two countries' prosperity, and it was argued that Japan, as the most successful moderniser in the non-Western world over the last century, could act as a conduit for the introduction of market forces and concomitant Western managerial practices into China.[4]

To this end, in a statement targeted at Japanese businessmen, Jiang Zemin has promised to improve China's investment environment in order that foreign trade and economic cooperation with Japan, especially, may be encouraged and advanced management techniques absorbed. Two results of this policy may be cited. In August 1988 during the visit of then Japanese Prime Minister Takeshita to China the Chinese–Japanese Investment Protection Agreement was signed, by which Sino-Japanese joint ventures were to have legal and related rights similar to those enjoyed by Chinese enterprises. While these rights were later extended to all foreign-invested enterprises, the agreement was at the time unprecedented. Similarly, in 1990 a Chinese–Japanese Investment Promotion organisation was established, following a counterpart on the Japanese side. Yet according to the Chinese official view, no country should be allowed to impose its will or economic development model on others. The Sino-Japanese relationship was not exclusive; on the contrary, China should draw on technological and managerial expertise from a number of countries. Ultimately, however, *vis-à-vis* the Sino-Japanese relationship, the Chinese have more options than Japan. Certainly, in the short term, China could become more heavily dependent on Japanese capital and technology. But Japan is resource-poor, and in search of new markets, of which China is potentially the largest in Asia. It is possible, too, that Japan may become increasingly reliant on Chinese food imports, and in times of war it is vulnerable to naval blockade. The Chinese for their part seek to utilise Japanese capital and technology to enter the ranks of developed countries but they do have other alternatives in cooperation with Western countries.

In addition, once this status is achieved, the Chinese will be increasingly able to dictate the terms of economic cooperation with Japan.

China's investment priorities: infrastructure

Foreign investment in China reflects the priorities outlined in the Industrial Plan discussed earlier, as well as targets in the Eighth Five Year Plan (1991–5) and its ninth counterpart (1996–2000), a key feature of which is the reform and technological renovation of state enterprises in order to sell quality high-tech goods on world markets as China moves from policies of import substitution to an export orientation. To this end the Chinese aim to attract at least US$25 billion in foreign capital over the period 1992 to 1997, most of it directed at high-technology and service industries.[5] In October 1993 the State Planning Commission stated that incentives for foreign investment would not now be provided through regions such as the Special Economic Zones, which had in any case been originally set up as laboratories to test new economic policies before their introduction to the rest of China; now the targeting would be through broad categories of industries. In brief, investment was to be encouraged in six fields: (1) general agricultural development and technology relating thereto; (2) the development of infrastructure and mining; (3) petrochemicals, together with the key industries of the 1990s, automobile manufacture and construction; (4) technical renovation of existing factories; (5) companies exporting finished products of high added value; (6) projects relating to new technologies or new facilities using existing resources or recycled resources.[6]

A *sine qua non* of the successful absorption of foreign manufacturing investment is the creation of a viable infrastructure. But such development is normally beyond the capacity of private initiative and is essentially a central government enterprise only possible through state input, loans from foreign countries or aid from international organisations. It is in this area of indirect investment that the Japanese are playing a major role in China's economy and the extent of their contribution here may be contrasted with the relatively lower volume of Japan's direct investment, that is in manufacturing or services. It is to be noted that in the 1990s the bulk of direct investment in China has come from Hong Kong which in 1992 accounted for 60 per cent of the total while Japan was in third place with 7 per cent, preceded by Taiwan and followed by the United States and Germany. The caveat must, however, be entered that some investing Hong Kong companies were Japanese subsidiaries and so to that extent Japan's input may have been underestimated.[7] In contrast, Japan's indirect investment is much greater. At a national level and within a comparative perspective China has accepted loans from a number of countries and international organisations. In 1988 and 1989 between 41 and 42 per cent of loans to China came from Japan; in contrast, the World Bank's contribution was between 16 and 17 per cent. These two sources thus accounted for about 60 per cent of the total.[8] Similarly, it was estimated that as of early 1993 over half of all official aid to China came from Japan.[9]

The major conduit of Japanese loan aid to China has been the Overseas Economic Cooperation Fund (OECF) which now accounts for 60 per cent of Japan's total bilateral overseas development assistance. The OECF's long-term credit to borrowing countries is offered at more attractive rates and lenient terms than is the case with commercial loans. The average interest rate on OECF loans to China, for example, is 2.5 to 3.5 per cent, with repayment spread over thirty years, including a ten-year grace period. In theory, all OECF loans to China are untied, that is a company from any country can bid for any project, though, for reasons suggested later, Japan's companies are often advantaged.

The focus of OECF loans to China has been infrastructural development and, significantly, it is calculated that the share of foreign investment in China's expenditure in this field rose to 13 per cent in 1992 from an equivalent figure of 2 per cent in 1982, a trend likely to continue and concurring with the aid donor's overall policy.[10] There is little doubt that China's capacity to sustain its impressive double-digit annual growth is heavily dependent on ability to upgrade infrastructure. Contrary to the glowing national developmental image, much of China is extremely primitive; there is a dearth of good roads, railway and port facilities are antiquated, and civil aviation facilities are severely overstretched and have an unenviable safety record; consequently, trade and industrial growth are impeded. Moreover, China's economic growth as a whole is further hampered by energy shortages, exacerbated by the railway's inefficient transport of coal, and a technology-starved communications network. Aware that massive improvements in the transportation, communications and energy sectors are the *sine qua non* of global economic power status, the Chinese leaders have been continually opening infrastructural sectors to foreign bilateral and direct investment. The problem is that in the short term returns, especially for private investors, are minimal, and so further incentives will need to be provided. Transformation of China's infrastructure will thus take time and money. Analysts provide staggering estimates of financial needs. A Hong Kong source suggested that China would need at least US$233 billion between 1994 and 2000 to modernise its transportation, power and communications systems to keep pace with economic expansion. Estimated needs for modernisation of the power and communication sectors over the same time span are US$66 billion and US$56 billion respectively. In summary, infrastructural development will depend heavily on ability to attract foreign investment for key projects.

At both the state bilateral and private levels the government accordingly began inviting foreign investment for infrastructural projects as well as related technology and equipment to augment state-allocated funds.

Attention will now initially be directed towards bilateral loans. Japan's national motives have been briefly discussed and undoubtedly China's infrastructural development opens a huge market for Japan's suppliers for many years to come. That is why OECF funds have been targeted at China and East Asia generally. Nearly 80 per cent of OECF's cumulative commitments over the past twenty years have been extended to East and Southeast Asia. Although aid to the region may have declined in proportion to OECF total world aid in recent years, Asian countries still accounted for nearly 65 per cent of loan commitments in the early 1990s. China had received about US$8 billion in OECF loan commitments by December 1992, representing about 10 per cent of the agency's total disbursements, being second only to Indonesia's 19 per cent.[11] Additionally, the OECF was the largest foreign lender to China during the 1980s, providing more financing each year than either the World Bank or the Asian Development Bank. Since 1991, however, funds disbursed by the World Bank have exceeded those of the OECF.

To date China has received four main OECF loans, if that recently under negotiation is included. As indicated, in general the focus has been on infrastructural projects; when the Minister of International Trade and Industry visited Beijing in August 1992, for example, energy, environmental protection and technology transfer were noted as priorities, with Japanese financial and economic cooperation being offered in large-scale exploration of oil and natural gas resources in west China. Extensive bilateral governmental consultation has preceded each loan package.[12] The initial OECF loan package to China, the First Yen Credit, was launched in 1980. It provided US$7.43 billion, mostly to finance railway and port projects aimed at reducing coal transportation bottlenecks in Shandong and Shanxi provinces. The number of OECF-funded projects increased to seventeen under the terms of the Second Yen Credit, beginning in 1984. Several projects under this US$3.51 billion package have already been completed. Again, reflecting the priorities of the Seventh Five Year Plan (1986–90), concentration was on telecommunications, power, underground railway, and water supply projects. The Second Yen Credit has also proved a harbinger of the deregulation and opening up of the service sectors to foreign participation; among its projects was a scheme to install computer-driven price and information networks for Beijing, Shanghai, Guangzhou and other cities to assist the central government in designing an integrated economic planning system. IBM Japan, a wholly owned Japanese subsidiary, was a successful bidder on the tender to supply mainframe computers. IBM Japan is now a major supplier of computers to Japanese aid projects, demonstrating the opportunities that the knowledge garnered by aid agencies may bring to national companies. Under the Third Yen Credit the OECF pledged US$6.2 billion to fund forty-two projects between 1990 and 1995. The use of loans was negotiated bilaterally on an annual basis. In 1994, for example, loans were earmarked for fifteen projects in communications, the power industry and agriculture.[13]

The Fourth Yen Credit to China was being negotiated in 1994 and early 1995 and is likely to exceed the third in total moneys. In contrast with the annual timescale of the previous loans, a 'three plus two' plan was being proposed to break the previous five-year lending timescale into two parts. Under the new plan the two countries would first negotiate the project's lending volume for the first three years, with the lending schedule for the remaining two years being decided by talks on an annual basis. Given the developing pace of China's economy, the new schedule will enhance flexibility. The loan will cover the period of China's Ninth Five Year Plan and be focused on infrastructural development, agriculture and environmental protection. Significantly, in view of growing regional and personal wealth disparities, some of the moneys will be allocated to backward inland areas.[14]

A powerful feature of loan negotiation has been the rapport developed between the respective parties. There is regular contact between Chinese and Japanese leaders, as provided for under the conditions of the Long Term Trade Agreement. In addition, some such personal contacts between the Chinese and the Japanese date from the 1930s and reinforce Japanese knowledge of the general economic terrain. This kind of liaison has enabled the Japanese to become privy to the mechanisms and content of China's national planning, and consulting firms in Japan have advised China's officials about development programmes, albeit often informally. In this setting Japanese loans to China are channelled via the Chinese Ministry of Foreign Trade and Economic Cooperation (MOFTEC). Three corporations under the

Ministry, the China National Technical Import Corporation, the China National Machinery Import-Export Corporation and the China National Instruments Import-Export Corporation, usually handle the tenders for which private companies bid, coordinate the technical feasibility criteria and evaluate the bid documents. Bids are conducted through international competitive bidding practices and advertised in relevant publications like the *China Daily*. The Bank of China handles disbursement procedures and repayments.

In summary, Sino-Japanese official coordination facilitates the funding of developmental priorities, especially in sectors like transportation. For example, railway, road, bridge, port and airport projects make up thirty of the fifty-seven projects either completed or scheduled in China, accounting for over 50 per cent of the OECF's total lending to the country. Power projects are the next focus, absorbing 14 per cent of all OECF loans to China to date, while commodity loans and telecommunication projects occupy third and fourth places (see Table 3.1). These emphases are likely to continue.

Table 3.1 OECF lending to China: sector shares

1 Transportation	53.6%
2 Electric power and gas	13.0%
3 Commodity loans	10.3%
4 Telecommunications	7.4%
5 Financial-intermediary loans	5.6%
6 Agriculture	5.5%
7 Social Services	4.3%
8 Irrigation	0.3%

Source: Based on OECF (as of October 1992), as quoted in the *China Business Review*, May–June 1993, p.31

OECF loans, however, are not the only source of funding; indirect investment and other sources of Japanese official assistance will now be examined. For example, China has also benefited from Japanese government gratis aid amounting to US$880 million since 1980, and this has been used to improve agriculture, medicine, health care and the environment. In Guizhou Province, for example, a 1.5 billion Japanese yen gift for a water supply project has provided 1.06 million rural people with hygienic drinking water.[15]

Another agency, the Export-Import Bank of Japan, signed an agreement in early 1994 to provide up to US$500 million as an untied two-step loan to the Bank of China to finance industrial projects in Shandong and Hainan.[16] Japanese financial institutions have also collaborated with international lending organisations; in March 1994 it was announced that Japanese commercial banks, under the leadership of the Asian Development Bank, would channel US$380 million through the Bank of China to develop power stations and petrochemical production. Additionally, for similar objectives, the Bank of Tokyo has decided to participate in fifteen-year joint loans to the Chinese government totalling US$470 million and initiated by the World Bank.[17] Finally, the Chinese are increasingly having recourse to bond issues to finance development. In July 1994, for example, the Chinese launched two yen-denominated bond issues on the Japanese market. Worth about US$750 million in total, the bonds were intended for state-financed projects. Nomura and Daiwa Securities were to be the lead managers to sell the five- and ten-year Chinese government bonds on the Japanese market, with the Long Term Credit Bank of Tokyo acting as the chief commercial bank for Japanese investing in the bonds.[18]

Such capital projects can only be financed from the national exchequer and foreign indirect investment but the Chinese are nevertheless incurring a huge debt in consequence. In the past China's debt service ratio has been kept within internationally acceptable limits but the rise of the yen, from 100 to 85 against the dollar, in the early months of 1995 had substantially increased the value of the loans as well as the repayment burden.

The role of Japanese companies in infrastructural projects

For national security and sound economic reasons the Chinese leaders have been reluctant to allow foreign companies to enjoy any controlling stake in the running of infrastructure and public utilities. China's leaders have clearly stated a national policy that prohibits foreign investors from exclusively operating and controlling infrastructural projects that closely affect the lives of the Chinese people. China's Ministry of Power Industry, for instance, published in 1994 provisions stipulating that foreign investors are not permitted to have more than a 30 per cent equity interest in a power plant, regardless of whether they are buying into existing facilities or entering into a joint venture with a Chinese partner to build or operate a new one. Similar restrictions exist with regard to foreign investment in ports and wharfs. What the Chinese do favour, in order to retain national control of projects, is the build-operate-transfer (BOT) system. Under this system, the key issue is that of term-limits, given that infrastructural projects are notorious for only offering long-run returns on capital. A foreign investor entering into a cooperative joint venture with a Chinese partner has the right not only to construct and operate the infrastructural facility but also to use the underlying land required for operation. The local party is responsible for providing the land use, construction and operation rights, while the foreign partner coordinates the design, construction and financing of the facility. In most cases the funding consists of a mixture of equity capital and project finance.

There are certain advantages for the foreign partner in that during the contract term the cooperative joint venture company has the sole right to operate the facility and collect tolls or charges. Nevertheless, at the end of the cooperation period all rights and assets of the joint venture company together with the facilities are transferred to the Chinese partner at no cost. Thus the shorter the cooperation term, the less attractive the BOT investment is to the foreign investor. Clearly, greater incentives have to be offered to foreign partners.

Accordingly, in some cases, mainly wharf and highway projects, involving long construction periods, foreign investors have been allowed to build into their contracts provisions permitting the joint venture term to be extended, should a project not be completed on schedule and returns thereby deferred. Secondly, the Chinese have offered tax concessions in order to offset the statutory 12 to 15 per cent rate of return, that is the maximum profit permitted each year, expressed as a percentage of total investment in a project, a level considered low by foreign investors. Such concessions must also compensate for the fact that the Chinese actually dictate the rate of return through their control over prices of fuel, raw materials and other inputs, as well as state direction of public utilities. Preferential tax treatment, then, applies, and investors in infrastructure are allowed to collect a return on total investment, that is registered capital plus loans, and are also permitted to deduct principal payments from taxable income, thus facilitating a higher rate of profit. The third incentive is term length, which varies according to the diverse categories of infrastructural projects. For road joint ventures, for instance, the maximum is thirty years from the date of establishment, not when the highway is actually opened. In contrast, coal-fired power plants are limited to twenty years while their hydroelectric counterparts are given thirty years, rationale in these cases being that where the fundamental interests of the Chinese public are affected, foreign investors should be given a long enough term as an incentive to invest but not so long that they have no inducement to cut costs and raise efficiency.[19] A number of sectors where the participation of Japanese companies has been significant will now be analysed.

Japanese companies and the energy sector

The energy sector is a prime example of where deficiencies in infrastructure have the potential to impede economic growth. In fact, of course, China's energy shortages are due to the ambitious economic policies pursued since 1978 and, if such accelerated growth continues, the chances are that demand for coal and oil will be increasingly difficult to meet. In a post-1949 context the Chinese have been heavily dependent on coal for power generation. In terms of tonnage of energy produced in 1980, coal accounted for 69 per cent, oil for 24 per cent, natural gas for 3 per cent, and hydroelectric power for 4 per cent; by 1991 the share of coal had risen to 74 per cent and hydroelectric power to 5 per cent, while that of oil had dropped to 19 per cent and natural gas to 2 per cent. Most coal is produced in state-run mines but the industry as a whole suffers from rising construction costs, a slow pace of mechanisation, a lack of funds, rigid price structures and, perhaps crucially, an overburdened transportation system. Clearly, greater coalmine efficiency is necessary to raise productivity, and technology has been sought from, for instance, Japan, Great Britain and Germany. But coal alone cannot satisfy the increasing demands of transportation and economic development in general, and the energy battle must be fought on a number of fronts.

From the early 1960s China's oil production gradually grew, and has accelerated since 1978, consumption surging because of greater use of cars, the development of industries like petrochemicals and renewed emphasis on mechanisation in agriculture. Simultaneously, China's main domestic oilfields which went into operation in the 1960s and 1970s are now entering the later stages of stable yields, and new sites have yet to be brought into full production. Given increasing oil consumption in the wake of economic restructuring, the Chinese leadership has embarked on intensified exploration and development, through foreign investment.[20]

The logic discussed earlier concerning government control over infrastructure in general applies with special force to the petroleum sector. As a result, China's leaders have only reluctantly and slowly allowed foreign participation in oil prospecting. It will be some time, however, before new fields come on stream, and meanwhile shortfalls have to be made up by imports requiring precious foreign exchange. In fact, the leadership may well become resigned to increasing oil imports; as suggested above, energy shortages are the penalty for economic success and are a mandate for the deregulation of the sector. Foreign analysts have estimated that each percentage increase in gross domestic product (GDP) leads to a corresponding 0.7 per cent increase in the consumption of oil products. Domestic production cannot keep pace with consumption. Moreover, to gain the market advantage, China has since the 1970s been exporting petroleum, especially to Japan. All omens point to the need for rapid development of domestic production to satisfy domestic demand, reduction in imports and promotion of exports.

The Chinese leaders' strategy is to develop new fields and through technological renovation to enhance oil recovery on existing sites. Recognition of the industry's need for capital and technology has led the government to expand the number of areas in which foreigners may explore. Optimism about prospects is reflected in the increasing number of exploration contracts signed in 1993 and 1994.

Development of petroleum resources in China, however, rests on a very narrow base. The oldest fields at Daqing in northeast China date from the early 1960s. Most oil has come from the northeast but in the 1980s and 1990s output increases have fallen drastically. By the early 1980s the sector was being opened to Western and Japanese capital and technology, without the Chinese government surrendering overall control over the industry. To these ends a new organisation, the China National Offshore Oil Corporation (CNOOC), was established in 1982, mainly to oversee exploration of offshore sites, to which foreign companies were initially restricted. During the 1980s and 1990s CNOOC has conducted a number of bidding rounds, driving a hard bargain by which foreign concerns bear exploration costs and any fields are jointly developed with CNOOC. While most contracts have to date been concluded with American companies, the Japanese stake is increasing, both offshore and onshore, as examples below will indicate.

The first areas open for bidding were in the South China Sea. Though initial results were disappointing, several oil and gas fields are now in production. A number of fields successfully prospected there through cooperation between Chevron, Texaco and the Italian company AGIP will now be exploited by CNOOC under US$56 million loan funding from five Japanese banks.[21] Recent bidding has centred on the Bohai Gulf and the South China Sea. The Bohai Gulf already produces over 1 million tons of oil per year, mainly from CNOOC's own wells, but Texaco, British Petroleum and the Japanese National Oil Company are now involved in the area's exploitation and development. Moreover, in August 1992 the Japan–China Oil Development Corporation signed two contracts to explore sections of the northern Bohai Sea. In addition, the Sino-Japanese Bohzong oilfield in Bohai Bay has been in operation since 1990. Offshore production, then, is a long-term prospect but it is likely that onshore sites, especially in new sectors, will provide most of China's oil production in the foreseeable future.

Given declining production at existing fields like Daqing, Shengli and Liaohe, the Chinese, in a departure from tradition, decided to open a number of areas in south China to foreign participation in 1985. In 1991 the Japanese National Oil Corporation signed an agreement to explore for oil in southern Jiangsu Province. But the most promising onshore region would appear to be the Tarim Basin in the western province of Xinjiang, in spite of inaccessible terrain and a lack of transportation infrastructure. In 1993 the Chinese initiated the first rounds of bidding for sites in the Tarim Basin; previously, Japan's National Oil Corporation had won the right to survey but exploration was still denied to foreign companies. The first award for exploration, announced in December 1993, was given to a consortium led by Esso-China (EXXON) which included Sumitomo Corporation and the Japanese-owned Indonesia Petroleum Limited. In February 1993 Texaco, together with Agip, Elf, the Japan Energy Corporation and Japan Petroleum Exploration, won rights to explore further sectors of the Tarim Basin.[22] Similarly, a further Tarim contract, signed in December 1993 by China's National Petroleum and National Gas Corporation (CNPNGC), Esso of the United States and the Japan–Indonesia Petroleum Company Limited, under Sumitomo Commercial Company Limited of Japan, covered prospecting over a 72,000 square kilometre area. The contract period is eight years, during which the foreign companies will bear the entire cost and risks of exploration. Upon discovery of oil, the parties will undertake joint production and share the product in proportion to the capital investment of each contributor. The above are the first onshore petroleum contracts concluded through international bidding, and are representative of the strategy to develop western oil resources, formally adopted in early 1994.[23] Finally, Japanese companies are already active in China's downstream petroleum sector; in this connection may be cited Mitsui Corporation's joint venture with a state oil subsidiary in Tianjin, and Itochu International is involved with Chisso (Japan) and the Shanghai Petrochemical Company Limited to establish a plastics and resin plant, both agreements having been signed in 1993.

It may be concluded that, as the Japanese import nearly all their oil, a stake in China's petroleum industry may well prove a long-term asset.

Environmental protection

Environmental protection is another infrastructural sector in which Japanese aid agencies and private companies have taken a long-term perspective, providing assistance and winning contracts which benefit both Chinese and Japanese industries alike. Environmental protection, of course, knows no national boundaries, and since the 1980s the two countries have cooperated within the overall context of Northeast Asia as well as in China itself. Japanese government loans have, for instance, financed clean drinking water projects in the eastern province of Guizhou during the period from 1991 to 1994.[24] The main focus of Japanese government environmental aid to China has nevertheless been industrial. So often it is developed countries which speak stridently about the evils of pollution, while developing nations are more immediately concerned with economic growth at whatever cost. Various pressures, however, have led to Chinese consciousness of environmental dangers. As discussed in the previous section, Chinese officials have been under strong pressure to increase power generation capacity to meet growing demand. Over the next decade China plans to build as many as a hundred new power plants, most of which will be coal-fired. Unfortunately, due to capital constraints, officials have not been able to insist on high-cost flue gas desulphurisation systems which can reduce pollution. But the Japanese are currently adapting technology which developing countries like China can afford. Support of environmental protection through bilateral assistance is a new departure for Japan in China; during the 1980s most OECF funding was being directed to other infrastructure projects.

In the 1990s this situation began to change. Three factors were catalysts for new Japanese policies to assist China's environmental protection: greater consciousness of need on the part of the Chinese, thereby making it easier for the Japanese to designate funds for particular projects; the lure of future business opportunities for Japanese companies; and, finally, China's growing use of coal increased the threat of acid rain.

Since 1991 Japanese government support for environmental research, through the Overseas Development Assistance (ODA) programme and the MITI, has proceeded on two fronts: long-term training to develop human resources and technology transfer. Once again the time-honoured close relationship between the Japanese government and business comes into operation.

There are two major sources of training for Chinese environmental experts. In 1991 the Japanese announced the establishment of the Japan–China Friendship Environmental Protection Centre in Beijing, financed by Japan's ODA, where members of Japan's Environmental Protection Agency are to train Chinese provincial officials. This will in turn aid the transfer and commercialisation of cleaner and more efficient technologies which are being developed under the auspices of MITI's Green Aid Plan, which began operating in 1992. MITI in this way sponsors demonstration projects throughout China in order to enhance the energy efficiency of large consumers like steel plants, thereby reducing sulphur emissions. A key role under the Green Aid Plan is also played by industrial associations like the Japan Society of Industrial Machinery Manufacturers and the Japan Iron and Steel Federation: they assist in negotiations with the Chinese government and liaise with China's officials over specific needs, thereby developing strong personal networks in the country as a whole. Moreover, in representing member companies, they coordinate training visits for Chinese engineers, dispatch Japanese personnel to China and provide detailed information about relevant technologies.

These programmes advantage both parties. The Chinese are being offered a range of affordable intermediate technologies. Whether those technologies are further developed in China in coming years will be greatly dependent on OECF loans. The benefits accruing to Japanese companies are manifold: the costs and risks associated with adaptation and testing are underwritten by aid moneys, and such projects also offer the possibility of long-term partnerships with Chinese domestic manufacturers. There is also the prospect that joint ventures and licensing agreements may result.

The scenario as a whole will undoubtedly aid Japanese exports in the long run, especially where there is competitive bidding. OECF loans to China are untied and thus open to international competition; the systems developed in China through the Green Aid Plan, however, could give Japanese firms and their local partners a significant price advantage in future bids. Moreover, this MITI source of funding is secure and long term.

In summary, then, Japan's aid not only stands to benefit the environment in China and Northeast Asia as a whole but provides Chinese manufacturers with low-cost technology which can be utilised for both Chinese domestic markets and those of other developing countries. In turn, Japanese companies whose technology is used for the manufacture of such environment-related equipment are likely to reap handsome dividends. Once again, as in other markets, the Japanese seek an early presence to guarantee a long-term market share.[25]

Other sectors

Energy and environment are not, of course, the only sectors where Japanese participation is growing. A number of other sectors will now be briefly covered. China plans to spend about US$6 billion in developing ports and waterways in the next five years. In the early 1990s this sector was opened to foreign investment; overseas companies can now invest in and help manage joint ventures in the construction of wharfs and ports, and in certain cases wholly owned enterprises are allowed to operate waterways. The Japanese appear to be in the vanguard; loans from the OECF, as well as from the World Bank and the Asian Development Bank, have been given to the Chinese government for port and berth construction at Qinhuangdao, Dalian, Tianjin, Shijiazhuang, Shanghai, Ningbo, Lianyungang, Xiamen and Guangzhou.[26] Port development is now heavily dependent on Japanese aid financing, as is air traffic control equipment. In addition, other parts of the transport sector are receiving Japanese input. China's railways are operating beyond their capacity, carrying 70 per cent of the country's freight and 60 per cent of its passengers. Notably, in September 1994 a delegation from the Japan–China Association of Economy and Trade, a Japanese official economic group devoted to business relations, agreed to provide technical and financial support to China's US$8 billion bullet train project.[27]

Another major growth area is telecommunications where competition for market share is intense. The sector is relatively undeveloped, which to some degree hinders international business transactions. China, for instance, has 1.6 telephones per hundred inhabitants, as compared to an equivalent figure of 60 per hundred in the United States. The focal point of competition is the switching sector; the government is expanding and modernising its telephone exchanges by installing stored programme computers to replace the older electromechanical equipment. But in return for a share of the market the Chinese are demanding semiconductor lines; consequently the major Japanese player in this field in China, the Nippon Electric Corporation (NEC), is producing semiconductors in a joint venture at the state-run Capital Iron and Steel Plant in Beijing. While it does not yet have a large share of the market, NEC is one of the few foreign companies engaged in a joint venture in China to manufacture switching equipment.[28] The above treatment of infrastructure is in no way exhaustive but the investments selected are indicative of the Japanese stake in China's economy. Needless to say, development of such sectors is vital to China's economic expansion, and Japanese investment and participation in management may well dictate choices in favour of Japanese products in the years to come.

Summary: Japan's indirect investment and secrets of success

There is no doubt that through indirect investment the Japanese are well placed to take full advantage of market opportunities in China. Even though the OECF operates an open bidding system there, Japanese companies have fared well. There has been a number of successful Japanese bids in, for example, reservoir development. During the period from 1983 to 1993 Japanese companies claimed about 35 per cent of the contracts awarded for projects in China. Chinese firms won 29 per cent, followed by those of Hong Kong (13 per cent), the United States (3 per cent), France (1 per cent) and Germany (1 per cent) during the same period, with the remainder going to companies based elsewhere. Japan's share may again have been underestimated, however, as a number of contracts were won by Japanese subsidiaries in China.[29]

The secrets of Japanese success lie in effective reconnaissance. The two peoples share a historical perspective and, as mentioned earlier, the personal relationships among officials from both countries, developed over time, have given the Japanese insights into Chinese planning mechanisms and economic priorities. These have been invaluable for exploiting indirect investment to Japan's advantage. Japanese companies seeking contracts have been aided by excellent marketing intelligence. The sogoshosha or trading companies which help to organise consortia for aid projects in developing countries have extensive experience of international commerce. Japan's commercial representative offices, like embassies, are staffed by personnel fluent in the Chinese language and conversant with Chinese culture. Such is not always true of Western operations in China. Japan's indirect investment has thus benefited Japanese manufacturers, and created an environment conducive to economic growth. Against this background, Japanese direct investment in manufacturing and services in China is set to accelerate.

General overview: Japan's direct investment in China's manufacturing industries

Since the initiation of the open door policy China's officialdom has sought to provide a setting conducive to successful foreign direct investment. Perhaps a measure of success is the fact that China now absorbs about half of all such investment to developing countries worldwide.[30] Since the early 1990s there has been a number of changes in Chinese policy, the first being a shift from management of foreign investment by region to targeting by industry. In the 1980s, for instance, Special Economic Zones, like Shenzhen, were established to attract overseas companies by offering tax and other incentives, and the relevant local authorities were given devolved powers which have subsequently also been extended elsewhere in China. While such policies stimulated economic growth, they have also increased regional and social inequalities. The leadership consequently now favours more balanced economic development over the country as a whole. Meanwhile, other factors have been militating against a regionally focused policy; the zones, especially those in the southeast, are often focused on light industries but China has now reached the stage where the engine of growth, particularly in the context of an export orientation, demands re-emphasis on basic and heavy industries, the traditional geographical bases of which lie elsewhere.

Thus concrete steps are now being taken to encourage investment in particular industries. Additionally, hitherto many Sino-foreign joint ventures have been with private and collective enterprises. But now overseas cooperation is being sought in the state enterprise sector where a major priority, heavy industry, is concentrated. Chinese leaders are no doubt mindful of the argument that, even under a joint stock system, foreign input may be more amenable to state control than it is under purely private enterprise. In line with these industrial priorities, the authorities announced a policy shift in 1993: foreign multinationals with industrial expertise would now be encouraged through allowing them to set up branches, and thus more integrated operations, within China. They were at the same time to be given the opportunity to balance foreign currency flows among their constituent companies, facilitating domestic sales. The Japanese trading company, C. Itoh, was one of thirty major companies, including Philips and IBM, which had secured permission to set up operations as of 1994. These measures are an integral part of opening up the domestic market to China-based foreign manufacturers; in the 1980s they were obliged to export most, if not all, of their products. In addition, to ensure more balanced development nationally, the hinterland regions are being opened up and this in itself will help to create a unified market, as the distribution system is reformed. As a further incentive, therefore, foreign concerns are being permitted to invest in tertiary sectors like retailing, although wholesaling as yet remains closed to them. The promise of a domestic market for both producer and consumer goods is indicated by China's impressive economic performance; from 1978 to 1993 China registered an annual GNP growth of 9.29 per cent and average annual increases of per capita income for city dwellers and peasants of 6.34 per cent and 8.47 per cent respectively, after offsetting commodity price factors.[31]

Foreign investment in China over the years since 1979 will now be evaluated. In 1992, for example, China received a total of about US$58 billion in direct investment on a contract basis (4.9 times more than the previous year) for 48,764 projects (an increase of 3.8 times), and about US$11 billion on an implemented basis (2.5 times more). Investment was accelerating, as the number and value of the projects contracted for exceeded even the cumulative total for the period from 1979 to 1991. The size of the investment per project also grew, the average value of a contract in 1992 being US$1.19 million as compared to an equivalent figure of US$920,000 for the previous year. This trend towards larger-scale investment is likely to continue, given official encouragement of heavy industry and foreign multinationals, especially as since 1993 the latter have been allowed to set up branches in China. During the period from 1979 to 1993 the top four direct investors were Hong Kong (including Macao), Taiwan, the United States and Japan. Ranked by contract value, Hong Kong was the largest source of investment. But whereas investment from Hong Kong had tended to be small in size and concentrated regionally in Guangdong Province, in 1992 there was a trend towards input into inland areas and an increase in the number of large-scale projects. Similarly, Taiwan has been diversifying the location of its investment, with emphasis shifting from the south of China to the Yangtze River basin and the north. A survey by the ROC (Taiwan) Straits Exchange Foundation showed that investment by Taiwanese companies in the Shanghai region had soared from 108 companies as of July 1991 to 300 as of the end of December 1992. Major investment projects launched by United States companies included Motorola for semiconductors and cellular telephones, IBM for software development, and General Motors for small-sized trucks. These trends were also apparent in the activities of Japanese multinationals which were increasingly focusing on Shanghai and northeast China.[32]

A general picture of the extent of the investment discussed above appears in Table 3.2.

Table 3.2 Direct overseas investment in China: the top ten investors, 1979–1993

	Country	Number of projects	Pledged investment US$ billion
1	Hong Kong/Macao	114,147	150.9
2	Taiwan	20,982	18.46
3	United States	12,019	14.6
4	Japan	7,812	8.9
5	Singapore	3,122	4.8
6	United Kingdom	616	3.3
7	Thailand	1,399	2.1
8	Canada	1,540	1.8
9	Germany	569	1.4
10	Australia	1,309	1.2

Source: *Financial Times*, 7 November 1994

In this overview of foreign direct investment, which is playing a key role in boosting industrial output and enhancing the diversity and quality of exports, more detailed attention will now be given to the Japanese manufacturing presence according to location, size and industrial sector.

While relative to total foreign direct investment Japan's share fell from 6.8 per cent in 1991 to 3.7 per cent in 1992, in absolute terms there was considerable growth. On a value basis, Japan's investment in China is second only to its stake in Indonesia, as of the early 1990s. China's share in Japan's overall investment in Asia rose from 9.8 per cent in fiscal year 1991 to 16.5 per cent in 1992.

By location, according to Chinese statistics, Japanese investment is heavily concentrated in a number of major cities. At the end of 1992 the major site for Japanese companies was Dalian in northeast China with 394 ventures worth US$1,186 million. Japanese manufacturers have commented favourably on Dalian's infrastructure and the willingness of the city authorities to cooperate with foreign investors. In fact, this enthusiasm on the part of the local authorities has been encouraged by China's national leaders. Dalian might eventually become a new Hong Kong. With the assistance of MITI, many companies have been cooperating in the creation of the Dalian Industrial Park, construction of which began in October 1992. The park is a thirty-year project and an integral part of a Special Economic Zone. This is the first time that the Japanese government has been involved in a joint venture of this kind with China and the park has a high financial contribution from Japan's OECF, in addition to moneys from the Dalian local government and Japanese companies like Marubeni and Mitsubishi. The northeast will undoubtedly become a major focus of Japanese investment in coming decades.[33]

Reference was briefly made to the Chinese leaders' policy of balanced national development and there is evidence to suggest that Shanghai and its rapidly growing Pudong Zone may have been conceived of as a counterweight to the zones of the south, as it is nearer to Beijing and possibly more amenable to control by the central authorities. In any case, long a major industrial centre, Shanghai has attracted US$810 million of investment from Japan in 339 ventures. Japanese input in other areas of the north is as follows: 340 ventures in Beijing worth US$121 million and 262 in Tianjin worth US$367 million. Finally, the Japanese have staked US$555 million in 183 ventures in the Special Economic Zone of Shenzhen in southeast China. Given the pace of change, any figures are soon outdated, but the references above do give some idea of trends in Japanese investment which is now being more heavily concentrated in north China.[34] At the same time, however, Chinese sources note Japanese interest in hinterland cities like Chongjing, Wuhan and Xian, in line with Chinese official policies.[35]

It will be seen from Table 3.2 that Japanese investment is small compared to that of Hong Kong and Taiwan. Significantly, however, it looms larger than such figures would suggest in certain cities like Shanghai, where Japan's companies accounted for 14 per cent of projects and 19 per cent of total value as of mid-1993. Equivalent figures for Beijing were 14 per cent of the projects and 19 per cent of the value.[36] In addition, in Dalian Japanese investment accounted for 36 per cent of the projects and 46 per cent of the value.

These figures partially reflect the size of Japanese investors and their investment. Prior to the mid-1990s Japanese investors were predominantly small and medium-sized companies. Thus, in the post-1978 context, initially most Japanese input went into small enterprises with low technology, high-technology and large enterprises being largely neglected.[37] In a questionnaire conducted by one writer in 1989 and 1990, among eighty-two Japanese-invested enterprises that gave detailed replies, the investment value was less than US$4 million, and these accounted for 74.4 per cent of the total. The average amount for each investment project was only US$1.5 million. Thus, in summary, there were few large-scale investment projects, most of the enterprises being medium sized or small.[38] But large corporations are now moving into manufacturing in China. Certainly, the latter have been hesitant because the greater the outlay, the greater the risk. One pacesetter, however, has been the Fujian-Hitachi Company, a joint venture set up in 1981 to manufacture television sets; it is now moving into videos, cameras and semiconductors on site in China. Moreover, in tandem with trends in location and size, Japanese investment is increasingly shifting from a labour-intensive to a high-tech focus. In this connection one Chinese source praised Japanese companies for their transfer of technology to China.[39]

There is thus a wide range of Japanese companies manufacturing in China through some kind of joint venture or wholly owned concern. It must be remembered, too, that a company may engage in a number of separate ventures. The list provided in Table 3.3 is not exhaustive but demonstrates the ongoing trends suggested above. It will be noted that suppliers of electrical machinery are the top investors, followed by food, textile and chemical companies. The categories, of course, reflect movement in China's consumer markets, particularly for durable goods.

Amidst the hyperbole relating to the large number of contracts being signed by the Chinese with foreign investors and the improving

Table 3.3 Number of Japanese corporations in China, by industry

Category	Total number of companies	Cases of investment with more than 50 per cent Japanese capital participation
Electrical machinery	36	24
Precision investments	9	8
Automobiles	7	1
Machinery	6	4
Electric wires	2	2
Non-ferrous metals	2	1
Steel	5	1
Fisheries	6	2
Foodstuffs	17	3
Chemicals	13	6
Textiles	15	8
Rubber tyres	1	0
Other manufacturing industries	3	1
Construction	10	7
Distribution	6	2
Commerce	6	4
Trading companies	36	5
Total	180	79

Source: Yamaichi Research, *Japan Outlook*, July 1992, pp. 13–15. Reproduced by kind permission Yamaichi Research Institute (Europe) Limited

Notes: 1 Total number of companies represents the number of locally incorporated companies.
2 Cases of investments with more than 50% Japanese participation are locally incorporated companies with more than 50% ownership held by Japanese interests.
3 These are listed or over-the-counter companies.
4 As of March 1992.

environment in China, a distinction must be made between agreements and their actual implementation. Significantly, during 1993 it was estimated that about three-quarters of investment contracts entered into in China by small and medium-sized Japanese enterprises were implemented. There is also a high rate of profitability among Japanese concerns.[40] A questionnaire survey conducted by the Japan–China Investment Promotion Organisation in late 1992 shows that 73.5 per cent of Japanese investors in China were making profits, a number having recently moved from deficit to profit. The trading company,

Itochu, for example, stated that, as of November 1994, of its forty-three companies in China, only two were in the red.[41]

In conclusion, the foregoing suggests that, as the investment environment improves, China will become an increasingly important manufacturing base for Japanese companies. Japan's investment seems set to accelerate in coming years, with the further opening of the Chinese domestic market and the now permitted repatriation of profits. The motives of Japanese companies investing in China and their participation in the country's priority industries are the subject of the following section.

Investment in China's automobile industry: Japanese motives and Chinese incentives

In general, the main motives for Japanese investment in Asian countries, especially China, are the availability of cheap, though increasingly better-educated, labour, and the opportunity to target a growing domestic market, particularly because of greater discretionary income as living standards rise. In addition, in the case of China, Japanese investors in manufacturing will benefit from improved physical infrastructure, effected at least partially by Japanese loans. Since the 1980s the value of the yen has been rising, making Japan's exports problematic. But whereas Japan's investment moves in the European Community, into, say, automobiles and electronics, were prompted by protectionist barriers in mature markets, China's demand is nascent and Japanese manufacturers are keen to bid early against Western rivals. An added incentive has been that in other parts of Asia like Taiwan and Hong Kong higher wages have made production there less attractive to Japan's companies.[42]

The Chinese for their part seek cooperation in developing their priority industries, as existing state concerns lack both advanced technical and marketing skills. It is not intended, of course, that such foreign-invested ventures dominate infant industries like automobiles but that they act as models and pacesetters for reform of state concerns. To this end a number of macroeconomic measures have been taken to provide incentives and a more predictable environment for foreign investors. A case in point is China's new Company Law, passed in 1994, which, in targeting multinationals, contains a section entitled 'Branches of Foreign Companies'. This, in principle, permits a foreign company to establish on Chinese soil a branch office which can conduct a wide range of business activities. This could facilitate major investment by international firms; hitherto Chinese law has only allowed representative offices which may not engage in direct sales, marketing, post-sales service or direct investment projects, most of which have had to be set up as isolated ventures that need to survive without help from their parent company. A second significant departure is provision for the establishment of joint stock companies which issue stock to be sold at stock exchanges rather than as shares to be held by a limited number of shareholders. The majority of a joint stock company's promoters must be residents of China.[43] Stocks and shares are listed on the Shanghai Securities Exchange, which was opened in 1990 and mainly deals to finance large state enterprises, and the Shenzhen Stock Exchange, open since 1991, and generally focused on joint venture companies. Both are regulated by the Securities Supervision Commission. Notably, for one category, B shares, traded for foreign currency, dividends are issued in United States or Hong Kong dollars; they may be purchased by foreign investors, even though companies seeking to list such shares must receive approval from the People's Bank of China. The caveat must nevertheless be entered that foreign investors will still be inhibited from investing, especially in China's state enterprises, because of the lack of solid financial data, documentation falling far short of international standards, although the central government is likely to issue regulations conforming to world practice.[44] China's leaders hope that these markets will become a major source of capital for state enterprises. In summary, new company legislation and the activities of the two main stock exchanges are designed to facilitate the transformation of state enterprises through the medium of foreign funding; equally, foreign-invested enterprises are the pacesetters for these reforms.

Additional measures are also intended to sustain foreign interest. Since the 1980s company and income taxes have been evolving. Firstly, in 1983 in order to encourage investment flows, the Chinese signed a double taxation agreement with Japan. More importantly, however, in 1994 a new tax law made foreign and domestic enterprises subject to the same tax regime. Nevertheless, certain concessions to foreign enterprises remained; the new value added tax, one of the measures, replacing the old Consolidated Industrial and Commercial Tax, retains a number of exemptions previously enjoyed by foreign business. For example, equipment imported by foreign ventures and used to process materials under a processing contract are exempt, as are exports thereby produced.[45] Again, new income tax rules, effective from 1 January 1994, abolished previous rate differentials between foreign and local employees, and there is now a unified schedule applicable to both categories. Nevertheless, certain concessions remain; for instance, foreign employees are now entitled to an allowance of 4,000 yuan before their salaries are taxed, while the equivalent for Chinese employees is 800 yuan.[46]

Finally, one of the great areas of contention between the Chinese authorities and foreign investors since 1978 has been the remission of foreign exchange derived from commercial operations. The above-cited legislation relating to the operation of branches by multinationals may facilitate the sending of profits abroad, given the requirement of China's foreign exchange regulations that expenditure incurred in the importation of, say, raw materials for manufacture be balanced by revenue accruing from exported goods.[47]

It is against this background of growing concessions to foreign manufacturing investors that Japanese investment in China's automobile industry will be examined. Further development of automobile production is one of the priorities of the Eighth Five Year Plan, basic policy being for domestic manufacturers to make commercial vehicles like trucks while joint ventures with foreign makers are targeted at passenger cars. Previously, such manufacturing took place in a number of state enterprises but now production is to be increased in cooperation with foreign companies. Following Japanese precedents in other industries during economic takeoff in the 1960s, the automobile sector is being treated as an infant industry and, as such, worthy of initial protection against foreign competition; this amounts also to a policy of import substitution which is designed ultimately to facilitate the creation of an export industry. Thus in 1986 the Chinese imposed a system of import licences, quotas and high tariff rates on foreign-made vehicles. In 1994, for example, tariff ratios on passenger cars amounted to 220 per cent, among the highest in the world, although compatibility with the World Trade Organisation will demand gradual reduction of such penalties. The goal is to develop a competitive domestic industry although government support will mean shielding domestic producers from competition rather than restriction of foreign investment. In fact, as shown later in this section, it is through foreign participation that technology and resources are sought. In this way during the next decade emphasis will be placed on improving the efficiency of existing technology and the quality of existing products; an entirely domestically developed car will probably not appear in China until 2010.

The major stress then is on economic efficiency; China's car industry, mainly though not exclusively devoted to commercial vehicles in the pre-1978 period, was, like state enterprises in other sectors, sheltered by a seller's market. The Ministry of Machine Building Industry, the State Administration of Building Materials and the China National

Automotive Industry Corporation, under whose jurisdiction the car industry falls, have targeted joint ventures and technology transfer accords with Western component manufacturers to realise this aim.

A major impediment to efficiency, another legacy of the command economy, is the large number of manufacturers, all under state control but concentrated in a number of regions. The government intends to focus funding on a small number of large producers of automobiles in the state sector; the existing 120 or so factories will be reorganised into eight to ten major companies by the year 2000 and three or four corporate groups by the year 2010. Automobile production is to be concentrated in ten localities across the country. The industry will produce low-priced, mass market-orientated small cars, 3 million vehicles being the target by the year 2000.

In accordance with this policy of inducing efficiency, in 1986 the government invited foreign investment. By the early 1990s there were many European, American and Japanese companies producing a wide range of vehicles, including minicars, sedans, vans, buses and heavy trucks. In addition to equity investment, the foreign companies' contribution lies in technology and management knowhow, and they help to change corporate culture towards efficiency, low cost and quality. Based on joint ventures with foreign companies, the main producers are Changchun Audi, Shanghai Santana (Volkswagen) and Hubei Citroën, which each target an annual production of 300,000 cars by the year 2000. In addition, Beijing Jeep (Chrysler), Guangzhou Peugeot and Tianjin Charade (Daihatsu) each aim at annual production approaching 100,000 cars by the year 2000. The Japanese role is greatest in minicars, where Suzuki Motor of Japan, in partnership with Chang'an Equipment and Fuji Heavy Industries, aims at a yearly output of 100,000 vehicles of 1000cc engine displacement. The above-mentioned companies are currently the largest car producers in China and by 1992 were responsible for the bulk of output of such vehicles.

Specifically, such cooperation sought to address the following problems. Despite efforts at standardisation, productivity and quality vary across the country, and economies of scale are still being impeded by the dispersion of resources mentioned above. The Ministries also lack staff trained in research and development and in advanced production management techniques. Foreign investment is thus playing a role not only in enhancing quality and productivity but also in improving personnel management. The need, of course, is also to disseminate such expertise across China's car industry as a whole.

The presence of foreign investment and technology has wide-ranging implications for employment and diffusion of skills. A common complaint concerning Japanese investment in Europe in such sectors as car manufacture and electronics has been that only assembly operations are introduced, components being sourced in Japan, with local parts makers consequently damaged. This is why, of course, a number of European countries, with support in the European Commission, have insisted upon high levels of local components before the products of such Japanese ventures can be considered saleable in other countries of the Union without the addition of tariffs. Similarly, the Chinese, while maintaining tight control of vehicle imports, have sought to boost local content of vehicles made in China. To protect an infant industry, the Chinese authorities require domestic producers to include a minimum amount of local materials and value-added work in their final product. China's goals are even more ambitious than, for example, Europe's: all domestic producers assembling finished cars are expected to achieve 80 per cent local content within eight years of production, the objective being to force producers to buy materials and parts on the local market, thereby facilitating synergies and aiding supporting industries in China.

From foreign partners' points of view, however, there is the stated objection that quality and safety of components do not reach international standards. The technical progress of local component manufacturers has been impeded by captive customer–supplier relationships, a remnant of the old state-planned command economy. Because of bureaucratic and infrastructural barriers each vehicle maker developed its own circle of parts producers; consequently the parts industry became fragmented, with a large number of producers offering similar parts, none of which met international standards. As the resulting local supply networks were monopolies, competition was stifled, effective market size was limited, inefficient production perpetuated and high costs maintained. Sino-foreign car manufacturing joint ventures have thrown the inadequacy of supplier–customer relationships into sharp relief: because vehicle manufacturers do not buy outside captive networks, they are increasingly unable to satisfy not only quality but quantity of parts. In response, the Chinese are initiating measures to revamp the components industries, thus providing opportunities for foreign partners to bring their own suppliers to China. In the very short term this may prove crucial, as localisation of parts is necessarily slow because passenger cars require high-quality, value-added and complex components. Nevertheless, China operates a supplier qualification process which takes time, especially for overseas parts makers; consequently, Daihatsu, for instance, maintains a formal policy of two suppliers per component, one captive and one external. In 1993 the

Japanese company's locally sourced imports reached a value of 47 per cent. Increasingly, there are also Sino-foreign joint ventures in China's components industry, cases in point being Japanese input in the Shanghai Xiaoxi Automobile Lights Company Limited and the Xiamen Liyang Industrial Company Limited which produces cylinder liners. In short, then, the passenger car sector still relies primarily, though not exclusively, on imported parts, although by 1994 the Chinese were requesting Japan's investment in sectors such as pistons, engine valves and hydraulic equipment.

In summary, foreign, including Japanese, car manufacturers, have been attracted by the prospect of a huge potential Chinese domestic market; and certainly in the immediate term the industry will be orientated towards domestic demand rather than exports. Domestic sales, however, start from a very narrow base. In the past purchasers have been organisations rather than individuals, and in 1993 80 per cent of passenger cars were bought by government ministries. Private enterprises and foreign companies accounted for about 19 per cent of such sales. The individual owner segment, however, is expected to rise as discretionary income grows; nevertheless, the high prices of vehicles still put them out of most citizens' reach, with even middle-market domestically produced vehicles selling for around US$23,000.

To date four major Japanese car manufacturers have entered the Chinese market but this may well change as export opportunities grow, especially given the rise in wage costs where Japanese companies have invested elsewhere in Asia.[48]

It was asserted earlier that foreign investment was mainly solicited for passenger car manufacture. But it is worth noting that the Kyodo News Service announced in Tokyo on 2 May 1994 that Nissan Diesel Motor Company would manufacture large-sized lorries in China under a joint venture, the first of its kind, with Dongfang Automotive Corporation, based in Hubei Province. Responding to Chinese requests, Nissan Diesel also plans to contribute to the nurturing of Chinese vehicle parts makers by incorporating some local suppliers in the planned joint production.

The foregoing has examined Japanese technology transfer and capital input in China's automobile industry within the framework set by the Chinese authorities. In the following sections Japanese investment will be examined within the focus of labour relations in a number of companies in a range of industries; it is asserted that Japan's greatest contribution to China's modernisation may well be made in the sphere of management.

Background to case studies of Japanese-invested ventures in China: labour legislation

From the vantage point of early 1995 there is evidence to suggest that the incidence of labour disputes is increasing, especially in foreign-invested ventures, the strike over better wages and working conditions at Japan's National Panasonic Motor Factory in the Special Economic Zone of Zhuhai being a case in point.[49] At the time of writing the dispute was being resolved through mediation by the Zhuhai Municipal Government's Labour Bureau. Significantly, demands were for a pay rise which would have brought monthly wages, then US$90, in line with the US$120 earned by employees at other foreign-owned factories in Zhuhai, evidence of the increasing importance of differentials in wider recruitment. This, however, was but one of a number of strikes to hit Japanese-invested companies in Zhuhai since 1993, even though strikes are technically illegal and the government seeks to conceal such industrial action lest it discourage further foreign capital input.

There is nevertheless official Chinese concern. One source mentioned that there were thousands of recorded labour disputes from 1986 to the middle of 1994, many of them at foreign ventures and privately run enterprises. In July 1994 Zhang Dinghua, Vice-President of the All China Federation of Trade Unions (ACFTU), singled out increasing encroachment on the legal rights of workers in some joint ventures.

These phenomena may well be the penalty of economic success; higher wages in some sections of the workforce have led to greater discretionary income, in turn leading to higher demand for consumer goods and rising expectations. Worker unrest has prompted legislation: The Labour Law of the People's Republic of China was approved by the National People's Congress, China's main legislative body, for implementation in September 1994. In Chapter 2 of this book social security and labour mobility were discussed largely in the context of state enterprise reforms; concern in this sector is on foreign ventures, even though the new law embraces a number of measures already being implemented at regional levels and applicable to all companies.

The first feature of the ongoing reforms to be considered is the establishment of a labour market, the fundamental goal being to facilitate the movement of labour and its distribution based on supply and demand. In hiring and employment both workers and companies should have free choice. To foster such mobility, social security and unemployment benefit are to be improved. Labour contracts are already widespread; in this and in other areas foreign-invested companies are the pioneers, to be followed by state enterprises.

Secondly, the Labour Law is designed to adjust labour–management relations under a market economy, primarily through the encouragement of labour unions, which in turn will help protect workers via the tougher health and safety rules now being enacted. Chinese official calls for greater labour union membership are no doubt prompted by the incidence of exploitation in joint ventures chronicled in the media since 1992; according to available statistics, in 1994 workers in only one in four ventures were unionised, even though the total number of unions in that sector had reached 10,000. The ACFTU is currently campaigning for union membership in over half of all foreign ventures. The government has also laid down strict guidelines for resolving industrial disputes. Should negotiations fail, there is recourse to the offices of labour dispute committees, which include representation from the company, the workers and the labour union, or to regional arbitration organisations, composed of delegates from local governments, regional economic management authorities and labour unions. It will be noted that such dispute mechanisms are intended to enhance the role of labour unions.

A third linchpin in social security is wage system reform. While at the inception of foreign ventures such enterprises were obliged by law to set their wages at 120 to 150 per cent of the wage mean for state-owned enterprises in the same region and sector, now remuneration may be linked to labour productivity and business performance, and here wholly owned foreign companies have greater discretionary powers than Sino-foreign joint ventures. The latter's minimum wage, however, must not fall below the mean for state-owned enterprises. The ultimate objective of government is to allow all companies to set wages independently in a competitive market, but under broad state supervision to guarantee living standards in line with norms in particular regions, minimum wages being set locally by, for instance, municipalities. In the long run it is intended that negotiations between companies and workers, through an expanded role for the unions, will become the norm.

The final pillar of social security is labour insurance, divided into pension provision and unemployment benefit. While the central government is aiming to have a social security net in place by the turn of the century, retirement and unemployment benefits are currently managed regionally. Since 1991 contributions for pensions have come from government, enterprises and individuals. It is intended that ultimately this system, now in embryo, will be applied to all enterprises in China, including foreign-invested companies. Practices currently differ regionally. As a general principle, in the case of foreign-invested companies, funds are managed by the Chinese side, whether a business partner or a labour union, funds being built up within individual ventures. This system as it stands is unsatisfactory, with worker benefit entitlement often unclear. In some regions with a considerable foreign industrial and commercial presence, however, like Guangzhou and the Special Economic Zone of Shenzhen, labour insurance for all companies, including joint ventures, is being standardised through municipal regulations, and it is likely that such practices will be followed elsewhere.

Nationally developed labour legislation and social security could prove a mixed blessing for Japanese investors. On the one hand new benefit rules have increased the prospect of labour mobility and thus of recruitment from wider catchment areas; on the other hand, provision of welfare standardised in all companies according to law means that differences in treatment of workers will be reduced, making competition for qualified personnel even fiercer. Of course, unscrupulous foreign entrepreneurs who exploit the workforce will find it even more difficult to avoid, for example, expenditure on welfare, health and safety. While labour-management relations will in time come to be governed by standardised rules, providing guidelines in the handling of Chinese employees, low labour cost advantages may well be lost, as higher remuneration will have to be offered to attract qualified managers increasingly at a premium on the job market.[50]

Management models for ventures with Japanese investment

It has been suggested earlier that China is more and more a focus of Japanese investment, with large corporations, previously cautious, now shifting production facilities to that country. A recent survey of thirty-five Japanese managers representing twenty-nine Japanese companies in China, predominantly located in Shanghai but with some representation from such provinces as Liaoning and Guangdong, suggested that personnel management was the most important issue in running an enterprise in China. The study divided companies according to three models of handling human resources. The first is the 'segregation model', in which all personnel matters are left to the Chinese side, with the Japanese side merely supplying the technical experts. Such ventures often began with simple technical exchanges between partners but have since evolved into fully fledged ventures. The second is the 'positive commitment model' in which the Japanese side handles personnel matters together with the Chinese side based on joint equity. This is the most common model of Japanese ventures in China, some examples having evolved from the segregation model. Others are closer to the third model, 'full management'. Here the Japanese side maintains complete control over personnel matters. This type would be the main choice of Japanese investors, though to implant it successfully requires long experience of doing business with China. Ventures under the third rubric are often given wide initiative, precisely because they belong to industries of strategic significance and involve the transfer of technical expertise required by China. Japanese ventures have in many cases progressed from the segregation model through the positive commitment type to the full management system. In fact, there is a strong though not absolute correlation between, on the one hand, joint operations based on equity ratio, joint ventures and wholly owned companies and, on the other, the segregation, positive commitment and full management models.

Each model has its disadvantages. Sino-foreign ventures in the segregation category often trace their origins to technical exchanges created in the days of the friendship trading companies discussed earlier and represent the most rudimentary form of cooperation. The Chinese seek to acquire technology as inexpensively as possible, and, given the risky nature of the venture, the Japanese need to cut expenses in hiring personnel. Thus there has to be reliance on employees provided by the Chinese partner. A major problem, however, is that many such personnel were socialised under the command economy, lack initiative and are often not suited to handling technical renovation. In addition, Chinese engineers, having acquired knowledge of a new technology, consider it their own personal property and are reluctant to impart it to, say, production workers. In a traditional structure of this kind, technical experience is not related to promotion, so technological transformation is inhibited. Under this model the Japanese, in targeting the domestic market, only make progress in the long term. Ongoing Chinese market reforms, however, may go some way to solving this problem, and the model itself may become increasingly outmoded.

Under the positive commitment model Japanese partners become more interested in personnel affairs; Chinese enterprises themselves have been given more self-management powers, and they are now more willing to share authority with the Japanese in order to improve business performance. There is nevertheless the danger that the Japanese will attempt to introduce their own management styles too rapidly. At the root of problems encountered under this model are lingering socialist traditions. In the Japanese view the Chinese are obsessed by personal connections and lack any real corporate loyalty. This makes Japanese-style horizontal consensus building difficult because the traditional strong vertical command system in China weakened lateral communication. Without consultation and consensus Japanese managers have directly to monitor the workforce more closely than at home. Consequently, it is difficult to implement any performance-related promotion system, given the egalitarianism of the old command economy, and Chinese personnel officers, because of personal connections, have their own vested interests in the status quo. In such areas Japanese managers are improving systems of communication but it is noticeable that successful business performance is the best way of persuading Chinese employers to adapt to new ways of working. Ultimately, Sino-Japanese ventures are judged by business results. Nothing succeeds like success.

The full management model presupposes abundant experience of China on the part of wholly owned Japanese companies. Such companies have often previously operated successfully in Hong Kong and businessmen from the colony frequently act as intermediaries with the Chinese. The Japanese side has complete discretion in hiring employees, but this does not in itself, of course, guarantee harmonious labour relations. Chinese workers may have high expectations over salaries and working conditions and, if these are not handled sensitively, they may lead to charges of capitalist exploitation. In fact, labour disputes have been more prevalent in wholly owned Japanese operations. In addition, as the Chinese become more familiar with a market economy, there is likely to be less Sino-Japanese conflict over economic institutions and business systems. Nevertheless, new institutions bring in their wake new values. Thus as trends towards the full management model accelerate, cultural friction born of different behavioural patterns and value systems, for example in relation to innovation, entrepreneurship and strategic thinking, may become more prevalent.[51]

In summary, the three models, segregation, positive commitment and full management, are concerned primarily with the management of human resources. After a brief introductory section, case studies of Japanese ventures will be examined and tentatively placed in one of the above categories.

Introduction to case studies: adapting Japanese management practice to China

Effective management of business resources is the key to successful Japanese ventures in China. In the discussion of models it was suggested that the Chinese are naturally prepared to accept Japanese practice when it is seen to work, and the reputed strengths of Japanese companies have been given much weight in Chinese official literature. Chinese managers are therefore amenable to persuasion. For instance, there are two areas of practice in which the Japanese may be said to excel, training and consultation, to which brief reference has been made in Chapter 2. These were also the focal point of a report written by a Chinese manager after his secondment to a Japanese company and published in the journal 'Labour Economics and Human Resource Management'. The writer noted emphasis on continuous training, both on the job and by job rotation, even though this is supplemented by more formal instruction outside the company. This applies to managers and workforce alike and is a prerequisite for promotion; appropriate qualifications must be gained, whether through the company's own research centres or outside institutions.[52] Such training programmes, Japanese style, cannot immediately be introduced in Chinese ventures, yet training is very much on the agenda where the Japanese have invested in China. A case in point is the Nonfemet International Aluminium Company, a joint venture between China, Canada and Japan which went into operation in China's Shenzhen Special Economic Zone in 1990. Its general manager, a Canadian, adopting Japanese methods, decided to test the managerial competence of such senior staff as the deputy general manager, the chief engineer and the chief accountant by seconding them to the front lines of production and management. They were to be restored to their original positions on proof of demonstrated ability. Particular attention has thus been paid to personnel training; new staff have been selected for their entrepreneurial skills, a break from tradition in Chinese enterprises. In this success, on the job training has undoubtedly played a key role although this is also supplemented by sending staff above the level of section chief to Japan itself for training from one to four months.[53] Since 1991 selected production workers have also received instruction in Japan. The possibility of participating in a training programme in Japan itself has often proved a motivation for Chinese workers. A Sino-Japanese sock manufacturing venture, for instance, has sought to enhance long-term productivity by sending 10 per cent of the workers to Japan each year for a month's training session. As only the best workers are sent, employees are motivated to work harder in the hope of being chosen. As it is intended that all workers complete such a training programme, long-term productivity is favoured.[54]

Thus in such training there is great emphasis on multi-skilling, traditionally lacking in Chinese enterprises. In fact, rigid division of labour formerly inhibited cooperation among workers performing different tasks. Ultimately, with the encouragement of a new breed of more motivated Chinese managers, fully fledged Japanese-style job rotation in such enterprises will be instituted.

In the context of training, Chinese sources have also referred to job rotation, whereby workers and managers are seconded periodically, especially during their first years of employment, to various departments both to impart their own expertise to younger colleagues and to acquire all-round knowledge of the company's activities. Such multi-skilling also helps to instil commitment to the company and conformity, although in addition the above sources report trends towards encouraging creativity as a component part of training, given the greater need for innovation in high-technology industries.

A second practice deemed worthy of emulation is consultation. Traditionally Japanese companies have been market-driven, that is customer needs and specifications are seen as paramount, and this is where Japanese stress on manager–worker consultation comes into focus, particularly in the context of total quality control, a practice developed to make both sides identify with the customer's standpoint. Thus those responsible for each stage of the production process view colleagues further down the line as their customers; quality is everyone's concern, not merely that of inspectors.[55]

Regular consultation with the workforce is crucially necessary to achieve quality control. While the quality of Chinese workers still leaves much to be desired, standards are improving over time with greater labour mobility and motivation via better wages. Expatriate Japanese managers are persuading Chinese staff in joint ventures of the virtues of closer relationships with the workforce. Recognising the importance of 'face' in instituting limited forms of consultation with Chinese workers, Japanese joint venture partners have taken care to build rapport with their senior Chinese colleagues lest these feel threatened.

Evidence of the effectiveness of such consultation is provided by Fujian-Hitachi Television Company. In this joint venture, set up by Fujian Province and Hitachi of Japan, over 60 per cent of the proposals made by workers and staff in 1990 involved improvements in production operations and management, resulting in considerable resource savings.

These measures, however, are not just remedial but are the first steps in effecting that fundamental overhaul of Chinese management practices necessary if the Chinese economy is to meet the challenges of coming decades. Perhaps the most significant barrier to implementing such far-reaching reforms as the institution of on the job training and consultation is the fact that Chinese managers, even at the middle and higher levels, are unaccustomed, because of the legacy of the command economy, to undertake the strategic decision making characteristic of companies in market economies. But over time, with increasing Sino-Japanese economic cooperation and the emergence of a new generation of Chinese acquainted with international practices, such fundamental problems may be resolved.

In summary, while it is neither possible nor desirable for Japanese management practices as a whole to be introduced, such features as training and consultation have been very much on the agenda when Japanese companies have been involved in China.

Case studies of companies with Japanese investment

There are two main preconditions for the implementation of Japanese management practices in China: intimate knowledge of China's business culture, best acquired through extensive practical experience, and considerable control over human resource management, especially the recruitment of highly qualified managers and workers. Earlier reference has been made to the three models, two of which, positive commitment and full management, correlate with a high degree of control by the Japanese side over recruitment of employees. Given that it is a crucial element in business success in China, personnel management will now be examined in the context of five case studies, two in textiles and three in electronics.

Kanebo

Successful joint ventures with foreign partners are considered pacesetters for management reform in state enterprises. One success story is Kanebo, an example of Sino-Japanese cooperation. Kanebo set up a joint venture, the Shanghai Huazhong Stocking Company, in 1987. Kanebo, however, was no stranger to China, having made massive investment in the country before the Second World War. Significantly, it had reinvested two-thirds of its profits in China. Moreover, its post-1978 experience indicates that good public relations and labour relations are crucial determinants of success. First of all, the company's basic stance has been commitment to the modernisation of China through technology transfer and business management skills. Learning, however, is a two-way process; consultation with Chinese managers and the workforce is designed to unleash the latter's creative potential. In this connection it was an advantage that managers and workers transferred to the venture by the Chinese partner were of high calibre.

In addition, given the freer conditions under which joint ventures operate in terms of recruitment and remuneration in comparison to the state enterprises, motivation of Kanebo's Chinese workers has been high, with performance related to salary. A sense of identity with the company has been fostered, as has dedication to quality control. Products are already said to be superior to those made in Japan. The joint venture has an equity equally divided between Kanebo and the Shanghai Number 19 Cotton Fabric Factory. The board of directors includes four Chinese and four Japanese; 500 workers are employed. The joint venture itself decides where to sell its products; currently 25 per cent of production is taken by Japan, 45 per cent by Hong Kong and 5 per cent goes to other countries. Importantly, the remainder is sold domestically in China.

In fact, the huge Chinese market would seem to offer enormous potential to Sino-foreign joint ventures. Even more lucrative possibilities may open up as China's domestic markets are further liberalised; restrictions on further investment in retail outlets are already being lifted. It is advantageous, however, for joint ventures and foreign enterprises to manufacture high-quality products acceptable internationally and source their raw material in China itself, given that sales will be in foreign currency but costs in *renminbi*. They may thus reap exchange rate advantages. In turn, the benefits to China offered by such companies as the Kanebo joint venture are up-to-date technology transfer, high-quality goods and thus competitiveness on world markets.

In summary, Kanebo is a successful joint venture, with consultation between the two sides concerning production issues, and it thus falls within the positive commitment strategy.[56]

Kunshan Cellutane

Another example of a successful joint venture is Kunshan Cellutane, established in a town in Jiangsu, near Shanghai, in 1985, as a partnership between the Japanese company Cellutane and a local light industrial enterprise. Operations commenced in May 1986. The venture started with an initial capital of US$1.85 million, with equity divided equally between the two sides. The main products are polyurethane foam and secondary processed items such as Japanese-style floor chair backrests, mattresses, foldaway sofas and health mats. Two-thirds of its production is sold in China as foam material. The remaining one-third is further processed and exported to Japan, mostly as chair rests and backrests so as to generate foreign currency. Again, as with Kanebo, the secrets of success lie in continuing long-term commitment, as indicated by the Japanese chairman obtaining permanent residence in China. The joint venture has cultivated good local connections and been able to find suitable workers. Kunshan local authority regulations make it difficult to dismiss full-time workers for five years but the venture has retained freedom of initiative by employing only sixty-one full-time workers and using part-time workers and contract workers as additional labour. Such part-time workers are hired both on a long-term basis of more than a year and a short-term basis. By law the venture must renew the contracts of its part-time workers on an annual basis. As mentioned earlier, it has been a tradition for enterprises in China to provide accommodation but, as workers at Kunshan Cellutane are drawn from local peasants, they already have their own homes and thus the venture avoids such expenditure, although it has subsequently built some company housing through moneys from the special employees' fund. The company continually diversifies its contacts and this stands it in good stead in labour recruitment. Some contract workers, employed for six-month periods, are used as in-house sub-contractors. One worker may introduce other possible employees who often come from inland provinces. Thus whereas generally local labour was employed, the catchment pool is now diversifying, permitting greater choice, even though the workforce recruited may still need training.

As in Japanese companies in Japan, the Kunshan joint venture has placed a premium on training. Selected local employees are seconded to the Japanese head office for training on the job so that they may acquire proper work attitudes and a commitment to quality control. They have an incentive to learn; about twenty are in training in Japan at any one time and on return to China are rewarded with promotion to foreman.

Importantly, Cellutane's venture partner is headed by a local political leader whose links have been invaluable in dealing with various government formalities and facilitating connections with local authorities.

In summary, Kunshan Cellutane may be categorised as falling within the positive commitment model; the Chinese side has clearly been of assistance in personnel matters but good industrial relations, derived from Japanese practices, have made possible training programmes to improve the qualifications of local managers.

Canon Dalian

Canon, one of Japan's leading optical equipment manufacturers, has long seen the production potential in China for both domestic and international markets. After a number of links involving technical exchanges, Canon's decision to invest in Dalian was prompted by the need to avoid trade friction and encouraged by the superior infrastructure in the port's economic and technical development zone. Canon Dalian, a wholly owned Chinese subsidiary of Canon established in 1989, produces cartridges and other consumables for laser printers, photocopiers and office equipment. The Dalian operation is also being used as a test site for the recycling of cartridges. As of July 1993 the venture had 1,400 employees, many highly qualified, projected to increase in number to 3,000 or so by the mid-1990s. On advertising for managers in 1990, the company was swamped by 1,600 applications, of which 10 per cent were from university graduates and 30 per cent from the various categories of secondary school leavers.

In order to retain good managers, the company has provided certain incentives; fifty housing units have been built for middle management. The labour market in general is becoming increasingly competitive, and the venture has obtained permission from the labour personnel bureau to employ peasants from the surrounding rural areas, in addition to urban workers. Attractive remuneration packages for workers include bonuses distributed in the summer and at the Spring Festival in late January/mid-February, with an average of just under two months' salary being paid out. Furthermore, an amount equivalent to 64.5 per cent of the basic salary is being put aside by the company for retirement allowances, housing funds and medical insurance, a scheme managed by the labour union. Inflationary pressures, however, as well as a competitive labour market, may well necessitate frequent upward adjustment in salaries.

Canon Dalian is a wholly owned subsidiary, advertising publicly for employees and extending welfare provision to its workforce, and its success would seem to lie in effective human resource management. It is therefore to be classified under the full management rubric.

Huaguang Electronics Industries

Huaguang Electronics, approved in 1989, is a joint venture between concerns from Japan, China and Hong Kong. The Wuxi Electrical Equipment Factory owns 60 per cent of the venture, Koyo Electronics of Japan owns 30 per cent and a Hong Kong company owns 10 per cent. Koyo Electronics, in turn a subsidiary of the bearing maker Koyo Seiko, has numerous links with foreign companies. In deciding to invest in Wuxi, Koyo Electronics was influenced by a number of considerations, including the presence of other high-tech companies in the region and the high local educational level, essential for its operations. The main products are high-tech: programmable controls for machines. The Japanese partner is supplying the technology and, because of the need for high quality, only about 10 to 15 per cent of the components and materials are sourced in China itself. While the Japanese company was originally attracted to the potential of the Chinese market, which, as of mid-1993, took 60 per cent of the production, the remaining 40 per cent was exported to Japan to generate foreign currency.

The venture owes its success to a number of factors. While Huaguang Electronics Industries is only 30 per cent Japanese owned, actual management power is held by the Japanese side which has taken a long-term perspective. Highly qualified personnel have been attracted to work there; of 160 employees, 70 per cent are university or technical school graduates, and the remainder have come from secondary schools. In 1993, for instance, from a catchment pool including graduates from elite institutions like Shanghai Jiaotong University and the China Institute of Science and Technology in Hefei, the venture appointed thirty university graduates. In fact, it has proved less easy to find general workers, whose annual salaries at the venture are 7,000 yuan, bonuses included. In lieu of housing provision, salaries have been raised as an inducement for workers to stay with the company. The company's strategy accords greater importance to reinvestment than recovering investment; consequently, of profits, 30 per cent is allotted to dividends, 10 per cent to bonuses, welfare and development funds, 40 per cent to increasing registered capital and 20 per cent to internal holdings.

Clearly, a key to the company's growth lies in building and retaining a core of engineers with superior skills. This investment in the careers of Chinese managers may represent the coming of age of Japanese ventures in China. Given that the Japanese side holds management power, the introduction of Japanese-style practices is facilitated. From this perspective, Huaguang Electronics Industries follows the full management model.

Sumida Electric

Sumida Electric, a Japanese manufacturer of electronic coils, has moved its mass-production lines, because of cost advantages, to other parts of Asia, and two of its biggest operations are in the Chinese province of Guangdong. One is the Fanyu Consignment Processing Plant, begun in 1988, and the other is Dongwan (Taiping) Sumida Electric, established in 1991. The Fanyu plant is actually managed by the Japanese company's Hong Kong subsidiary, Sumida Electric Hong

Kong. The Chinese side provided the factory site and buildings as well as the workers. For production operations the Japanese side furnishes machinery, equipment and materials, while the Chinese side deploys the workforce and takes care of import and export procedures. Similarly, the Taiping Plant is a joint venture, owned 75 per cent by Sumida Electric Hong Kong and 25 per cent by the Chinese partner, Guangdong Dongwan Taiping Port Commercial Corporation. The Fanyu plant employs 3,000 workers, while the Taiping plant has 2,000.

There is a highly educated core management team of 214 staff, consisting of four Japanese, twenty Hong Kong Chinese, 110 Chinese university graduates and eighty Chinese technical school graduates. A feature of Sumida operations in China, as in the rest of Asia, is to use local managers to institute Japanese practices. One feature of note in its Chinese venture is the rapid promotion of Chinese university graduates to positions of responsibility in both China and Hong Kong. They are already represented among foremen, section chiefs and departmental heads. In addition, while to date there has been a division of labour, with increasing availability of Chinese experts it is planned to locate design functions, hitherto in Japan, together with production activities, in China, the only drawback being the elitist attitude of Chinese graduates who are reluctant to engage in consultation with workers on the factory floor.

A noteworthy feature of the Sumida plant is the use of Hong Kong Chinese not only in mediation with the local authorities but as supervisors of young Chinese managers. The Fanyu plant's Chinese partner, a local mayor, and the Taiping plant's Chinese partner, an official in the Guangdong Provincial Government and a female entrepreneur, are both personal connections of Sumida Electric's Hong Kong subsidiary.

The Hong Kong Chinese are the *de facto* managers of the Fanyu plant; on behalf of the Japanese they direct the Chinese university graduates who in turn supervise the general workers. Such delegation of authority to the Hong Kong Chinese may well prove the key to the ongoing profitability of Sumida in Guangdong.

Sumida has built on its experience in other Asian countries like Taiwan, Malaysia and Singapore and is now leasing space at its Fanyu plant to other Japanese firms initiating investment in China, and is at the same time offering consultancy services. Its Japanese clients can thus gain assistance in dealing with Chinese officialdom. As well as renting space, these Japanese companies, new to the Chinese scene, may thereby reduce initial investment and gain ready access to a reliable workforce through the offices of Sumida and its connections. The learning process is two-way, and the knowledge Sumida gains as a result of these services will equip it to move into new areas of endeavour and train its own employees in line with business trends.

In summary, the Sumida example highlights the importance of first-hand knowledge through local connections. To the extent that the Japanese side retains overall direction of personnel matters, while delegating authority to the Chinese and the Hong Kong subsidiary over recruitment and management respectively, Sumida Electric's plants in Guangdong fall within the category of positive commitment.

In conclusion, the analysis contained in the foregoing case studies has demonstrated that effective human resource management is the key to the successful operation of Japanese-invested companies in China. Japanese firms have been known for their long-term perspective which sacrifices short-term gains for future market share. Thus while the Chinese domestic market beckons, a number of firms studied above are exporting to satisfy current foreign exchange requirements. In time, of course, Chinese consumer demand will grow. The Japanese companies under consideration have improved their prospects by operating through Hong Kong subsidiaries and cultivating close relationships with some of the colony's entrepreneurs, whose services are invaluable in forging links with Chinese local leaders and municipal authorities. Such contacts are often indispensable when it comes to hiring suitable workers and managers. Three ideal typologies were used to categorise human resource management. The first is the segregation model, where all personnel matters are left to the Chinese side; this category is characteristic of technical tie-ups and simple joint operations in early stages of cooperation. Under the second model, that of positive commitment, the Japanese side handles personnel matters together with its Chinese counterparts on the basis of equity held; this is typical of joint ventures. The full management model, typical of wholly owned Japanese ventures, is where the Japanese have complete control over personnel and their deployment. That the last two models are becoming the most common of the three indicates the coming of age of Japanese ventures in China, although future delegation of authority to Chinese managers is not precluded and, indeed, is being positively encouraged, as the case studies show.

A key determinant of success is the selection of managers and workers who can be motivated. Recruitment of graduates is a step in the right direction but does not necessarily guarantee management potential. While it is neither necessarily desirable nor possible to introduce Japanese practices in their entirety, two features, training and consultation, are intrinsically valuable and a means of inducting managers and workers into a new corporate culture. Chinese managers, because of the vertical controls of the command economy, have often been loath to develop horizontal links with the workforce. Motivation in that direction, however, could include technological and management training in Japan, often coveted by Chinese managers, and such training visits often serve to reinforce identification with the values and norms of a Japanese company. After all, technology transfer and staff training are perhaps the greatest contributions the Japanese can make to China's development. Ultimately, of course, it is intended that Chinese employees play a greater role in management in Japanese-invested firms. Japanese companies have invested in China the better to secure both Chinese domestic and world markets but their chances of doing so are likely to be enhanced if, like Kanebo, they are also genuinely committed to the host country's modernisation. Targeting the domestic market will be considerably aided by ongoing distribution reforms, the subject of the next section.[57]

China's distribution system: opportunities for Japanese retailers

It is only recently that the distribution sector has been subject to reform and open to foreign participation. Previous sections have outlined industrial reforms, and in the transition from command to market, Sino-foreign joint ventures and wholly owned foreign enterprises have played a major role. As a reward, they may now place at least some of their products for sale in China instead of being required to produce solely for export. As China has come to play a greater role in international commerce which itself now looms larger in China's own economy, the country's foreign trade organs have been accorded greater independence from central government so that they may adjust more appropriately to competitive forces. Within this overall scenario China's consumer markets have matured; while attitudes associated with the older seller's market linger, distributors are having to satisfy greater consumer quality discernment and provide a wider range of foreign and domestically produced goods. In fact, in the face of these changes, the distribution system has come to appear increasingly antiquated; since 1992 the Chinese government has been inviting foreign investment in retailing and in 1994 began to allow, in exceptional cases, 100 per cent overseas ownership of retail outlets.

Announcing the official stance on distribution reform in June 1994, China's Minister of Internal Trade, Zhang Haoruo, was nevertheless at pains to assert that foreign participation should not mean overseas domination of the sector. Thus, while it was imperative to draw on the experience of the world community in developing retail business, especially chain stores, China would also pursue a policy of 'walking on two legs'. One leg was to bring in foreign capital by relaxing rules governing Sino-foreign joint retail operations, in order to further the modernisation of China's commercial system. The second leg was to select the best existing commercial enterprises in the major cities of China and reorganise them as chain store groups with Chinese characteristics, the implication being that, as in industrial sectors, foreign-invested ventures would become the pacesetters for reform of their state counterparts. Particularly worthy of study were the chain store practices of Japan; China's supermarkets, clothing stores, pharmacies, bookstores, photo processing companies and jewellery shops should all consider emulating Japanese experiences, where appropriate.[58]

For Japanese concerns, especially department stores, moves into the Chinese market are a continuation of a strategy targeting Southeast and East Asia since the late 1980s. Real estate prices and distribution costs are still likely to be lower in China and elsewhere in Asia than in Japan; in addition, Japanese department stores in China, like their counterparts in Hong Kong, may attract Japanese tourists who, because of the high yen, can buy Japanese products at prices which are low relative to those in Tokyo. Moreover, Japanese consumers in their own country have always helped to finance cheap exports but cartel arrangements which keep prices high in Japan are likely to be much weaker in Hong Kong and China. There is thus every incentive for Japanese retailers to operate in the Chinese market.

Since 1978 the Chinese leaders have staked their own legitimacy on improving living standards and enhancing the population's quality of life. High wage levels, providing they are justified by the enhanced competitiveness of China's economy, furnish greater discretionary income and purchasing power, themselves in turn incentives for further personal endeavour. Since the early 1990s there has been noticeably greater purchasing power among the population at large, even though in that respect there are striking regional disparities as well as urban–rural inequalities. Private enterprise, still heavily concentrated in the zones and cities of the southeastern seaboard, has undoubtedly been a major factor in raising incomes for owners, managers and workers. There has also been an increase in secondary income from part-time work due to the legalisation of sideline business, especially in service industries. Thus, while China remains a developing country, some of its coastal areas have a higher per capita income on a GNP basis than other Asian states. In 1993 income on that criterion in the cities of the south as well as in Shanghai, Beijing and Tianjin was within the range of US$804 to US$1,925, well above the US$666 per capita GNP of Indonesia. As for Shenzhen, one of the Special Economic Zones, its income was said to exceed the average in Thailand. China's economic reform policies are producing a new class of wealthy customers in the cities of the eastern seaboard. Greater income differentials are undoubtedly emerging but there is strong evidence that the majority are enjoying improvements in living standards. One indicator has been food consumption. Between 1978 and 1984 consumption of grain increased from 195.5 to 251.5 kilograms, while more meat, eggs and edible oil were consumed. Satisfaction of basic material needs among an ever greater percentage of the population has led to rising expectations. In fact, more households are able to afford electrical goods like television sets, washing machines and refrigerators, even though poorer sections of the population have profited less from the economic reforms of the 1980s and 1990s.

While consumer goods ownership is a useful indicator of potential markets, Chinese statistics may underestimate the purchasing power of the Chinese consumer. This is because in China housing, transportation and health insurance take up only 5 per cent of household income, although this may increase as private ownership of dwellings grows in the 1990s. Costs of food and education have also been low, although this seems set to change, as true market forces are allowed to operate, as in other sectors. In any case at present spending on the former three items falls between the 20 per cent and 40 per cent norm for Asian countries.[59]

The changing nature of China's consumer markets will now be examined in greater depth. The wealthiest class of Chinese consumers consists of those earning the equivalent of US$5,000 per annum, ten times the average annual income in China. Their lifestyle increasingly differentiates them from the rest of the population; they are the natural consumer targets for luxury items and imported goods, as they have travelled overseas and enjoy more leisure through shorter working hours. While this group only represents about 1 per cent of the population, it nevertheless sets standards of consumption, which are being enjoyed to a greater extent by a growing middle class. Although the average annual income of the Chinese population in general is low by world standards, because of the underestimation of purchasing power discussed above, possession of consumer durables places China in a middle category among states. This would apply, for example, to refrigerators and washing machines, of which ownership in China in the early 1990s has so far reached 35 per cent and 15 per cent of urban households respectively, according to Chinese statistics. Moreover, for television sets the figure is 70 per cent which places China among high-income countries.[60]

There are, however, stark contrasts between ownership of consumer goods as between the cities and the countryside. The non-agricultural residents of China, most of whom still live in the major urban centres, represent 20 per cent of the population but their consumption has reached 40 per cent of the country's total. But while the urban–rural gap may well be currently widening, increasing purchasing power in the countryside may herald future market potential when, as distribution is improved, supermarket and other large retail outlets are established in China's rural towns.[61]

Given that in the immediate future major Japanese-invested retail outlets will be in the cities, trends there are the major focus of this section. The most striking urban trend is greater consumer discernment: a transition from quantity to quality consciousness. An initial impetus has undoubtedly been the desire to replace products purchased in the days of inexpensive, poor-quality, uniform mass-production items made under the old planned economy. Moreover, consumers are now seeking more nutritious food, more comfortable clothes and superior workmanship in high-quality household appliances. For instance, there is evidence that consumers are increasingly demanding brand-name foodstuffs, often foreign, together with fresh fruit, not previously always available in great variety, aquatic products and wines. This is also in line with dietary changes made possible by greater discretionary income. While consumption of plant-derived staple foods has actually fallen, that of meat has increased. There is more variety, too, in clothing, for which spending per urban inhabitant in 1992 was over twice that of 1978, and international brand-name products are increasingly in demand.[62] This quality consciousness is, of course, an aspect of market competition, and it has been partly fostered by increased money supply which in turn has enhanced purchasing power. As the quality of some categories of consumer goods produced by the Chinese themselves is poor, foreign manufacturers with well-established brand names could in future enjoy differential advantage in China's markets.[63]

A further effect of this concern for quality has been the shortening of the product life-cycle for durable consumer goods. Domestically produced goods, often limited in variety and soon out of fashion, are losing out in popularity to foreign products and those of joint ventures. Such trends are discernible across a wide range of consumer goods;

high-quality stainless steel cooking utensils and electrical appliances are being sought, and plastic items will be increasingly favoured. Finally, as both worker and peasant incomes rise, there will be a good market for such consumer durables as electric heating, shower equipment, kitchen exhaust fans, microwave ovens, food processors, air purifiers, heating equipment for health care and other home appliances, providing, of course, that gas and electricity supplies can keep pace with the demand for power.[64] Moreover, as the market for some consumer goods like television sets becomes glutted in the cities, so consumer focus there moves towards air conditioners and cameras, and the latter two commodities are already comparable in price to the former. In certain respects it may be suggested that the consumer situation is comparable to that in Japan in the 1950s and 1960s, when the Japanese public were attracted by the appliances they saw in American homes on television. In Japan black and white television sets were gradually replaced by colour ones, and consumers started buying electric refrigerators and washing machines. Later, video cassette recorders and air conditioners became best-selling items. In the 1990s the population of China's southeastern coast can receive Hong Kong television and seek to emulate the lifestyles presented. Such products, like household electrical appliances, have been penetrating Chinese homes even faster than was the case in Japan in the comparable days of the 1960s and 1970s.

One of the most promising sectors of consumption in China is private housing, the construction of which is proceeding rapidly. In fact, however, China's private housing market is still in its infancy; under the command economy the state took responsibility for provision but market forces will now increasingly operate.[65] In many countries housing construction is a harbinger of various kinds of consumer demand, especially for electrical goods, furnishings and interior decoration. It is noteworthy that it is official Chinese policy to increase rural purchasing power to forestall social instability born of excessive wealth differentials. More importantly, perhaps, there will undoubtedly be rural migration to the cities; though already not without adverse effects, it will nevertheless expand markets for consumer goods.

Finally, in the context of retail outlet expansion, Chinese official forecasts make instructive reading. Statistics suggest that by the year 2000 consumption levels of those living in the villages will be equivalent to those of city residents in 1988. The structure of consumption is changing, especially in the urban areas of the southeastern coast. One feature, discussed above, is the greater variety of goods and quality discernment. It is pertinent at this point to introduce the distinction between short-term and long-term consumption: the former refers to everyday items like food and some essential consumer goods which, of course, increase in number with rising living standards; the latter includes consumption of services like housing, education and medical insurance. In the years to come long-term consumption as a ratio of Chinese residents' expenditure is set to grow. While under the old command economy the state looked after sectors like education and medicine, its role in these and other welfare areas is likely to diminish in relative terms, and individual households will increasingly take responsibility for such provision. Forecasts which do not clearly itemise spending on such welfare aspects nevertheless give an indication of future consumption trends. It is estimated that by the year 2000 the ratio spent on food will have fallen to 45 per cent, the amount used for clothing will be about 12 per cent, expenditure on commodities for daily use will rise to 19 per cent and the outlay for accommodation will increase to between 10 and 13 per cent, while spending on water, electricity, communications and incidentals will reach between 11 and 14 per cent. These figures are, however, only approximate and likely to be more typical of city dwellers than rural inhabitants in the foreseeable future but the trends are clear and will tend to follow those of other countries.[66] From the viewpoint of retailing, of course, expenditure on long-term items, as defined above, could leave less room for spending on consumer goods. An alternative and more probable scenario, however, could follow the early post-war Japanese trend where individual savings, intended to cover welfare and insurance, grew, but at a level which still permitted spending on consumer goods, to the long-term advantage of the Japanese economy. In that eventuality, Chinese consumer demand would seem set to expand.

So far, a rather optimistic appraisal of prospects for Japan's retailers in China has been presented. Nevertheless, a barrier must be surmounted before China's markets may be satisfactorily penetrated. Whether reliant on China-made goods or foreign imports or both, overseas retailers in China, especially if they wish to operate nationally, are dependent at least in part on the ongoing reform of the country's distribution system. Such reform began in the late 1980s and is only now being implemented on a national scale. Under the command economy, based on central planning, the state sector of industry had been predominant, and supply and circulation of commodities were virtually government monopolies. In fact from 1949 to 1978 China lacked the kind of independently focused economic activity characteristic of Western countries, since state-owned stores dominated retail sales throughout the country. In addition, goods circulated in a region were often produced there, and this inhibited the development of commerce on a nationwide scale, producing fragmented commodity circulation, with state wholesalers controlling specific regional jurisdictions. Thus distribution reform in the 1980s and 1990s has been designed to foster competition and create nationwide markets. To this end, as part of the Seventh Five Year Plan (1986–90), the CCP enunciated two basic principles governing the reform of the distribution system: firstly, wholesale markets were to be simplified to improve the flow of goods; and, secondly, producers were to be brought closer to customers. One barrier impeding the creation of a nationwide market is poor infrastructure and in 1994 China's Premier, Li Peng, enjoined local government to undertake the construction of better transportation, storage and circulation facilities to ease the shipment of foodstuffs from one end of China to another. Such channels, of course, also facilitate the transit of consumer goods, given the need in a free market economy to link production bases and marketing centres; this is an issue particularly relevant to foreign companies contemplating whether to export to or manufacture in China.[67]

Having discussed current objectives, progress to date is now examined at a time when China's distribution is in a period of transition. Prior to the reforms of the 1980s, distribution in China was tightly controlled by the central government via ministries dealing with categories of products and state-run commercial bureaux at local levels. As a major objective in market reform is to make producers more accountable to consumers, in contrast with the previous system distributors are now given the freedom to buy from any supplier and sell to any customer. Wholesalers from different levels of the old system are now able to compete with one another and, as indicated elsewhere, the prices of most products have been decontrolled. While the old-type wholesalers often remain quasi-state-run companies that contract to turn over a quota of profit to the state, they may retain any additional revenue. A number of private wholesalers has now emerged and these have been able to form cooperative relationships with Hong Kong and Western distributors which offer more effective channels for foreign producers. But any wholly independent foreign participation in wholesale distribution is likely to remain restricted in the immediate future. Importantly, the most lucrative markets in China for food, as well as other consumer goods, are in Guangdong, the southeastern province, Shanghai and Beijing. One source has suggested that in Guangdong non-state-owned wholesalers account for as much as 80 per cent of the value of all food distributed. While there are encouraging signs for foreign manufacturers targeting Chinese consumers, the slow development of a unified market means that suppliers still need to select a different partner in each local or municipal market that they wish to penetrate, as even wholesalers cooperating with foreign partners are unlikely to be strong in more than one region of China.[68] It must be stressed, too, that given the country's size, reform moves at different speeds in different areas, and is subject to implementation by diverse local authorities.

Certainly, problems with wholesaling facilities are a very real hindrance to the procuring of merchandise within China but this is by no means the only barrier to successful retailing by foreigners. There are limits, for instance, to the amount of high-quality products made in the country that can be sold on the domestic market, as most are still targeted for export. Moreover, there are few factories that can produce products of the quality required by, especially, Japanese retailers. Finally, the retail outlets frequently sell the same foreign brand products made by companies with manufacturing bases in China; consequently it is difficult to distinguish one store from another.

An alternative is to import but there are barriers here too. While decentralisation of foreign trade organs provides more channels of entry for imports and thus greater opportunities for foreign exporters, handling fees are still charged (even if these do not apply to retailers with direct import rights) and the central government still retains residual powers like foreign exchange controls and relatively high tariffs. Moreover, fixed import cycles and complex customs procedures, combined with slow physical distribution inside China, often combine to preclude synchronising purchases abroad with current market demand.

In spite of attempts by the national leadership to codify laws to encourage foreign economic cooperation, retail, like other trading activities, is still impeded by the lack of a credible legal framework. Traders are disconcerted by laws set up in the wake of actual developments in an *ad hoc* fashion; legal judgements are often seen to be based on the power of personal connections. There are also vague areas within the laws themselves which allow the old tension between central and local governments to surface. As indicated elsewhere, some local governments have become notorious for waiving regulations and granting tax concessions.

While considerable coverage has been given earlier to labour legislation, the power of connections is nowhere better seen than in labour–management relations. Joint venture partners and owners of wholly foreign enterprises alike are advantaged by strong relations with local Communist Party leaders and Chinese managers, especially in the deployment of staff within a company and the procurement of raw materials. Smooth operation is said to be easily achieved, when, for example, the vice-president of a joint venture is simultaneously company CCP secretary and leader of the trade union. Even good relations between national and foreign managers cannot change the legacy of the command economy overnight. One feature, a lack of long-term strategic thinking on the part of Chinese managers, has been mentioned before. In a Sino-foreign company, such attitudes frequently engender a desire for short-term profit, even at the expense of the enterprise's reputation. Again, especially in the case of retail operations, individual sales employees, used to the idea of a seller's market, have little concept of service and customer satisfaction. Effective selling, of course, is a cooperative effort, and in the service and other sectors lateral communication or group solidarity have often been impeded by the old vertical structure of authority. While labour mobility is generally desirable, the service sector has often seen excessive movement, as employees see the training and skills acquired as a passport to better employment elsewhere, preferably abroad.

Brief reference was made earlier to the desire to attract foreign expertise to reform retailing and the inducements offered through legislation. These are now examined in greater depth. In the early 1990s the government gave approval to joint ventures in retailing in a small number of major locations, as follows: the Shenzhen, Zhuhai, Shantou, Xiamen and Hainan Island Special Economic Zones (SEZs) as well as the cities of Beijing, Tianjin, Shanghai, Dalian, Qingdao and Guangzhou. Two such ventures were permitted for each location. Shenyang, Harbin, Nanjing, Wuhan, Chongjing and Xian were added to the list in 1994. Approval for such operation is, however, at the level of the central government, although small-sized ventures may be approved by local authorities of individual cities and districts. Amount of investment would appear to be the criterion; investment over US$30 million requires central government approval.

In June 1994 there was a policy watershed, with central government allowing, as exceptions, 100 per cent foreign-owned retail operations, which had been previously restricted under detailed implementing regulations. Undoubtedly, foreign retailers will be further encouraged. Until the 1994 law foreign participation in retail had been severely circumscribed, being limited to operations within private shops in hotels and apartment complexes. With large-scale investment now possible, a surge of Japanese and other Asian investment now seems imminent.

With this background, Japanese investment in China's retail sector will be examined. That investment has passed through a number of stages since the new legislation. The first Japanese retailer to enter China was Mitsukoshi which, from 1982 to 1984, operated a consignment sales store in Beijing's Temple of Heaven Park. It also provided technical guidance to the Beijing Department Store, one of the oldest stores in the city. Similarly, Seibu opened a shop inside the Tiantan apartment complex for foreigners in 1988. This again was an internal shop. In 1990 Mitsukoshi opened a comparable outlet in the Shanghai Huayuan Hotel. These operations predated the opening of the tertiary industry to foreigners, and so they were confined to running internal shops in premises under Chinese ownership; they were nevertheless harbingers of more extensive commitment by Japanese retailers.

The first major Japanese retailer to set up a joint venture in China was Yaohan which opened a supermarket with a sales area of 1,500 square metres in Shenzhen City, adjacent to Hong Kong, in 1991. This was, in fact, a special Chinese concession to Yaohan, in view of the cosmopolitan nature of the area. The precedent, however, was followed in 1992 by the opening of the service sector to other foreign retailers, albeit within certain limitations, investment sites being mainly in Shanghai, Beijing, Dalian, Tianjin, Shenzhen and other open coastal cities. Foreign retailers were still prevented from establishing nationwide store networks. In June 1994, however, as a further incentive the government announced a policy of approving the establishment of joint ventures with licences to retail nationwide, and this was followed in July by the establishment of the formerly prohibited 100 per cent wholly owned foreign retail ventures. Significantly, such rights have been secured by two companies, both Japanese: the superstore chain, Daiei, as a joint venture, and Nichiei, as a wholly foreign-owned enterprise.

These were major concessions on the part of the Chinese. Until 1994 the Chinese only permitted joint ventures and limited retail licences to specific cities, and this created difficulties in finding suitable Chinese partners. Thus, if a foreign joint venture partner wanted to establish a chain of stores, it was forced to find a separate partner for each city. Now Daiei and Nichiei may open up chain stores all over China, although this privilege has not yet been extended to other foreign companies.

Both Japanese concerns have formulated a strategy to try to circumvent the barriers posed by the existing distribution system. Daiei, for instance, seeks to acquire a licence for retailing and wholesaling operations on a national level, as well as permission to engage in export and import trade. Daiei would use such licences to open 10,000 stores throughout China, including superstores, with sales areas as large as 20,000 square metres, supermarkets, convenience stores and restaurants. Nichiei is to establish its wholly owned Mycal Dalian Company in Dalian. It also seeks to campaign for the simplification of various joint venture procedures to enable a local subsidiary to obtain treatment equal to that accorded to domestic Chinese firms. It has plans for joint ventures between its Dalian subsidiary and Chinese companies to set up large-sized shopping centres, hotels and supermarkets, about a hundred operations in total, thus opening up a wide range of business throughout the country. Meanwhile, Yaohan, one of the pioneers in the field, is using its Shanghai Number One department store as the flagship for joint ventures throughout China. Seibu is also developing its own China strategy.[69]

In conclusion, while it is evident that China offers a potentially lucrative long-term consumer market for Japanese and other foreign retailers, there are nevertheless formidable barriers to be overcome. Among these may be listed laws which are not enforced consistently across the country but are subject to local interpretation, currency exchange problems and high tariffs. In addition, labour–management relations are still heavily influenced by the legacy of the old command economy; sales staff are insufficiently motivated and there is too little lateral communication. Moreover, with rising expectations, employees are demanding higher wages and consider training as a passport to a better position with another company. There is also the question of merchandise procurement. There are too few quality products that can be sourced in China and too little differentiation among competitors, while imports await lengthy, complex procedures conducted through Chinese trade organs. Most importantly of all, merchandise, whether produced domestically or overseas, must pass through a distribution system which, while in the process of reform, is not truly national, and will remain a serious impediment to the establishment of nationwide retail chains. The answer, of course, is for foreign ventures to set up their own distribution networks.

Summary

In summary, this chapter has examined Japanese investment in a number of China's economic sectors. Of crucial importance are the national motives of the two partners which are, of course, inextricably bound up with their relations in the context of East Asia as a whole. In addition, the two economies are to a large degree complementary: China needs Japanese capital and expertise, while for Japan China would seem a huge potential market, in view of growing protectionist barriers elsewhere like those in the European Union and NAFTA. One of the major priorities in China's industrial plan is the development of infrastructure and in such a sector financing is, because of cost, out of reach of private enterprise. Usually, such financing is the province of aid agencies. Here Japan's OECF has been active, providing a series of loans targeted at transportation, communications and power. This is properly classified as indirect aid, although it is to be noted that a number of Japanese companies are participating in infrastructural projects in, for instance, the petroleum sector. Similar opportunities exist in, say, environmental protection.

Japan's government officials have continually fostered close personal relationships with their Chinese counterparts, some extending back to previous days, and this, together with excellent reconnaissance and linguistic competence on the part of Japan's diplomats, has facilitated inside knowledge of the workings of, particularly, China's planning institutions, and aided cognisance of its industrial priorities. Sino-Japanese cultural affinities are also an asset. Thus, the Japanese have been advantaged over Western rivals in both indirect and, to an extent, direct investment.

The Japanese have invested in a wide range of manufacturing industries; again the close relationship between business and government in Japan has been of benefit, and sectors like automobile manufacture, one of China's priorities, offer long-term potential.

An educated and highly motivated labour force is crucial for the success of Japanese or any other ventures, and China's labour legislation has been implemented as a way of improving labour–management relations. Given that management of human resources is a major key to success, case studies of Japanese ventures in China have been presented to indicate adaptability to particular circumstances. In general, the segregation model is typical of preliminary technical tie-ups involving joint operations, while the positive commitment model corresponds to a fully fledged joint venture and the full management model is normally characteristic of fully owned Japanese ventures. It is to be emphasised that the full management model which gives the Japanese side the greatest freedom of manoeuvre in labour–management relations also facilitates the introduction of such Japanese management practices as on the job training and consultation. These in turn could equip Chinese managers for greater responsibilities and decision-making powers in such enterprises in the years to come.

The final section considered Japanese investment in distribution, a sector where reform has lagged behind that in agriculture and industry.

As in the latter, the Chinese seek to avoid foreign control, although foreign retailing ventures are clearly seen as models for their Chinese counterparts, just as Sino-foreign-invested ventures are seen as the pacesetters for the reform of state enterprises. Given rising personal incomes and greater purchasing power, China offers potentially lucrative markets, and consumer demand is soaring, especially in the cities of the eastern seaboard where retailing by such well-known Japanese names as Yaohan has been concentrated since new Chinese legislation was passed in 1992 and 1994. Moreover there is greater consumer discernment, whether in food, clothing or consumer durables, favouring high-quality joint-venture and foreign products. These trends are comparable to those in Japan during the 1960s and 1970s.

But Japanese participation in the market is still restricted, and there remain formidable barriers to the creation of a nationwide network of stores by overseas retailers, the foremost obstacles being difficulties in the passage of goods, whether locally sourced or imported, through China's antiquated distribution system.

To date the Japanese government has been prominent in granting loans and assistance to China. In statistical terms Japan's direct investment in China seems much less significant, however. Nevertheless, its influence and effectiveness are greater than at first sight. Although in the 1980s Japan's companies were often said to be reluctant to build up China as a competitor on world markets, since the early 1990s Japanese high-tech investment in Chinese ventures has been increasing. In addition, the Japanese have selectively targeted centres like Dalian and Shanghai, where their stake accounts for a considerable proportion of total investment. Moreover the rate of Japanese contract implementation is high and most of Japan's investments are profitable. Finally, a number of overseas Chinese companies from Hong Kong, the major investor in China, are subsidiaries of Japanese concerns.

The Japanese are investing in the long-term potential of China's vast market; the Chinese for their part seek to diversify their sources of funds. Investment by Japanese companies is now growing in a wide range of industrial and tertiary sectors. This is already having a crucial impact on the Sino-Japanese trade which is the topic of the next chapter.

4   Japan's role in China's world trade

China's export priorities and trading enterprise reform

The Chinese leaders' emulation of Japan's economic policy, discussed in previous chapters, has had a strong impact on the strategy, content, direction and commodity structure of China's trade with Japan itself and the rest of the world. Currently, however, China's trade policy, pursued in accordance with a key element of the Japanese strategy, export orientation, is facing a number of major challenges. While a basic principle is to maintain a rough balance between imports and exports, China suffered a deficit in its world trade in 1993 and 1994. Chinese officials have blamed the creation of regional blocs and resulting protectionism, claiming that Western countries are unilaterally imposing restrictions and unreasonable sanctions on Chinese trade.[1] Nor has China's export drive been helped by accusations of dumping, generally defined as selling goods in foreign countries at below domestic cost. Nevertheless at the root of the deficit are more fundamental structural economic problems which only China's policy makers can solve. The fact is that the country's exports are becoming too expensive, especially in competition with goods from other Asian countries at similar stages of development, one cause being the relatively high value of the yuan or *renminbi*. A recent devaluation of the yuan to 8.7 to the US dollar helped China's exports to grow by 31.9 per cent in 1994 but any further official depreciation may well be ruled out because of increases in state foreign exchange reserves in 1995. Moreover, the appreciation of the yuan since its sudden fall in value at the beginning of 1994 has put pressure on China's exporters but the government, which must balance a number of economic priorities, dare not devalue too quickly because of inflationary pressures. Furthermore trade deficits are being caused precisely because of the upward movement of manufacturing costs as wages, especially, have risen, reducing China's traditional cheap labour advantage; export expansion is thus more difficult.[2] The Chinese must move out of a vicious circle: if the country is no longer advantaged in labour-intensive products, then the best option is to target value-added goods but, to do this, capital equipment must be imported, and this can only be paid for by ever increasing exports.[3]

China's drive for export competitiveness is to proceed on three fronts. In the words of Wu Yi, Minister of Foreign Trade and Economic Cooperation, the basic principle is to attain a rough balance between imports and exports. Such balance is to be achieved by export expansion rather than import restriction. Advanced technology and equipment, together with other goods in short supply on the domestic market, will be imported but luxury items severely limited. Significantly, 80 per cent of China's foreign exchange comes from exports, a prerequisite for the country's modernisation. Thus the first aspect of trade policy is the encouragement of sales of capital-intensive high-tech quality products instead of labour-intensive ones. The consequent rise in added value is intended to offset losses caused by high export costs: products sent overseas will increasingly include technology-intensive machinery and electronic products as well as complete sets of equipment.

Secondly, foreign trade is stimulated by macroeconomic measures, the first of which is the exchange rate mechanism. Reform of China's foreign exchange management system began in 1994, steps being initiated to unify the former dual exchange rates, with the ultimate objective of making the *renminbi* into a fully convertible currency. This unitary system, to be based on a floating exchange rate, according to market supply and demand, will be more economically realistic and especially advantageous to exporters among China's foreign-invested enterprises. In the past foreign ventures were required to register their capital at the official exchange rate, while profits remitted abroad were calculated at the market rate, the latter being higher than the former; under the new rules overseas investors in China stand to benefit. In place of the old swap centres, specifically designed to enable foreign ventures to obtain scarce foreign exchange, the banks will now play a greater role by implementing a system of settling accounts and selling currencies. In addition, the requirement by which foreign trading enterprises must submit a portion of their foreign exchange income to the state has been abolished, giving them greater control over their own resources. Foreign exchange reform, of course, also reflects the need to provide the kind of transparency demanded by GATT and the World Trade Organisation – which the Chinese leaders hope to join – as well as the increased role that foreign trade plays in China's GNP.[4] Another incentive for exporters is extension of credit through the newly established Import-Export Credit Bank, the main function of which is to furnish loans to support the export of China's capital goods.[5]

The third element, potentially the most decisive key to successful exporting, is foreign trade management reform. Until the post-1978 reforms the major industrial enterprises as well as the wholesale and retail distribution systems were virtually state monopolies; similarly, until the reforms of the 1980s, the conduct of foreign trade was subject to central government control and planning. Just as industrial enterprise and internal distribution reform have been designed to enhance efficiency, so also is restructuring of foreign trade management intended to inject competitiveness; once again a role for foreign-invested companies is envisaged. From now on market forces rather than administrative levers will determine the conduct of foreign trade.

The predominant trend is towards management of foreign trade through organs independent of the state. While the main focuses in this study are the ongoing reforms initiated from 1994, changes in foreign trade management have been in progress since the 1980s, and these will be briefly summarised before attention is turned to the structures now being created as well as those projected for the future. Under the pre-1978 Maoist command economy policies of self-reliance were adopted, foreign trade being seen as an adjunct to domestic economic activity. Essentially, international economic relations were handled by a number of import-export corporations centralised under the Ministry of Foreign Trade and Economic Cooperation (MOFTEC). The reforms of the 1980s brought considerable decentralisation and as these took ever greater effect, new product-specialised trade corporations were set up under the aegis of the central ministries responsible for industrial production rather than under the Ministry of Foreign Trade. Significantly, this gave Chinese traders specific expertise relating to import or export products. In addition, there was devolution of initiative to the regions; provinces and cities could now form their own foreign trade bodies and approve some import and export contracts. Since the late 1980s decentralisation of foreign trade administration has accelerated, with provinces being given autonomous trading rights for a number of commodities, although there remains conflict, born of divergent interests, between the centre and the regions. In addition, such changes have not meant that China's trading enterprises are becoming independent; they are still subject to direction by the state, whether nationally or locally.

Nevertheless, since 1994 China's policy makers have determined that such enterprises be reformed in line with the market economy; like their industrial counterparts, they are to lose their monopoly position and be exposed to market forces in a move away from the central planning model. New provisions are enshrined in China's Foreign Trade Law which went into effect in July 1994. It means that administrative fiat is to be replaced by macroeconomic controls in the transition from a command to a market economy in the foreign trade sphere, and is thus a sign of the Chinese government's commitment both nationally and internationally to free trade. As China's foreign trade companies become independent entities, MOFTEC will serve as their regulator rather than their state owner, the law being the mechanism through which this sector may be guided in the national interest. Moreover, the law contains clauses that reflect the central government's unease with losing too much control over China's external trade. For example, the law ostensibly places limits on free trade by giving the state residual powers to restrict or prohibit the import or export of goods and technology when issues involving national security, balance of payments, and health and safety are involved. In addition, the government has abolished mandatory planning in order to liberalise the management of imports and exports but a few commodities of crucial national importance will be subject to central control. While every country ultimately retains such power, in China's case there is as yet no independent judiciary, and MOFTEC writes and administers the rules governing its own activities. Moreover, the new law does not specify any time limit for MOFTEC to review or terminate such restriction on trade. But officially the law commits the Chinese to free competition among their own trading enterprises and on international markets.

One of the most significant provisions of the law is that relating to foreign trading enterprises, designated as the only bodies authorised to engage in the import and export of goods and technology. Importantly, the law does not mention national requirements for foreign trading enterprises, implicitly opening the door to participation by overseas companies to compete with the Chinese, in this sphere as in others. It is, however, stipulated that to qualify as a foreign trading enterprise, companies must already have a track record in the import-export business and, as there have hitherto been severe restrictions on foreign participation, this requirement will for the time being limit the number of overseas firms eligible as well as the scope of business in which they can engage. This is another example of maintenance of government control over the trade sector.

Domestic trading companies thus have a head start over potential foreign competition, although in the long term it may be that foreign-invested companies can provide the expertise to resolve such bottlenecks in the service sector as financing, transportation and tele-communications.[6]

Meanwhile, however, the reform focuses on enhancing the competitive position of foreign trading enterprises on both domestic and international markets. As in the industrial sector a crucial prerequisite is better management, especially now that the 7,000 firms which formerly held a state monopoly will soon have to compete on equal terms with the 100,000 that have been gradually granted trading management rights over the last decade. The objective is to enable all to participate more fully in international markets. In addition, like their international counterparts, trading enterprises are to be responsible for their own profits and losses.

Evidence suggests that there may already be too many trading companies entering the market, and even greater competition will result in future, as various import-export trading rights are further extended to more manufacturing enterprises and science and technology units, as well as some domestic commercial and materials supply companies, the implication being that the full rigours of the market be allowed to operate, even if this results in bankruptcy. A premium will thus be placed on the creation of a modern management system: new personnel deployment methods and remuneration packages are to be introduced, with labour contracts and payment in US dollars earned from settlement in foreign exchange, designed as incentives for staff and workers alike. Thus, in summary, improvements in decision making and leadership are intended, as in the industrial sector, to lead to streamlining and therefore greater competitiveness.[7]

While monopolies are being curtailed, increased competition seems likely to lead to greater economies of scale, a trend being positively encouraged by the MOFTEC Minister Wu Yi in statements introducing the Foreign Trade Law. Large-scale operations are to be achieved through the diversification of products handled; this contrasts with the former situation when, under the ministries, in spite of centralisation and state monopoly, foreign trading enterprises tended to deal in only a narrow range of commodities. Such diversification is nevertheless seen as assisting the development of their main operations and by-products, and is to be furthered by close cooperation between the trading firms and China's manufacturing companies and agricultural sector, the ultimate goal being the creation of enterprise groups combining commerce and production and cutting across different regions. Such links built on complementary strengths are seen to be internally advantageous, as well as furthering China's international competitiveness. These enterprise group partnerships will be facilitated by a shareholding system, currently at an experimental stage and similar to that envisaged for state enterprises in the production sector. While at the time of writing it is only possible to speculate concerning the long-term development of the reformed trading enterprises, ongoing organisation of enterprise groups in Beijing, according to the above pattern, highly praised by the MOFTEC Minister Wu Yi, would seem to be akin to the sogoshosha, or trading companies, linked to the keiretsu or conglomerates in Japan.[8] Chinese economic journals are replete with articles extolling the success of the Japanese trading companies, particularly their great reconnaissance and information-gathering capacities. The role of the sogoshosha in Japan's post-war economic growth must not be underestimated; they located strategic raw materials for the industries of resource-poor Japan, while simul-taneously exploring new markets, especially in the less accessible countries of the then Communist bloc. Their intelligence has also proved invaluable as Japan's multinationals have targeted local pro-duction in Western Europe and North America. The creation of enterprise groups around China's trading enterprises may perhaps be seen as a prelude to the further development of the country's multi-national companies, which are said to have had an auspicious begin-ning. Up to 1991, 1,683 Chinese directly invested enterprises had been established in over a hundred countries. A special department is to be established to oversee the activities of Chinese firms abroad.[9]

In summary, trading enterprise reform under the rubric of China's first Foreign Trade Law is intended to enhance export competitiveness and thus enable the country to pay for advanced technology and capital plant imports. As in the case of the state industrial sector, management reform as well as changes in personnel deployment and remuneration are intended as incentives to greater efficiency. Finally, enterprise group creation around trading enterprises and the development of multinationals are themselves modelled on Japan's post-war experience.

The evolution of China's world trade

While it is as yet too early to assess the long-term impact of trading enterprise management reform, the impact of decentralisation of de-cision making in this sector and in secondary industry since the 1980s has been reflected in China's world trade performance. In fact, a recent World Bank report commented favourably on the reforms, stating that these had made China's trade system in practice more open than its high nominal tariff rates, import controls and other non-tariff barriers might suggest. Openness of the economy may be measured as the ratio of

China's trade to GNP in current prices; this increased from 38 per cent in 1993 to 45 per cent in 1994, indicating a greater degree of reliance of the national economy on foreign trade. In addition, in 1994 China ranked eleventh among the world's trading nations and regions as opposed to thirty-second in 1978. In terms of exports alone, growth has been remarkable. China was the world's thirteenth largest exporter in 1991; it had taken twenty-sixth place in 1980. Moreover, in terms of value, according to preliminary statistics of China's Administration of Customs, its foreign trade volume reached US$236.7 billion in 1994, a 20.9 per cent increase over that of 1993. Of China's total foreign trade volume in 1994, exports amounted to US$121 billion, 31.9 per cent higher than in 1993, while imports reached US$115.7 billion, an increase of 11.2 per cent over 1993. China thus moved from deficit to surplus.[10] Growth in absolute terms of China's world trade is shown in Table 4.1.

Table 4.1 China's trade with the world ($billion)

	Exports (FOB)	Imports (CIF)	Total	Balance
1987	39.4	43.2	82.6	-3.8
1988	47.5	55.2	102.7	-7.7
1989	52.5	59.1	111.6	-6.6
1990	62.1	53.4	115.5	8.7
1991	71.9	63.8	135.7	8.1
1992	85.0	80.6	165.6	4.4
1993	91.8	104.0	195.8	-12.2
1994	121.0	115.7	236.7	5.3

Sources: For 1987–93, China's State Statistical Bureau, as quoted in *The China Business Review*, May–June 1994, p. 59; 1994, preliminary statistics of China's General Administration of Customs (*SWB*, 1 February 1995)

Since the 1980s overseas investment has been encouraged to spur the technological transformation of China's industry and in the 1990s foreign ventures have been playing a growing role in China's imports and exports. In early 1991, for example, wholly foreign-owned companies, Sino-foreign cooperative enterprises of various kinds and Sino-foreign joint ventures were already accounting for 20.4 per cent of China's two-way trade, with the greatest increase in exports coming from the first category. Goods processed with imported raw materials represented the largest proportion of the total exports of those three categories of foreign enterprise. But in the 1990s such foreign concerns have been moving beyond processing and assembly, also producing capital goods and more sophisticated consumer items. Again, in 1991, according to China's customs statistics, export items produced by overseas-funded firms, including machinery, textiles, clothing and shoes, for instance, were showing marked increases, with electrical equipment sales outside China rising by 58.8 per cent and valued at US$1.62 billion. In turn, of course, such export growth necessitated more imports of both capital goods and natural resources, such as electrical machinery, electronic devices, raw materials and chemicals as well as cloth for the textile and garment industries. In 1994 total foreign trade by the three categories amounted to US$87.65 billion, a 30.7 per cent increase over 1993, accounting for 37 per cent of China's total trade as against 34.3 per cent in 1993.[11]

Much has been written of the growing wealth differentials between the southeastern coast and the hinterland, and the Chinese official policies on investment in the 1980s only accelerated such trends. As discussed earlier, however, in the mid-1990s there has been a shift from emphasis on regions to stress on industries, while at the same time new sites for foreign investment in Shanghai's Pudong Zone and the northeast as well as the hinterland are being strategically targeted. Undoubtedly, however, foreign investment has been contributing to wealth disparities in the country as a whole, and in the short term at least these seem set to widen. A partial indication of such socioeconomic inequality and the role of foreign investment in China's trade is the contribution of regions to exports: in 1994 the overseas sales of the eleven provinces and cities on the east coast increased by 34.2 per cent, while those of the hinterland rose by 24.3 per cent. In absolute terms, of course, there was export growth in both the above regions, with the coast starting from a higher base level but the differential has widened.[12]

In summary, foreign ventures in China, still mainly located in China's coastal cities and Special Economic Zones, are boosting the quality and value of China's exports.

A Japan External Trade Organisation (JETRO) source estimated in early 1994 that China was only able to increase exports of purely domestic products by US$140 million in 1993; foreign ventures, however, accounted for 27.5 per cent or US$25.2 billion of total exports. Thus it is mainly foreign ventures which currently give China its potential for export growth.

Most significantly, on the basis of the above statistics, it can also be seen that foreign ventures are contributing to the evolving commodity composition of China's trade. Between 1980 and 1992 the proportion of finished products among China's export commodities increased by a wide margin, with the share of machinery and electronic products rising

Table 4.2 Commodity composition of China's imports and exports (per cent)

| | Exports | | Imports | |
	1980	1992	1980	1992
Primary products	49.7	18.3	34.8	16.4
Finished products	50.3	81.7	65.2	83.6

Source: China's State Statistical Bureau

from 9.4 per cent to 24.7 per cent. As China's manufacturing capacity grew, Chinese imports of finished products also increased, with the share of machinery and electronic products rising from 25.6 per cent to 38.8 per cent. The commodity composition of China's two-way foreign trade is summarised in Table 4.2.

For exports, these trends have continued in the mid-1990s; the proportion of industrial manufactures as a whole in China's total exports increased from 81.8 per cent in 1993 to over 83.7 per cent in 1994. The export value of mechanical and electronic products was US$32 billion, an increase of 40.9 per cent, and higher than the growth rate of all exports. Exports of light industrial consumer products also grew in 1994. For example, the export of garments was valued at US$23.72 billion in 1994, a rise of 28.7 per cent over figures for 1993. Textile and related product exports reached US$11.83 billion in 1994, an increase of 35.8 per cent over 1993. Shoe exports were valued at US$5.7 billion, a rise of 12.9 per cent over the previous year. Toy exports were valued at US$3.06 million in 1994, an increase of 16.5 per cent over 1993.[13]

Thus export figures indicate continuity and earlier import trends were also maintained in the mid-1990s. There were, however, slight adjustments. In 1994, for example, the proportion of industrial manufactured products among total imports decreased from 86.3 per cent to 85.8 per cent, a variation partly reflecting the restrictions on the purchase of luxury items from abroad; these had earlier been growing. Thus imports of steel products fell by 24.3 per cent, oil products by 25.4 per cent and small cars by 51.3 per cent. But there was a considerable increase in high-technology products like means of production, electric equipment and telecommunications facilities. The importation of telephone switchboards was valued at US$1.81 billion in 1994, an increase of 76.7 per cent over 1993. Significantly, China was importing more raw materials; cotton imports, for instance, increased in volume from 10,000 tonnes in 1993 to 500,000 tonnes in 1994. In summary, commodity composition trends are themselves a reflection of China's current stage of economic development.[14] As China moves out of the ranks of the poorer developing countries, exports of manufactures will increase as those of primary products decline in importance. Imports will still reflect China's need for capital plant but purchases of primary products from overseas may continue to rise.

China's trade strategy must necessarily take account of price movements in international trade, and this will in turn increasingly influence the geographical direction of China's trade. It was suggested earlier that a consistent feature of China's foreign policy has been support for developing countries, and Chinese sources are full of references to the unfair advantage allegedly enjoyed by developed countries in international trade. According to the Chinese, between 1981 and 1991 the average prices for primary products on world markets dropped by 31 per cent and those for minerals and fuel by 41 per cent and 43 per cent: these are often the domain of the developing countries. Prices for exports overall from such states fell by 41 per cent over the decade. In contrast, prices for finished products jumped by 31 per cent overall over the same time span, with those from developing countries rising by 14 per cent and those from developed countries by 53 per cent. The most rapid rises were for machinery and electronic products, mainstays of more mature economies. From these statistics, it may be seen that the Chinese economy will be more advantaged as it moves towards high-tech value-added products, although it will still need to import capital goods for some years to come.

In fact, this changing commodity composition is already affecting the geographical direction of China's trade. In terms of the regional composition of imports and exports, China's trade volume with Asian countries has developed rapidly, with the proportion rising from 58.3 per cent in 1984 to 66.5 per cent in 1992. Consequently, the proportion of trade with other regions has fallen by varying degrees because of the rapid development of China's trade with East and Southeast Asia. This trend derives from two factors: the increasing proportion of manufactures in China's exports, for which there is a market in the region, and the growing weight of Asia in world trade. Overall, there is a suggestion that China's reliance on foreign trade with the developed countries of North America, Europe and Japan has diminished.[15]

In any case it has always been a cardinal principle of Chinese policy 'to use barbarians to control barbarians' and, in a trading context, to diversify both sources of supply and markets. To dilute trading risk China's traders are said to be targeting Russia, Latin America, Southeast Asia, the Middle East, Africa, Taiwan and Macao. China is currently heavily reliant for trade on a few developed countries and regions; statistics for the General Administration of Customs show that

Japan, Hong Kong, the United States and the European Union accounted for 66 per cent of China's total imports and exports in 1994. Hong Kong and the United States were ranked second and third respectively in terms of their trade with China. In fact, the United States absorbs more than a third of China's exports while facing a heavily protected market in China itself. Others in the ranks of China's top ten trading partners in 1994 were countries from the European Union (of which Germany was the largest) and Taiwan, South Korea, Russia, Singapore, Australia and Canada. All the top ten partners recorded increases in trade with China in 1994, except for Russia, whose exports to China decreased by 33.8 per cent, while China's exports to Russia went down by 41.2 per cent, both admittedly from a narrow base. China's top trading partners appear in Table 4.3. Attention is now turned to trade with Japan which has overtaken Hong Kong as China's largest trading partner.[16]

Table 4.3 China's top trading partners: 1993

Nation	Total trade (US$ billion)	Percentage of total
Japan	39.0	20
Hong Kong	32.5	17
United States	27.7	14
European Community	26.1	13
Taiwan	14.4	7
ASEAN	10.7	5
South Korea	8.2	4
Russia	7.7	0.4
Others	–	19

Source: China's Customs Statistics, as quoted in *China Business Review*, May–June 1994, p. 59
Note: Hong Kong's share in China's trade may have been overestimated in view of re-exports.

Officially, Hong Kong alone receives 54 per cent of China's total exports. But, according to the World Bank, adjusting for re-exports raises the US share of Chinese exports from 8.7 per cent to 25.6 per cent and the European Community share from 9.2 per cent to 19.2 per cent, while the Hong Kong share shifts back to a mere 6.2 per cent. For details, see the *Financial Times*, 18 November 1993.

Sino-Japanese trade

Sino-Japanese trade has its own special characteristics but in general it follows the world trends outlined above. Nevertheless, the nature of trade and investment between the two countries, together with economic complementarity and cultural affinity, suggests that Japan will in coming years prove the most important contributor to China's modernisation. As stated, Japan is China's greatest two-way trading partner; significantly, in 1993 China became the sixth most important destination for Japanese exports. As a result, China moved to second place after the United States in Japan's two-way trade.

According to Japanese Finance Ministry sources, two-way trade was worth US$37 billion in 1993, Chinese exports being valued at US$20.565 billion, a rise of 21.3 per cent, and imports US$17.273 billion, an increase of 44.6 per cent. While China's trade surplus was reduced, Japan suffered its sixth successive annual deficit with China. The proportion of imports from Japan to the total volume of China's imports had increased from 14 per cent in 1990 to 22 per cent in 1993. In addition, the proportion of China's total export volume heading for Japan over the same period had risen from 14.51 per cent to 17.2 per cent, indicating the importance of such trade to both countries.[17] According to the latest Japanese statistics Sino-Japanese trade reached US$46.24 billion in 1994, a 22.2 per cent increase over 1993. Japan exported US$18.68 billion worth of goods to China in 1994, an 8.1 per cent increase over the previous year, and imported products valued at US$27.56 billion from China, an increase of 34 per cent. Thus trade was again in China's favour, the Japanese deficit being $US8.88 billion.[18]

Focus is now on commodity composition of Sino-Japanese trade which has been strongly influenced by the priorities of China's post-1978 open door policy and subsequent Japanese investment. The discussion below mainly concerns the latest developments in two-way trade as of 1994 but current trends were already in evidence in the early 1990s, and data for those years will first be briefly reviewed. Continuing increases in Sino-Japanese trade in the early 1990s reflected a number of factors. Japan and other countries have assisted with improvement and development of China's industrial production facilities, and yen loans especially have aided infrastructure and increased energy resources. Consequently, the structure of Sino-Japanese trade has followed the world pattern examined above. Thus Japan has been buying more processed goods and, generally speaking, fewer primary commodities from China. The share of finished products in China's total exports to Japan grew from 40 per cent in 1978 to 58 per cent in 1991. Composition was similar in 1992, with better-quality light industrial and electronic goods being prominent. In addition, precisely because of ongoing infrastructural expansion and industrial development in China, imports from Japan were growing in sectors like telecommunications and high-performance consumer electronics, reflecting China's rising living standards.[19]

These figures and proportions follow the structural changes in China's economy, and the commodity composition of Sino-Japanese trade in the 1990s will now be examined in more detail. In 1992 and 1993 there was a boom in construction in China accompanied by a sharp rise in investment in fixed assets. The key construction projects of the Eighth Five Year Plan (1991–5) brought demand for machinery and equipment. In 1993, for example, the main products in which Japan experienced export growth were ferrous metals, which rose 101.4 per cent in value to US$2.965 billion, with steel products especially in evidence. Exports of communications equipment grew by a similar figure but fewer electrical consumer goods were sold to China, perhaps because of local Chinese production and government attempts to restrict luxury imports. There were spectacular rises in transport equipment, especially buses and trucks, though Chinese customs restrictions on passenger car imports began to bite. Purchases of other machinery and equipment also grew rapidly; this category as a whole accounted for 57.5 per cent of all Japanese exports to China.

Trends in China's exports to Japan in 1993 followed the pattern set in 1991 and 1992. The share of manufactured goods in total sales rose by 5.4 points from the 63.7 per cent of 1992 to reach 69.1 per cent in 1993. In fact, manufactured goods exports rose by 31.4 per cent, China thereby maintaining its position as number two among suppliers of such products to Japan. For example, garments and their accessories, which accounted for 44.5 per cent of the imports of manufactured goods from China to Japan, rose by 30.1 per cent. China's share of Japanese clothes imports reached 51.2 per cent by value. More importantly, because of changes in China's economy, there was a major growth in machinery and equipment exports, and their percentage in Japan's manufactured goods imports rose from the 10.3 per cent of 1992 to 12.6 per cent of all exports to China.

Main examples were audio-visual equipment, distribution and control equipment as well as computer central processors (digital) and such precision equipment as electronic copiers.

In addition, although it is argued that primary products as a whole are playing a decreasing role in China's foreign trade, minerals and fuels are still prominent in China's exports to Japan. In 1993 these exports fell but largely because of China's own growing domestic fuel demands and the effects of the Japanese recession. Nevertheless the Japanese are largely dependent on fuel imports, and as new Chinese mines and wells are brought into operation, China's exports to Japan could increase.[20] But China's raw material exports to Japan in general have been falling, for example cotton for textile production.

Sino-Japanese trade composition in 1994 has confirmed these trends. There is, however, one sector which needs further consideration. During the 1990s there has been growth in food products developed for export to Japan by Japanese, Taiwanese and other ventures in China. Japanese agriculture has long been protected but in 1994 there was a striking increase in rice imports by Japan. China was the greatest exporter of rice to Japan in the first half of the year. Discernible is a shift towards China as a major source of food in the future, in spite of that country's own expanding needs. Thus, while Sino-Japanese trade will become ever more horizontal (with similar kinds of industrial products to exchange), rather than vertical (with raw materials provided for manufacturers), one primary sector, food, is likely to loom larger in China's exports to Japan.[21] A general overview of the data presented above for the composition of Sino-Japanese trade appears in Tables 4.4–4.7.

The main determinant of this trade pattern is Japanese investment, both indirect and direct. Japan's exports to China have been stimulated by indirect investment; a number of key construction projects listed in China's Eighth Five Year Plan, like transportation systems, are being financed by Japan's OECF, as discussed earlier. In addition, some agricultural schemes are also being supported by OECF. A case in point is a plant being constructed in southwest China's Guizhou Province for the manufacture of chemical fertiliser, a crucial element in raising grain and other agricultural yields. By the terms of an

Table 4.4 Trends in Japan–China trade (in US$million)

Year	Exports (A)		Imports (B)		Total (A) + (B)	
1981	5,095	(0.3)	5,292	(22.4)	10,387	(10.5)
1982	3,511	(−31.3)	5,352	(1.1)	8,863	(−14.7)
1983	4,912	(39.9)	5,087	(−5.0)	9,999	(12.8)
1984	7,217	(46.9)	5,958	(17.1)	13,175	(31.8)
1985	12,477	(72.9)	6,483	(8.8)	18,980	(43.9)
1986	9,857	(−21.0)	5,652	(−12.8)	15,506	(−16.2)
1987	8,250	(−16.3)	7,401	(30.9)	15,651	(0.9)
1988	9,476	(14.9)	9,859	(33.2)	19,335	(23.5)
1989	8,516	(−10.1)	11,146	(13.1)	19,862	(1.7)
1990	6,130	(−28.0)	12,054	(8.1)	18,184	(−7.5)
1991	8,593	(40.2)	14,216	(17.9)	22,809	(25.4)

Source: Compiled by Yamaichi Research Institute on the basis of Customs Clearance Statistics, Japanese Ministry of Finance (Yamaichi Research, *Japan Outlook*, 1992, p. 13)
Note: Figures in parentheses represent percentage change from the previous year.

Table 4.5 Sino-Japanese trade, 1992–1994 (in US$ million)

Year	Exports	Imports	Total
1992	16,953	11,949	28,902
1993	20,565	17,273	37,838
1994	27,560	18,680	46,240

Sources: (1992) *China Newsletter*, 1993, no. 104, pp. 23–4; (1993) *ibid.*, 1994, no. 109, p. 21; (1994) *Xinhua News Agency*, 26 January 1995, as reported in *SWB*, 8 February 1995

Table 4.6 Export trends to China, by item (in US$ million)

	1990		1991	
Chemical products	751	(−4.7)	1,072	(42.7)
Steel	1,059	(−54.4)	1,364	(28.9)
Machinery	1,034	(−35.2)	1,497	(44.8)
TVs	241	(−14.8)	423	(75.5)
VCRs	288	(10.4)	410	(42.0)
Communications equipment	110	(−28.7)	125	(13.3)
Four-wheeled vehicles	146	(−12.0)	341	(134.4)
Two-wheeled vehicles	16	(−76.8)	48	(215.9)
Auto parts	54	(11.4)	107	(100.3)
Precision instruments	96	(−17.0)	143	(49.4)
Total	6,130	(−28.0)	8,593	(40.2)

Source: Compiled by Yamaichi Research Institute on the basis of Customs Clearance Statistics, Japanese Ministry of Finance (Yamaichi Research, *Japan Outlook*, 1992, p. 13)
Note: Figures in parentheses represent percentage change from the previous year.

Table 4.7 Import trends from China, by item (in US$ million)

	1987		1991	
		% share		% share
Foodstuffs	1,282	17.3	2,446	17.2
Materials	1,071	14.5	1,145	8.1
Crude oil	1,553	21.0	1,767	12.4
Total of non-manufactured goods	4,460	60.3	5,954	41.9
Clothing	833	11.0	3,234	22.7
Steel	128	1.7	511	3.6
Machinery	63	0.9	824	5.8
Total of manufactured goods	2,941	39.7	8,262	58.1
Total	7,401	100.0	14,216	100.0

Source: Compiled by Yamaichi Research Institute on the basis of Customs Clearance Statistics, Japanese Ministry of Finance (Yamaichi Research, *Japan Outlook*, 1992, p. 13)

agreement signed in November 1994 between China's National Technical Import and Export Corporation and Mitsui Engineering Shipping Corporation, together with Mitsubishi Heavy Industry of Japan, the two Japanese companies will provide production equipment. When completed the factory will become the world's largest producer of chemical fertiliser.[22]

Direct investment, on the other hand, is a spur to two-way trade; Japan's manufacturers benefit from sales of capital plant and, most importantly, technology, the country now accounting for 28 per cent of China's imports in that sector by value, while Japanese ventures in China export finished products back to their own country as well as worldwide.[23] A rising proportion of textiles, metal goods and computer software being shipped to Japan is made in factories with Japanese investment.[24]

It may appear that the above has presented a rather sanguine view of Sino-Japanese trading relations but these have not been without friction. While, for example, there are now fewer complaints about Japanese reluctance to transfer technology to China, some of Japan's companies on occasion do not seem loath to export poor-quality equipment to China. In 1992, for instance, Zhejiang Light Industrial Products Import and Export Corporation of Hangzhou filed a lawsuit against a Japanese firm for supplying machines in poor condition. Failure to obtain damages in full after Chinese and international arbitration prompted the Zhejiang Company to bring the case before a Japanese district court.[25]

More fundamentally, perhaps, the Chinese have attacked as unfair Japanese tariff duties, quota levels and other limitations imposed upon Chinese exports to Japan. Japan's MITI for its part, in a strange irony, given frequent criticisms of Japan on world markets, in 1992 accused the Chinese of dumping: the latter had been selling ferro-silicon manganese, an ingredient in making steel, at unfairly low prices, thus causing damage to domestic Japanese producers and contravening the principles of GATT.

Such friction is to a growing extent due to China's commercial success. For example, according to Japanese statistics, a quarter of Japan's cotton cloth imports came from China in 1993, and Japanese enterprises have been lobbying their government to restrict such imports.[26] In the face of these moves Chinese officially inspired sources have shown awareness of such potential for future trade friction, recommending commodity composition changes as a long-term solution. Thus Chinese exporters must target Japan's markets with quality products, in order to compete against Japanese and South Asian goods.[27] In conclusion, then, the key to equitable trading relations would seem to lie in horizontal trade.

Summary

This chapter has evaluated Sino-Japanese trading relations within the overall context of China's economic priorities and world trade. Chinese policy is to export more value-added goods to pay for capital plant and machinery, thereby reducing the external deficit. To achieve this goal the Chinese are taking such measures as unifying exchange rates to provide incentives for foreign ventures. In addition, China's trading enterprises, hitherto monopolies under state direction, are being made independent entities, in order that competition should facilitate the movement of imports and exports. The intention is also to achieve economies of scale. But while new independent foreign trading enterprises are being encouraged, it is unclear whether the participation of overseas companies will be permitted in this sector. In any case Chinese trading companies with a track record will have a head start. Foreign trading management reform has additional ramifications: enterprise groups, linking commercial activities and industrial production, are being encouraged, and these are modelled on the Japanese keiretsu or conglomerates which themselves bring together these functions. China already has multinationals investing abroad, and the reconnaissance function, typical of Japanese trading companies, is at a premium.

The principles governing trading management reform are enshrined in China's Foreign Trade Law which came into force in 1994. Ostensibly, the document is committed to free trade, yet the Chinese leaders are reluctant to surrender control over the sector. In addition to having, in common with all other countries, the prerogative to prohibit or restrict certain imports or exports, albeit within international rules like those of GATT, MOFTEC, untrammelled by an independent judiciary, writes and administers the rules governing its own actions.

Post-1978 economic reforms, especially the decentralisation of decision making, have stimulated growth, and China is more reliant than ever on international commerce, as indicated by the ratio of such trade to GNP. Foreign ventures have contributed to that growth and have helped to transform the commodity structure of China's foreign trade, with more finished goods and fewer primary products now being exported. Both capital plant and equipment and primary raw materials for processing are being imported in greater quantities. Foreign ventures are contributing considerably to China's export drive as a whole.

While having their own special characteristics, Chinese trading relations with Japan have followed the general trends in China's world trade. Stimulus has been provided by Japanese investment ventures in China which, while buying capital goods from Japan, have also exported goods back there. Commodity composition is evolving in line with the developments discussed earlier but there is still potential for trade friction in sectors like textiles. Though still a contentious area, Japanese technology transfer to China is increasing. Sino-Japanese trade is becoming horizontal; that is, differentiated goods are being exchanged. There may well also be a potentially lucrative market in Japan for China's agricultural products.

In economic terms, however, the destinies of the two countries are being more and more influenced by market developments in Asia as a whole. In the years to come Sino-Japanese economic relations will increasingly be conducted in the context of sub-regional integration in East Asia. These topics will be the focus of the next chapter.

5 Greater China: sub-regional economic integration

China's regional policy

The Chinese leaders' policies towards regional integration in East Asia are both economically and politically motivated. Chinese sources argue that in the decades to come China's economic destiny will be inextricably linked to that of East and Southeast Asia. While Western markets are not precluded and will continue to play a role in China's development, their share in China's total trade could be reduced if protectionist sentiments continue to grow in Europe and North America alike; witness friction over China's textile sales to the latter, not to mention United States unease over intellectual property rights in China.[1] Thus, in line with their time-honoured principle of trade diversification, the Chinese continue to condemn Western exclusivity, claiming commitment to free trade throughout the world and especially in East and Southeast Asia. Any regional economic integration under the Greater China concept should not be exclusive but open to all countries both within and outside the region. The Asia-Pacific has the highest growth rate of any region and, given Japan's economic superpower status and China's gradual ascent to the ranks of developed countries, its weight in the world economy is likely to increase. To quote a Chinese journal, the East Asian sector of that region, encompassing Japan, China, the two Korean states, Taiwan and Hong Kong, accounts for 7.8 per cent of the world's land area, 26.1 per cent of its population, 20.24 per cent of its GNP and 14.5 per cent of its import-export trade. In addition, in 1990 for example, 53.5 per cent of China's total two-way trade was with Japan, North Korea, Taiwan and Hong Kong, and the same states accounted for 58.5 per cent of China's inward investment. These details are summarised in Tables 5.1, 5.2 and 5.3. Comparative figures are also provided in Tables 5.4 and 5.5.

It is becoming less and less accurate, however, to speak of China as

Table 5.1 East Asian economies

Country	Population (hundred million)	Land area (10,000sq. km)	GNP (US$ 100 million)	Import-export value (US$100 million)
Japan	1.2361	47.7	31,900	5,217.5
South Korea	0.4238	9.9	2,317	1,347
North Korea	0.2240	12.3	528	N.A.[a]
China	11.4333	960	3,605.3	1,154
Taiwan	0.2013	3.6	1,503	1,184.7
Hong Kong	0.0581	0.1	629.68	1453[b]
World total	52	13,500	208,000	61,863
Ratio to East Asia total	26.1%	7.8%	20.24%	14.5%

Sources: *World Economic Yearbook* (1991); *World Resources Yearbook* (1991)
Notes: [a] North Korean figures are not available.
[b] Hong Kong imports and exports include transit trade.

Table 5.2 East Asian countries' trade with China

Country	Trade total (US$100 million)
Japan	165.99
South Korea	N.A.[a]
North Korea	4.83
Hong Kong	409.1
Taiwan	34.83[b]
TOTAL	1,154.4
(China's imports and exports to all countries)	
Share of East Asian countries	53.5%

Sources: *China Statistical Yearbook* (1991); *China Foreign Trade Yearbook* (1991)
Notes: [a] There are still no official statistics for South Korea. Another source, *News Review Seoul*, gave the figure of $4.4 billion for two-way trade in 1991 between China and South Korea. See Chong-sik Lee and Hyuk-sang Sohn, 'South Korea in 1994: a Year of Trial', *Asian Survey*, 1995, vol. XXV, no. 1, pp. 28–36.
[b] The Taiwan figure refers to indirect trade.

Table 5.3 East Asian countries' investment in China

Country	Total investment (US$100 million)
Japan	20.36
South Korea	N.A.[a]
North Korea	0.01
Hong Kong	77
Taiwan	10[b]
Total overseas investment in China	183.5
Share of East Asian countries	58.5%

Sources: *China Statistical Yearbook* (1991); *China Foreign Trade Yearbook* (1991)
Notes: [a] There are still no official statistics for South Korea.
[b] The Taiwan figure refers to indirect investment.
Tables 5.1–5.3 appeared in 'The East Asian Economy and the Economic Development of China's Coastal Region', *Tequ yu Kaifa qu Jingji* ('The Economy of the Special Zones and Development Zones'), 1994, no. 4, pp. 78–80.

Table 5.4 Direct investment in China by major investing countries/regions (contract basis)

Country	1992		1993		January–June 1994	
	Number of contracts	Value (US$ million)	Number of contracts	Value (US$ million)	Number of contracts	Value (US$ million)
Hong Kong/ Macao	31,892	41,531	50,868	76,753	13,378	26,361
Taiwan	6,430	5,543	10,948	9,965	2,218	2,546
US	3,265	3,121	6,750	6,813	2,228	2,445
Japan	1,805	2,173	3,488	2,960	1,428	1,855
Singapore	742	997	1,751	2,954	712	1,972
UK	126	287	348	1,988	131	1,514
Republic of Korea	650	417	1,748	1,557	888	789
Total	48,764	58,124	83,437	111,436	25,450	37,482

Sources: Ministry of Foreign Economic Relations and Trade, China, as quoted in *China Newsletter*, 1995, no. 115, p. 18.
Notes: Totals include investments from other countries.

Table 5.5 China's top trading partners, 1994

Nation	Total trade (US$ billion)
Japan	47.9
Hong Kong	41.8
United States	35.4
European Community	31.5
(Germany)	(11.9)
Taiwan	16.3
ASEAN	13.2
South Korea	11.7
Russia	5.1

Source: China's customs statistics, as in *China Business Review*, May–June 1995, p. 56

an economic entity although it is undoubtedly still a cultural and political one. The economically advanced coastal region as a whole, including the eleven provinces and cities of Liaoning, Hebei, Tianjin, Shandong, Jiangsu, Shanghai, Zhejiang, Fujian, Guangdong, Guangxi and Hainan, has experienced spectacular growth; in 1990, with 24.7 per cent of China's land area and 38 per cent of its population, the imports and exports of such areas represented 64.3 per cent of the country's total. Earlier reference was made to the high growth rates and living standards of coastal areas and cities like Guangdong and Shanghai, which in fact form part of a virtuous circle. Most of China's imports and exports either originate or pass through such coastal regions and most overseas sales of Guangdong, for instance, are destined for the Asia-Pacific. In turn they are able to attract investment and advanced technology transfer from other parts of East Asia; in 1989, for instance, Hong Kong, Macao, Taiwan, Japan and the United States together accounted for 92.2 per cent of direct investment in Guangdong Province. As a result, parts of Guangdong have attained growth rates not only higher than the rest of China but faster than Singapore, South Korea, Hong Kong and Taiwan during these countries' early development in the 1970s.[2] Thus China's open door policy is already facilitating mutual dependence between its coastal regions and economic interests from Taiwan, Hong Kong and Macao.

The Chinese leadership is aware of the limitations as well as the potential of such cooperation which is seen, first of all, as part of the global trend towards regional development. Nevertheless, in the CCP view it is said to differ from economic associations elsewhere in that cooperation between the major partners takes place within territories of the same nation, with varying social and economic systems. Moreover, Chinese sources are at pains to emphasise that present cooperation is driven by commercial interests which, although with official encouragement, have come together voluntarily and not under government auspices. The resulting economic complementarity that optimises resource use and production, with cooperation between the mainland, Taiwan and Hong Kong, contributes to stability throughout the Asia-Pacific region. The association is not exclusive, the three parties having previously developed their own trading links with the rest of the world. Furthermore, perhaps for ostensible diplomatic reasons, the Chinese leaders, while welcoming investments from overseas Chinese entrepreneurs as far afield as Singapore and Malaysia, reject any intention of creating a greater Chinese economic sphere, and enjoin their compatriots abroad to contribute wholeheartedly to their countries of residence.

Nevertheless the leadership in Beijing is mindful of the fact that Hong Kong and Taiwan have provided a disproportionate share of investment in South China; in addition, greater economic integration could result if these two territories were reunited with the mainland under CCP rule. Therefore, in spite of official reluctance, it is possible always to see a hidden agenda in statements emanating from Beijing. In fact, there is little doubt that the CCP leaders have used the promise of further trade and investment as incentives for political consensus, especially from Taiwan's establishment. A Taiwan source claimed access to a CCP internal document which allegedly asserted that mainland trade with Taiwan was designed to force commercial and industrial circles on the island to pressure the ROC government towards acceptance of unification on Communist terms, by which the island's leaders would give up their claim to be the government of the whole of China, even though this has been expressed less stridently in recent years.[3] For their part the ROC leaders have been ambivalent about growing trade and investment links with China: they see these as economically desirable but are aware of their political implications and constantly seek an undertaking from the CCP leadership concerning a renunciation of the use of force to reunite the island with the mainland. The issue has been further complicated by the attempts of the Taiwan authorities to regain their seat in the United Nations, on the grounds that in practical terms the 21 million inhabitants of the island remain unrepresented in international bodies, while accepting that the ROC and the People's Republic of China are two sovereign states, neither subordinate to the other. To the leadership in Beijing this would mean acceptance of a two China policy by the back door or an independent Taiwanese state, neither of these options being acceptable to the Communist regime.[4]

Such political ramifications are also part of the CCP leaders' stance regarding Hong Kong. The Chinese leaders have long been preparing for the return of the British colony to China's sovereignty in 1997; in 1993 they announced the establishment of a fifty-seven-member group, believed to be a government in waiting for Hong Kong. More importantly, perhaps, China's stake in Hong Kong is considerable, with investment in manufacturing and services, while the colony's economy as a whole is increasingly being integrated with that of south China.[5] On issues like that of airport construction in the colony, the Chinese authorities have often appeared obstructive and yet they undoubtedly see the continuing stability of Hong Kong as in their long-term interests. While their actions after 1997 are impossible to predict, current statements from Beijing speak of the colony as a key mediator in Chinese trading and investment relations with the Asia-Pacific, and of its role as an international banking centre being enhanced on its return to their national sovereignty.[6]

Hong Kong is ideally placed to assist the economic development of China's southern region. Hong Kong has long been skilled in manufacturing and now its focus is increasingly on services; both are needed by China. The latter's priorities also include energy, communications and information services. There is potential for collaboration between science and technology parks at Guangzhou and Shenzhen on the one side and Hong Kong's institutes on the other in high-tech and commodity production. In the next twenty years or so the basic thrust will come from the new high-tech enterprises of the Pearl River Delta designed to forge synergies with bodies outside China in fields like information sciences, biotechnology and new materials. In addition to input from Japan, major investment in these sectors will come from Hong Kong and Taiwan.[7]

In summary, this section has briefly examined China's southern regional policy and it is in such a context that much of the country's development will take place. The south, however, is not the only focus, and the logic of cooperation with other East Asian states applies also to other parts of China. It is to the definition and scope of such nationwide links that attention is now turned.

Definition and scope of the sub-regions

In the early days of the open door policy in the 1980s regional policy was focused on encouraging foreign investment, initially from Hong Kong and Taiwan, in the Special Economic Zones of the southeast, notably Shenzhen, next to Hong Kong, Zhuhai, adjacent to Macao, and Xiamen, opposite Taiwan. Major foreign activity was thus confined to the provinces of Guangdong and Fujian. There are strong political and economic reasons why, in the 1990s, the Chinese leaders are promoting economic integration between East Asian states and other parts of China. In addition, it was noted earlier that strategy was being concentrated on industries rather than regions as such, and re-emphasis on sectors like steel and automobiles itself suggests a move away from stress on the assembly and processing orientation of the southern Special Zones and towards the northeast. In political terms the leadership in Beijing has been apprehensive concerning the growing independence of provinces like Guangdong, problems with revenue sharing having been noted. In a related sense, the growing economic disparities between a prosperous southern coastal region and a poorer hinterland threaten social stability and national cohesion. Current policy thus retains stress on foreign investment in sub-regions but calls at the same time for more balanced national development.

A Chinese source quoted above divided China into major economic areas, with the southern coastal region, including its hinterland connections, in turn cut into sectors. The southern coastal area is itself split into two: the first section includes Shenzhen, Guangzhou and Zhuhai, thus encompassing the province of Guangdong; the second includes Xiamen and Fuzhou, embracing much of Fujian. In the early 1990s the government concluded that because of the growing necessity for heavy industry, the southern coastal region, which in large part had been the base for consignment processing for Hong Kong, could not serve as the leading model of development for this decade and beyond. It was appropriate, however, that the region should continue to achieve growth on its own, through foreign investment and the market mechanism. The two sectors of the southern zone each draw different sources of foreign investment: that of Shenzhen and Guangzhou cooperates with interests from Hong Kong and Macao to export value-added goods, while that of Xiamen and Fuzhou has its main links with Taiwan.

But regional development elsewhere was now to receive priority, an example being Shanghai, for the purpose of this discussion the second major economic area. Given its traditional status as a major port and an industrial centre, Shanghai is now designated as a key centre of production and a huge market, given its population of 15 million. Thus, in contrast with Guangdong, Shanghai has sufficient industrial infrastructure, technical knowhow and manpower as a result of previous industrialisation and is located at the centre of the distribution network traversing north and south and east and west; in addition, it is linked with the vast potential markets of the hinterland and along the Yangtze River. In 1991 the development of the Pudong district of Shanghai was named as a key national project, to receive substantial state assistance.

National fiscal deficits, however, precluded such funding, and therefore it was decided to stimulate private sector development. The municipal government was permitted to sell land to private developers and used the proceeds to fund the project, in which independent entrepreneurs were allowed to participate. Intended for Pudong and the old Puxi district, which is being redeveloped, is the creation of a Singaporean-type advanced city-state, functioning as a centre of information, banking and trade, side by side with industry. In fact, within the environs of Shanghai there is already a division of labour; as the presence of foreign investors has led to soaring labour costs and office rents, so labour-intensive manufacturing operations have relocated from the suburbs of Shanghai to areas in nearby Jiangsu and Zhejiang provinces. Consequently, the entire lower Yangtze River delta is being transformed into a concentrated centre of industry, with enterprises ranging from information technologies to textile manufacturing. When Hong Kong reverts to China in 1997, it may lose some of its importance as a banking and financial base to Shanghai, which will become one of the leading service and manufacturing centres of East Asia by the early years of the twenty-first century. In summary, then, this eastern coastline area, embracing Shanghai and the provinces of Jiangsu and Zhejiang, is already technologically advanced and is set to play a major role in the economic takeoff of both the coast and the adjacent hinterland. In linking with other economies of East Asia, the area will utilise high technology and service industry expertise in sectors like banking from Japan, Hong Kong and Taiwan.

Thirdly, since the early 1990s another coastal development region has been forming in north China; this is adjacent to the Bohai Gulf and includes the Liaodong Peninsula and the cities of Dalian and Shenyang in Liaoning Province, as well as the Shandong Peninsula and its cities of Yantai and Qingdao. It also encompasses Beijing and Tianjin. The region, a centre of China's heavy industry, partly built by Japan in pre-war days, is now receiving investment from Japanese and South Korean companies, which are also being followed by their component suppliers. This region could become East Asia's major centre of production for basic industrial materials and parts. Nor does official policy neglect the hinterland on China's western borders. Xinjiang Province, Inner Mongolia and other areas on China's borders are currently expanding trade and other economic links with neighbouring countries, even though regional integration, as discussed above, is as yet precluded.

Finally must be added the proposed Tumen Development Zone, not yet in existence, but offering enormous potential for cooperation involving Japanese and South Korean capital and technology as well as abundant Chinese and Russian natural resources. Given the domestic markets of the major players, such cooperation could serve as an engine of growth not only for Northeast Asia but for the Asia-Pacific region as a whole. This zone is given separate coverage in a later section.[8]

Economic complementarity: motives and advantages

In addition to regional policy, a number of international and Chinese domestic factors form the setting within which the motives of companies from Japan, Hong Kong and Taiwan for investing in China and the advantages attaching thereto may be assessed. With the ending of the cold war and the fall of Communist regimes in the Soviet Union and Eastern Europe in the late 1980s came the discrediting of the role of public ownership in national economies. This enhanced the position of private enterprise, especially in Asian countries, which could increase capital flows across national borders, taking advantage of the elimination of barriers in the international economy due to the collapse of the global cold war structure. The leader in capital flows has been Japan which, faced with a rapid rise in the yen since the Plaza Accord of 1985, has increased its investment abroad to reduce costs, a policy then followed by other industrialising countries like South Korea, Taiwan and Singapore. What has resulted is the free movement of production facilities in East Asia. Consequently, a number of competitive productivity centres has emerged, creating a regional market without regard to differences in political system such as between China, South Korea and Taiwan.

Initially, the flow of private investment, albeit under government encouragement, was directed at the ASEAN countries of Southeast Asia in the mid-1980s. But the cost advantages of investment there were soon lost with soaring wages, and as its open door policy gathered momentum, China became increasingly attractive as an investment site. As discussed immediately above, investment went first of all into processing in the Special Zones of Guangdong but in the 1990s it has been extended to Shanghai, the Yangtze River delta and the coastal region along the Bohai Sea. This acceleration of investment has been fuelled by further inducements offered by the Chinese, namely allowing foreign input in financing, retailing and real estate as well as other service sectors, together with the opening up of the domestic Chinese market to foreign venture products. Additionally, permitting land sales and usage rights has increased the fiscal resources of local governments, thereby promoting regional development. More significantly, foreign entrepreneurs are now allowed to engage in real-estate dealing and the construction of infrastructure such as railways, roads and housing. The resulting enthusiasm of East Asian entrepreneurs, especially overseas business groups, reflects optimism concerning the future potential of China's economy.

While private enterprise has been supreme in effecting East Asian cross-national capital flows, it has already been argued that less and less of the Chinese economy is amenable to direct central government control. Much has been written of private concerns in the cities and Special Economic Zones but less about town and village enterprises operated locally, some of which have joined in ventures with foreign capital. Such rural enterprises have developed outside the central planning framework and are playing a leading role in the transition from command to market economy. They provide employment and increase purchasing power in the rural areas. Acting as sub-contractors they play a major role in the development of the coastal areas as well as the adjacent hinterland. In fostering joint ventures, capitalists from Japan, Taiwan and Hong Kong aim to use rural enterprises as bases to complement production in their own countries and cut costs, thereby gaining market share in China, which is in turn becoming an integral part of the division of labour in East Asia. In the past rural enterprises have been hamstrung by the weak fiscal, technological and market bases of the countryside, and thus benefit from the stronger business foundation and more diverse business opportunities offered by city enterprises, a number of which have, for example, Hong Kong investment input. In turn, foreign entrepreneurs benefit from low production costs.

In short, in accordance with the 'flying geese' theory, the East Asian economy has been growing, with a succession of countries moving into the lower end of production vacated by their predecessors. While China, given its regional diversity, does not fit neatly into this pattern, incentives offered through official policy and by private, especially rural, enterprises, are being avidly accepted by East Asian investors. The motives of capitalists from Japan, Hong Kong and Taiwan will be addressed in turn.

Japan

Japan's role in China's economic sub-regions is informed by the strategic thinking of Japanese companies. The rapid appreciation of the yen since 1992 has forced Japanese manufacturers to reconsider their domestic and overseas business strategies. It made economic sense to reduce production at home when there were growing differentials between the domestic and overseas prices of goods manufactured in Japan on the one hand and those produced abroad on the other. In addition, Japanese goods were increasingly at a price disadvantage *vis-à-vis* newly industrialising countries like South Korea and Taiwan. For much of the 1980s Japanese companies were able to overcome yen appreciation through a strategy of product differentiation, that is by shifting production of export products to countries closer to their markets and with lower production costs, while they would produce domestically consumer products for Japan itself. Thus higher value-added products were made in Japan, whereas lower-price mass-production goods were made in manufacturing centres elsewhere in Asia. In the 1990s the Japanese have begun to import production for consumption in Japan from their manufacturing bases in, for example, China. Production of ever higher value-added products is being shifted overseas in the interests of cost effectiveness. The trend in China, as in ASEAN countries, is for the expansion of facilities so that electrical and electronic products made locally are of sufficient quality to satisfy the discerning Japanese consumer.

In the past, when manufacturing in China, as elsewhere, companies sourced components from Japan. Now, however, integrated production from upstream to downstream has become a key issue in cutting costs, and companies are consequently trying to transfer technology to overseas manufacturing bases in order to produce higher-quality products there. A case in point is the movement of semiconductor silicon wafer production to achieve integrated local production of VCRs and air conditioners. Additionally, with growing integrated manufacturing, design and development functions are also beginning to be located abroad.

In China, for instance, Japanese firms have defined the two objectives of building integrated production bases and preparing to penetrate the ever growing Chinese market. They are nevertheless finding difficulty in sourcing materials locally because of quality requirements. There have been cases of Japanese appliance manufacturers securing parts not only from within China but through affiliated companies in Taiwan, thereby building an East Asian supply network. There is thus an increasing division of labour emerging among manufacturers in the region. Sometimes parent companies persuade Japanese sub-contractors to set up operations overseas in tandem with their own investments. Furthermore there has been a tendency for small and medium-sized Japanese parts manufacturers, which lost orders when Japanese electrical, electronic and transport machinery assemblers began to move overseas, to start investing in China to save their markets.

China, like other states and territories in East Asia, is thus becoming a global base for machinery manufacture. There is therefore a growing division of labour among the countries of the region, each of which is at a different stage of development, but this scenario diverges from the model of the 1980s, by which less developed states tended to follow in the footsteps of the more advanced. There is now greater diversity and interdependence. The roles of Japan and China in this pattern of regional integration will now be examined. The Japanese have long been transferring textiles and electrical and electronic equipment manufacture overseas but their economy is now entering a new phase. Smokestack industries like steel, cars, paper, synthetic fibres and ethylene are less suited to Japan's current pioneer mode and, as in the case of machinery assembly, costs are now forcing them offshore. These trends are leading to the 'hollowing out' of the Japanese economy. It is very likely that in future the Japanese will produce small lots of diverse customised products to serve increasingly sophisticated domestic markets and concentrate on research and development. But as less competitive Japanese industries have gone offshore, countries like Taiwan and ASEAN members have suffered ballooning deficits with Japan because of its advantage in key components and machinery exports. This is not the case, however, with China which enjoys trade surpluses with Japan. One way in which the Japanese may reduce that deficit is by transferring more high technology and capital plant to China, even though this in time may build that country into a major competitor. Meanwhile, in the short term, the states of East Asia, like Taiwan, may improve their current account balance by supplying key components, developed through association with Japanese companies, as well as applied technology, to China, thereby completing the circle of an East Asian economic division of labour.[9] This, in turn, furthers the integration of China's sub-regions with the rest of East Asia; significantly, accumulated investment by Japan, Hong Kong and Taiwan together represented 58.5 per cent of China's total up to 1990, and of that percentage the greatest part was absorbed by the coastal provinces and cities.[10]

In line with this East Asian division of labour, Guangdong in China's southern coastal area is now moving into capital- and knowledge-intensive sectors. There is increasing scientific and technological content in key industries like cars, aircraft and human-made satellites, as well as chemicals, a trend now being encouraged by both the Chinese and Japanese governments. In fact, Japan's ODA is now playing a key role in the technological transformation of Shenzhen, one of Guangdong's first Special Economic Zones. In 1986 the Shenzhen-Japan Joint

Committee was established as the setting for conducting trade, investment and technological transformation between the two countries.
Meetings alternate between Shenzhen and Japan, and representatives
from the latter include personnel from economic research institutes,
trading companies and banks; the stated aim of the committee is to
develop Shenzhen in the interests of fostering East Asian economic
stability. Shenzhen is to become a pioneer for the rest of China in testing
sectors like banking and communications, and, in conjunction with
Hong Kong as the latter reverts to China, act as a commercial centre
for the rest of the region. Trade between Shenzhen and Japan is to be
diversified, the former having progressed from the labour-intensive
manufactures of the past to value-added exports, the key to which is the
training of scientific personnel from China and overseas. An environment conducive to foreign investment is thereby created. Shenzhen, an area dedicated to traditional pursuits like farming and fishing
as recently as the late 1970s, now enjoys some of the highest personal
incomes and living standards in China, and, now emerging as one of
the major consumer markets of the region, will be a prime target for
Japanese manufacturers.[11] In summary, Shenzhen's future will hinge
not only on the Japanese connection but relations with Hong Kong; the
next section discusses the colony's investment in the sub-regions of
China's coast.

Hong Kong

Economic complementarity has spurred Hong Kong's investment in
China's southern coastal region. The colony is increasingly dependent
on the service sector, and its industrial leaders have valuable experience
of manufacturing and possess abundant capital. Like their overseas
Chinese counterparts in Singapore, they find that economic restructuring at their home base and the liberalisation efforts of the Chinese
government have presented them with golden entrepreneurial opportunities for expansion across the border. Hong Kong, then, has become
a conduit for the infusion of funds into China from overseas Chinese
interests throughout Asia. Thus Chinese-controlled enterprises in
ASEAN countries have channelled substantial investments to Hong
Kong and, largely through their subsidiaries in the British colony, to
China itself. In fact, overseas Chinese entrepreneurs, both from Hong
Kong and elsewhere in Asia, now comprise the largest group of
investors in China in terms of both the number of approved projects
and the amount of committed funds. China, on the other hand, has
abundant labour – especially in view of the unemployment caused by

the rationalisation of agriculture since the late 1970s – and natural resources but lacks capital plant and manufacturing skills. The perfect venue for cooperation between Hong Kong and Chinese interests, particularly in Guangdong, has been the rural enterprise, broadly discussed earlier. In macroeconomic terms the growth of the rural enterprises offers a testing ground for the conversion of China to a true market economy; it may also hasten the development of the rural areas. In the long run the rural enterprise may well facilitate the movement of capital in China but concurrently it is providing an avenue for investors in Hong Kong disadvantaged by rising costs, to establish viable production bases. It is Chinese official policy to improve the infrastructure of the coast and create an environment conducive to ventures between foreign capital and rural enterprises. Such ventures are now becoming an integral part of the East Asian division of labour.

Until recently Hong Kong was an important Asian production base but rising costs have gradually led to the shifting of production to China. In general, in such ventures, the Hong Kong company maintains control over management, planning, design and sales functions, while production is delegated to the local Chinese side. One formula is the establishment of wholly owned Hong Kong factories through capital investment; another is for local rural enterprises to be used as subcontractors. One example of each type follows.

An instance of a wholly owned Hong Kong venture is the Shishi Development Enterprise, a garment manufacturer, which began operations in 1988. Its head office is in Hong Kong. The venture has a number of factories not only in Shishi City but in Shenzhen, Xiamen and Guangzhou. The main factory at Shishi has about 500 workers who produce jackets and shirts. The Hong Kong head office decided to invest in China because of lower costs, particularly wages, and to increase production. Like other foreign-invested ventures, the Shishi Development Enterprise follows plans and designs set up by the Hong Kong head office. Raw materials are either supplied from the colony or procured in China. While half of the production is sent to Hong Kong, the rest is sold in China, as the company takes advantage of a growing Chinese domestic market. The enterprise is thus both a consignment process and a domestic Chinese manufacturer.

In contrast, the Nanjing Knit Garment Company of Nan'an County, Quanzhou City in Fujian, the province immediately north of Guangdong, was established as a joint venture among Hong Kong, Japanese and Chinese firms. Half the investment was provided by the Hong Kong and Japanese sides, and the rest by the Chinese. Of the Hong Kong and Japanese equities, Hong Kong's Nanji Enterprise accounted for 51 per cent and Yamaichi 49 per cent. Of the Chinese equities, the foreign economic relations and trade committee of Nan'an County holds 70 per cent and other local interests 30 per cent. The main products of the Nanjing Knit Garment Company are weft knits. As is often the case with such joint ventures, the planning, designs and raw materials come from Hong Kong and increasingly nearly all the products are exported to the colony rather than being placed on the Chinese domestic market. They are then re-exported to Japan and Europe. In June 1993 the company had over 1,000 employees processing 80,000 garments a year.

The Hong Kong partner, Nanji Enterprise, is typical of investors in China's light industries. Founded in 1963, its investments date from 1981 and it has factories in Beijing, Shanghai and Shenzhen as well as in Fujian. It is now a corporate group managing over twenty directly run factories and joint ventures engaged in a number of industries ranging from garments to flower cultivation.

The two examples cited above are representative of Hong Kong-invested ventures and fall under the category of rural enterprises, since they are located in the countryside, and in terms of land provision and labour deployment are subject to local authority regulation. They enjoy tax incentives. In fact, rural enterprise development in south China is increasingly reliant on Hong Kong capital and more and more closely linked with the international economy.

In addition, Hong Kong concerns are acting not only on their own account but as mediators for foreign companies. There have been instances where the latter are direct investors in China controlling their own production but may present plans and designs to Hong Kong companies and place orders with them. Hong Kong manufacturers take responsibility for production control. The same is true of Sino-foreign joint ventures. Hong Kong concerns receive consignment orders from a foreign company and then arrange for a Chinese factory or rural enterprise to process the raw materials into products. The goods are then delivered to the foreign concern. Demand for such services provided by Hong Kong companies is likely to grow. Firstly, they offer superior reconnaissance, are abreast of China's economic policy, familiar with the workings of the Chinese bureaucracy, and know how to work such mechanisms as the exchange rate system. Additionally, they are steeped in Chinese culture, and China's business etiquette is second nature to them. Perhaps most crucially of all, Hong Kong businessmen have cultivated good connections with local governments, essential for securing energy supplies and land rights, and are often related by blood to country and village leaders in south China.[12]

But while rural enterprises offer great investment potential, Hong

Kong entrepreneurs have not neglected the cities and Special Economic Zones of Guangdong. In an interview in 1992 the Shenzhen Party Secretary, Li Hao, admitted that without foreign funds and experience Shenzhen's achievements in the 1980s and 1990s would not have been possible. Thus while foreigners' private motives had been commercial, Shenzhen benefited from scientific, technological and management knowhow from capitalist countries. While Japan's role in this process has been assessed earlier, the key to the future prosperity of Shenzhen is now said to be cooperation with Hong Kong interests; competition and mutual advantage are alike inherent in the economic complementarity of the two territories, according to the Chinese leadership.

Hong Kong's preponderant role is demonstrated by its 85 per cent share of foreign funds invested in Shenzhen. In fact, the vast majority of the more than 7,000 existing enterprises in Shenzhen is operated by Hong Kong entrepreneurs; ventures include processing with supplied material on the basis of drawings and samples, assembly with components provided and compensation trade.[13] Hong Kong's companies have thereby been able to compete in price terms on world markets; for Shenzhen the colony's capitalist experience has been invaluable in helping the zone to formulate laws and administrative regulations conducive to the development of private enterprise.[14] In future, as with Japan, Shenzhen's partnership with Hong Kong is to be enhanced through cooperation in the development of high technology. This makes sound economic sense as, given the rise in costs of land and wages, labour-intensive industry is a less and less attractive proposition.

An important consequence has been a fall in manufacturing employment in the colony, as low- and semi-skilled jobs have been moved to China. Hong Kong's manufacturing labour force, 890,000 in number and 37.5 per cent of the employed at the beginning of the 1980s, had been reduced to 655,000 or 23.4 per cent of employees at the end of 1991. China has in turn benefited from the creation of millions of manufacturing jobs.[15]

So far in this description Hong Kong's contribution has been evaluated in terms of finished manufacturing operations; attention is now turned to the colony's role as a capital market. Accelerated economic integration between Hong Kong and China has been reflected in the activities of the colony's stock exchange. In addition, many Hong Kong-based companies are now looking beyond light industrial manufacturing in south China and seeking opportunities for investment in heavy industries and infrastructure. Such interest is welcomed by China's policy makers whose reform programme has been designed to lessen the dependence of state enterprises, mainly in the heavy industrial sector, on central government support. In the 1990s such ventures have been encouraged to convert themselves into joint stock companies, of which there are now about 5,000 in China as a whole. While some have limited shareholding to employees and supervisory investors, others have been prepared to approach the open market, issuing stocks to domestic and overseas individual and institutional buyers. But China's inefficient overmanned heavy industry needs a massive injection of funds and, with the tightening of Chinese government credits, modernisation is only possible through funds derived from stock exchange listing. There are two methods: back door and direct listings. In the 1990s a number of Chinese state enterprises have sought back door listings, that is they have gained access to the Hong Kong Stock Exchange by taking over listed but inactive companies in the colony and then injecting their own assets into them. In 1992 five Hong Kong-registered Chinese companies gained a direct listing on the colony's stock exchange; these included the China Travel Service and Guangzhou Investment, their shares being heavily over-subscribed. The major impetus, however, came in late 1992, when nine Chinese state enterprises were given official authorisation to seek direct listings. These enterprises, from separate regions of China, were for the most part involved in heavy industry and their listing reflects a drive on the part of both the Chinese and Hong Kong governments to make the Hong Kong Stock Exchange a source of capital for China's modernisation. Six of the originally selected nine companies were listed under the H share rubric. The share offers for the companies, which also included China's famous Chingdao Brewery, were so successful that in 1993 they accounted for 43 per cent of the funds raised by the top ten listings of the stock exchange, and in 1994 the Chinese authorities permitted more of the country's companies to seek listings.

There is nevertheless a number of formidable barriers to be overcome before the broad range of Chinese companies may be listed on the Hong Kong Stock Exchange, one being Chinese accounting methods which still do not conform to international requirements, and need lengthy adjustment. But in the long term, growth in the representation of Chinese joint stock companies will result in still greater integration between the mainland and Hong Kong economies. The composition of listings will change, and by the year 2000 the market could be dominated by large Chinese industrial enterprises. In addition, Hong Kong's investors could increasingly help to fund China's vast energy, transportation and infrastructure projects, even though, needless to say, such investments are not without risk.[16]

Hong Kong's contribution to China's infrastructure is already considerable. Until recently it was largely confined to Guangdong and the
Pearl River delta, one example being the recently announced financing
of the Yantan container port, to be one of China's five strategic ports,
on the west coast of Shenzhen. The US$86 million first-stage develop-
ment will be owned by Hong Kong investors and a Shenzhen company,
the former providing 70 per cent and the latter 30 per cent of the funds.[17]
An exclusively Hong Kong project, ten years in construction and
costing US$1.2 billion, was a 123-kilometre motorway between Guang-
zhou and Shenzhen opened in 1994, an accomplishment of the conglomerate Hopewell Holdings Limited, led by its managing director,
Gordon Wu, with the help of his connections with the Chinese
government and overseas Chinese companies.[18]

Another Hong Kong concern has been active in infrastructural
development in south China. In 1992 an international consortium, led
by Kumagai Gumi (Hong Kong), a subsidiary of the Japanese construction giant, announced plans to build a power plant in China's first
privately funded free port and industrial park, located in the 11-square
kilometre economic zone at Yangpu on Hainan Island, formerly part of
Guangdong but now a separate province. The power station, for which
the German company Siemens will supply generating equipment and a
distribution network, is crucial for the development as a whole, likely
to cost US$2.3 billion over the next fifteen years, making it China's
single largest foreign investment project. Furthermore, Kumagai Gumi
has the right to develop and market the land in the Special Zone for
seventy years. Kumagai is to form a consortium of multinational
corporations to fund the Yangpu Development Company, which it is
intended will then sign a contract with the central government for the
right to sub-lease and mortgage the land in the zone. Currently, Yangpu,
as Shenzhen once was, is an undeveloped area inhabited by fishermen
and farmers, and it is calculated that project construction will employ
350,000. For this project Kumagai Gumi will finance the building of
sewers, roads, telecommunications, residential living and other infrastructure necessary to make the zone into a modern industrial city with
huge employment potential. But even though manufacturers moving
into the zone will enjoy tax concessions and exemption from most
export and import tariffs, it is still debatable whether this, together with
the promise of cheap labour, is sufficient to attract other foreign
investors. Given, however, that the central government leaders now
envisage similar ports, there is clearly a political will to ensure
success.[19]

In summary, given the limited scope of Hong Kong itself, its

entrepreneurs and industrialists have invested both in China's manufacturing and infrastructure, which in turn will further East Asia's sub-
regional integration. In fact, Hong Kong's manufacturing investment in
Guangdong and other parts of China has already brought changes in the
two territories' trade structure. While until the 1970s Hong Kong's
foreign trade consisted mainly of local exports from its industries,
mostly textiles and other light industrial goods, once China's open door
policy had been initiated, there was remarkable growth in re-exports
going through, though not stopping in, Hong Kong. For example, in
1978, re-exports accounted for only one-quarter of Hong Kong's total
exports, but in 1993 this rose to 80 per cent.[20]

Discussion of sub-regional integration would not be complete without reference to China's investment in Hong Kong. China is now a great
influence on the colony's economic life. The highest investor, it poured
in about US$20 billion in 1993, as much as Japan and the United States,
respectively the second and third largest, put together. The number of
Hong Kong companies owned by China's state-run firms rose from 400
to 1,000 in 1991–4. Major Chinese players include China International
Trust and Investment Corporation (CITIC, the mainland investment
company); its Hong Kong offshoot, CITIC Pacific, has enjoyed ex-
ponential growth and spectacular profits. The latter has a stake in
Cathay Pacific, the colony's main airline, and joint control with the
Swire Group in Dragonair, another regional airline. It has also invested
in sectors like housing and telecommunications, as well as essential
services ranging from waste disposal to power plants. Apart from
growing economic influence in preparation for 1997, China may gain a
number of other advantages from investment in Hong Kong. Chinese
managers can learn about advanced foreign technology, crucial for the
renovation of China's own state enterprises. Finally, Hong Kong is a
window on the world, enabling China's companies to observe world
market trends and develop better information channels.[21]

Taiwan

Taiwan, an island of 21 million inhabitants and seat of the Republic of
China (ROC), which still claims sovereignty over the whole of China,
is one of Asia's post-war economic miracles. A crucial ingredient in that
success has been the double role of Japan: as a pre-war colonial power
which helped to lay an invaluable physical infrastructure, and in latter
decades as an investor in, especially, Taiwan's processing zones,
providing input similar to its stake in China in the recent past. By 1993
Taiwan had a per capita income of US$16,000 and at the current rate

of progress will have joined the ranks of developed countries by the turn of the century.

It will be seen, however, that Japan's trade with and investment in Taiwan has been a mixed blessing for the ROC. As a late-developing country the ROC administration has been inclined to follow the Japanese model of development, though with necessary modifications, given different population and market size on the island. In fact, the Taiwan economy, at an earlier stage, has been more export-orientated. The two partners' different levels of development have meant a measure of economic complementarity. Accordingly, economic relations have reflected a vertical division of labour. The Japanese have moved declining, less competitive industries offshore; Taiwan at the same time has been moving into such sectors and technologies. This has led to growing Japanese investment on the island but a concomitant adverse trade balance for Taiwan, with increasing inputs of Japanese machinery and equipment. For example, from 1952 until the end of 1991, Japan's direct investment in Taiwan amounted to US$4.2 billion, accounting for 32.7 per cent of the island's total from overseas. During that time Japan made 2,181 technology transfers to Taiwan, or 60.4 per cent of the total from abroad, an indication of heavy reliance on one partner. But if such a link has been crucial to Taiwan, it has become less important to Japan. Since the mid-1980s the share of Japan's investment in Taiwan in its total investment has been declining. In 1985 investment in Taiwan accounted for 1.19 per cent of Japan's direct overseas investment which totalled US$12.2 billion. In 1989 Japan's direct investment had reached US$67.5 billion but only 0.95 per cent was invested in Taiwan. Thus while Japan's investment abroad expanded 5.5 times, the share of its investment in Taiwan dropped by 20 per cent. Simultaneously, however, the proportion of Japan's investment in China to its total in Asia has been increasing.

In certain respects Taiwan has undoubtedly been advantaged by Japanese investment. Economic and technological cooperation has enabled Taiwan's manufacturers to purchase more raw materials, components and equipment from Japan. Moreover, reliance has increased as Taiwan has entered more high-tech sectors. But most export products made with Japanese technology and components have been sold not to Japan but to Western countries. Consequently, Taiwan's foreign trade deficit with Japan has been growing.

Firstly, this phenomenon is largely due to the nature of Japanese investment and the size of Taiwan's export companies. Small and medium-sized entrepreneurs are the main producers of export goods, many being original equipment manufacturers (OEM) for big Japanese companies which manipulate their raw material supply and sales channels. This effectively means Japanese control. Given Taiwan's stage of development, its manufacturers choose Japan as an OEM partner because Japan's products are high in quality and competitive in price.

Secondly, despite its protestations to the contrary, Japan's markets have been notoriously difficult to penetrate. Customs and inspections systems are rigorous and time-consuming; distribution, compared to that of Western countries, is outmoded and, though in the process of reform, is multilayered and complex. Success in Japan's domestic markets demands extensive long-term reconnaissance. Furthermore, Japanese companies investing in Taiwan aim at exploiting the island's market or using it as a base to manufacture or process products targeted at the United States. In this respect they differ, for example, from American-invested projects which export back to the United States. Taiwan not only suffers a trade deficit with Japan but its companies find it equally difficult to invest there.

In fact, in spite of Taiwan's much vaunted economic success, its level of research and development remains relatively low and foreign input is still necessary for industrial restructuring. Consequently, Taiwan relies on technology inputs from Japan. The electronics industry illustrates this dependence. Although in 1982 electronics was designated a strategic industry, only a fraction of parts and components are made domestically. In some domestic sectors 80 per cent of these are imported, especially from Japan. Furthermore, it is estimated that 90 per cent of Taiwan's inputs of integrated circuits, essential for information electronics, are met by imports. As a result of such dependence, economic development has been uneven and there has been only limited scientific and technological progress to be transferred to industry as a whole. Instead there have been profit-making sectors which have absorbed foreign technology and capital, producing more exports, but there has been no spin-off to other industries.

To address these economic weaknesses, national strategy is focusing in the short term on reducing trade imbalances, while the long-term solution is acknowledged as being industrial restructuring and a more positive role in regional integration. Significantly, one objective is investment in China. The twin aspects of this strategy will now be considered in turn.

In brief, Taiwan's trade deficit with Japan has been a longstanding problem; it rose from US$4.8 billion in 1987 to $9.7 billion in 1991. Measures taken to reduce it include the establishment of the Taiwan Trade Centre and the Joint After Sales Service Centre in Japan; attempts have been made to persuade Japanese manufacturers in Taiwan to sell their products back to their own country. Moves have been set in motion to diversify import sources. One key to reducing dependence on Japan has been to upgrade Taiwan's industry as a whole, by raising product quality, improving industrial design, strengthening inspection systems, encouraging manufacturers to develop their own technology, enabling them to make key components independently, and developing new sources of investment. In introducing the above measures, the Industrial Development Bureau of the Ministry of Economic Affairs is promoting the manufacture of key products to ensure the independence of the island's industry in a bid to solve the trade deficit long term.

Meanwhile, however, Taiwan's deficit with Japan must be seen in the context of the island's world trade as a whole. In the 1980s, for example, its trade deficit with Japan was offset by its trade surplus with the United States. As the trade deficit with Japan increased, so also did the surplus with the United States. But since 1987, as Taiwan's deficit with Japan continued to climb, its surplus with the United States has in general been declining. A palliative, however, has been growing direct trade with Hong Kong. In addition, indirect trade with China is becoming more important to Taiwan's economy. In 1992 such trade was worth US$17.2 billion and the two connections accounted for 12 per cent of Taiwan's total. Moreover, the trade surplus with Hong Kong and China for that year reached US$13.6 billion, much higher than the US$7.8 billion with the United States. By the end of 1993 Taiwan's surplus with Hong Kong and China exceeded $15 billion. Furthermore, most importantly, Taiwan's trade surplus with the latter two partners in the 1990s has been approximately equivalent to its deficit with Japan, thereby helping to maintain its overall trade balance.

The above has examined Taiwan's recent measures to improve export performance but attempts are also in train to adjust economic relations with Japan as a whole. The fact is that industrial and product upgrading – a prescription for Taiwan's survival and development – is still dependent on Japan, 80 per cent of its imports from there being machinery, equipment and components. In addition to exploiting new markets in Japan as discussed above, the government of the ROC seeks to adjust the industrial structure to reduce reliance on Japan, diversifying foreign markets and exploiting new overseas sources of technology and equipment. Nevertheless in the short term at least Taiwan will continue to be dependent on Japanese investment. Nor will there be a radical change in the unfavourable trade balance, even though it may stabilise because of ultimate limits to the size of Taiwan's market. What is required is a fundamental restructuring of Taiwan's economy, assessed within the wider context of growing economic relations between the island and China, a scenario which offers hope of reducing reliance on Japan.[22]

Taiwan's economic restructuring and its relations with China are, however, inextricably linked to East Asian sub-regional integration. The Asian Development Bank, for example, noted that Asian nations are depending increasingly on trade with the sub-region formed by Taiwan, Hong Kong and China. Recently, a report by the American consultancy firm McKinsey, commissioned by the ROC government, stated that Taiwan is well placed to play a key role in sub-regional integration in a number of spheres: manufacturing, financial services, telecommunications and transportation. Given its highly educated, disciplined labour force, Taiwan is well equipped to attract high-tech manufacturing plants and to create research and development centres for value-added products. Taiwan, given discretionary income, also has an attractive, though limited, domestic market. The island already has a vigorous stock market, a potential basis for becoming a regional financial centre. Taiwan's geographical location makes it an ideal focus for telecommunications and media. Similarly, it has potential as a transshipment and distribution centre for sea cargoes and as an airline hub for both passengers and freight. Sub-regional integration, however, suggests complementarity and Taiwan has a number of rivals. A feasibility study by the Industrial Development and Investment Centre, under the ROC's Ministry of Economic Affairs, suggested that while Taiwan had greater advantages in manufacturing than either Hong Kong or Singapore, they could well prove fierce competitors in a bid to become the Asian hub for research and development. Furthermore, Taiwan lags behind both territories in its legal system and administrative efficiency, and this could prove a handicap in the promotion of financial services. Finally, the main barrier to Taiwan becoming a communications hub for the sub-region is the lack of direct transportation links with China: Hong Kong controls a large proportion of transshipment to China, and handles container cargo very efficiently; even in the event of direct transportation links across the Taiwan straits, Hong Kong would continue to play a major role.

There are thus a number of prerequisites before Taiwan can become a major hub of the region. Before Taiwan's officials can reach their goal of turning the island into a regional operations centre for the Asia-Pacific, foreign multinationals must be given greater inducements to invest. Like China, Taiwan, until the 1980s, had a protected command economy, including a major government role in economic enterprise; sophisticated macroeconomic controls have only been used in the

1990s. Streamlined banking and tax systems are crucial to attracting foreign investment. In addition, restrictive government regulations must be reduced, administrative efficiency enhanced and public facilities like harbours, roads and airports improved, even though little can be done about the high land costs in Taiwan which are lower than Hong Kong's but higher than Singapore's.

Another area of concern is financial services where Taiwan lags behind Hong Kong and Singapore because of too many restrictions and the slow pace of liberalisation. The Central Bank of China, Taiwan's main financial arbiter, supports liberalisation but with a step-by-step approach in order to protect local financial markets and their vested interests. The framework for financial liberalisation has been broadened; in 1992 fifteen new private commercial banks began operating in what was once a public sector domain, and new financial instruments, including a futures market, were authorised. Further measures being considered include relaxation of curbs on inflow and outflow of capital, broadening the scope of local financial services and encouraging more foreign investment in Taiwan's markets. Liberalisation of markets in both commodities and services will in any case be a prerequisite for membership of the new World Trade Organisation. Finally, improved seaports and airports are as essential for transforming Taiwan into a regional transportation and telecommunications centre as they are for attracting foreign investment in manufacturing. Together with the macroeconomic and liberalisation policies listed above, the ROC government has been spending US$300 billion on infrastructural development, and in the first three quarters of 1994 foreign investment totalled more than US$1 billion, a 25 per cent increase over the equivalent period in 1993. Of that investment about US$290 million came from Japan, registering growth of 39 per cent over the previous year's equivalent period, and the Japanese were the biggest investors over that time, followed by those of the United States. Significantly, the greatest increases in foreign investments were in service sectors like finance and insurance. It is impossible, however, for any country to rely exclusively on services, and Taiwan manufacturing, increasingly high tech, will continue to loom large in the national economy. While such issues of economic strategy are always contentious, observers both within the ROC and outside are agreed that Taiwan cannot become a sub-regional centre unless direct economic and transportation links with China are developed.[23]

Intensified direct economic links with China may be crucial for Taiwan's future as a regional centre but it is unlikely that the ROC will encourage its industrialists to think in these terms alone. As will be shown later, there are alternative investment possibilities in the countries of Southeast Asia. Nevertheless, China is undoubtedly a lure for both business people and official policy makers. The importance that trade with and investment in China is officially accorded was demonstrated by a report issued in July 1994, at the end of its second conference, by the Mainland Affairs Council of Taiwan, assessing the factors that are likely to influence cross-straits ties in the years ahead. A major recommendation was that the government make plans over the following twelve months to end the ROC's ban on direct transportation links to the mainland. ROC President Lee Teng-hui reiterated shortly after the conference that there would be no political surrender; closer economic relations were to be promoted to further mutual interests, establish bilateral trust and thereby gradually attain the goal of peaceful reunification, but on the ROC's, not Communist, terms. In addition, direct transportation links were seen as enhancing Taiwan's position as an economic and communications crossroads in the East Asia sub-region on Hong Kong's return to Chinese sovereignty in 1997.[24] These developments must be seen against the background of political change in the ROC since the beginning of the decade. The first landmark was President Lee Teng-hui's statement in April 1991 that the state of emergency, imposed in February 1948 during the Civil War between the Guomindang and the Communists, would end on 1 May 1992. In practice, this meant that the Chinese Communist authorities were officially recognised as the legal political entity governing the Chinese mainland. Shortly prior to this, and by way of preparation, the Mainland Affairs Council of the Executive Yuan, Taiwan's cabinet, had been launched in October 1990, followed by the creation of the Straits Exchange Foundation. The Council was in charge of coordinating and implementing policies towards the mainland; the Foundation had responsibility for promoting private exchange and protecting the interests of people on both sides of the straits. The Foundation, under official auspices, has a number of functions, the most important of which are the processing of documentation relating to the entry and exit of travellers from both sides of the straits, arbitration in trade disputes and the promotion of scientific and cultural exchanges. The Foundation is, however, an administrative body, being subject to the supervision of the Executive Yuan, and not involved in policy making. In December 1991 the government in Beijing launched a parallel private intermediary organisation, the Association for Relations across the Taiwan Straits, to handle exchanges with Taiwan. Basically, the creation of the Foundation has been to put on a firmer footing the movement of private individuals which has been permitted since the

1980s but, more importantly, also to facilitate commercial intercourse across the straits.[25]

To date, in a technical sense, trade and investment relations with the mainland have been illegal but, while prior to the 1990s they were connived at by the authorities, there are now signs that the government is actually encouraging such contacts. For example, whereas government officials had previously been allowed to travel to China in a private capacity, since February 1994 they may now participate in, for instance, cultural and educational exchanges as, in effect, official representatives, a hidden agenda being the desire to facilitate government-to-government economic relations.[26]

Such motives have also been indicated by veiled references to the compatibility of the economic systems of Taiwan and China, carried by the island's journals and extensively quoted in mainland publications. Taiwan's economic journals, like their mainland counterparts, extol the virtues of private enterprise. Thus, prior to being separated from state control, public enterprises in Taiwan are said to have been inefficient, not cost effective and lacking entrepreneurship. Once privatised, however, such companies, under the guidance of the profit motive, will be better equipped to cooperate with China's state enterprises which are passing through a similar transition. A division of labour will thereby be possible, and in January 1995 the ROC's Economics Ministry for the first time gave approval for the participation of technologists from the mainland in Taiwan's development. In fact, some mainland strengths in military technology have civilian applications but China needs Taiwan's capital to exploit such advantages. In summary, the ROC authorities envisage exploiting strengths to mutual advantage and using technological synergies.[27] A number of concrete instances indicate this trend. In January 1995 the ROC's Economics Minister P. K. Chiang addressed the Cross Taiwan Straits Iron and Steel Development Seminar, declaring that the island's steel industry, with its world-renowned production technologies, abundant capital and marketing experience, could make a contribution to upgrading its counterpart in China. Other speakers referred to complementarities between Taiwan's production experience and advanced technology and China's skilled workforce.[28]

Unlike the steel industry, securities markets are in their infancy in both China and Taiwan. The Second Mainland-Taiwan Symposium on Securities and Futures Legal System opened in Beijing in January 1995. At the meeting topics under discussion included over-the-counter trading, credit trading, disclosure of information and risk control, the aim being to boost governmental exchanges between the two industries, especially given the growing stake of Taiwan's companies in China's economy.[29]

Nevertheless government and business in Taiwan no longer speak with one voice, especially in relation to economic cooperation with the mainland. Private investment by Taiwan's concerns in China is attaining its own momentum and the government is increasingly responsive to business pressure. Prior to their investment in the mainland, Taiwan's companies' productivity gains contributed to the island's economic growth, and there was a community of interest between business and government. But now there is a triangular relationship between the government of the ROC, Taiwan's companies and China. Taiwan's firms are concerned with profits but the island's political leaders must balance cross-straits relations with overall national security interests, global priorities and regional role.[30]

Furthermore, as suggested earlier the Chinese government for its part seeks to use the incentives of trade and investment to achieve political unification with Taiwan, legitimised by the concept of 'one country two systems', the formula to be applied to Hong Kong on its retrocession to China in 1997.

Thus Taiwan's current official policies towards economic relations with the mainland are partly a response to the business lobby. In general, over the past months the ROC authorities have been implementing more flexible trade policies but, fearing the economic leverage which the Chinese leaders in Beijing could exert, have been more reticent concerning investment on the mainland. The investment tide, however, is proving difficult to stem. But while prepared to be more flexible on economic relations with the mainland, the Ministry of Economic Affairs has simultaneously been drafting a three-year plan to promote trade and cooperation with Southeast Asian countries. This is part of the government's southern strategy of eliminating investment barriers and expanding trade and technological cooperation with ASEAN member states and the area formerly known as Indochina, the initial targets being Vietnam, Indonesia and Malaysia, even if as yet Taiwan's stake in that region does not approach its level of investment in China.[31] Nevertheless in early 1994, on the trade front, the International Trade Bureau of the ROC Economics Department announced new measures which really amounted to opening the Taiwan market completely to mainland goods within two years. Gradually, methods for listing negative factors and facilitating exemptions for mainland goods will go into effect. Until now the importation of mainland goods has required an import licence issued by the National Trade Bureau. Reform will pass through three stages: initially a visa system will operate, then a system of listing negative factors will be implemented, and finally free trade will be instituted. The government's role will thus change from using business to helping businessmen and manufacturers develop markets. Earlier Taiwan's Economics Ministry had proposed direct trade between, for instance, Kaohsuing in Taiwan and Xiamen in China, and between Keelung and the mainland province of Fujian, which would cut costs. In addition, there is a suggestion that a US$9 billion industrial zone be built, including a new port at Yunlin on the western coast of Taiwan, opposite Xiamen, in preparation for the opening of direct shipping services.

There is a number of reasons for Taiwan's more flexible cross-straits trade policy. The first relates to membership of the World Trade Organisation which Taiwan cannot join if it prohibits or restricts the importation of goods from mainland China for political reasons. The second concerns Taiwan's world trade balance. In July 1994 the Ministry of Finance announced that in the previous year Taiwan had a US$7.88 billion foreign trade surplus, US$10.59 billion less than for 1992. But there was a US$16.72 billion surplus with Hong Kong, an increase of 22.7 per cent over the year before. Much of this surplus is accounted for by the fact that Taiwan's mainland trade passes through Hong Kong; thus exports to China contribute heavily to the island's favourable balance of world trade. Thirdly, overall, encouraging imports from the mainland will advantage Taiwan's economy. Although giving mainland commodities a more open market will reduce the trade surplus with China, Taiwan will be able to obtain cheaper raw materials and semi-finished products which will improve the international competitiveness of the island's own exports. Moreover, if Taiwan's mainland investment increases, more of its semi-finished products can be produced in China, with resulting cost benefits.

The ROC government, however, is more ambivalent about mainland investment. There are two fears: the first, that Taiwan's industry will become a vacuum or, in popular parlance, 'hollowed out'; and the second, that there will be excessive dependence on China. Taiwan's government officials and industrialists alike are aware that direct investment in the mainland facilitates the exploitation of cheap land, labour and resources, and can also take advantage of a huge Chinese market. Such investment, however, could put the ROC at a disadvantage in any future political negotiations.

In summary, Taiwan's officialdom has little choice but to accept increasing trade with and investment in mainland China, although it seems likely to continue to promote an economic stake in Southeast Asia as a counterbalance. Economic links, of course, have attained their own momentum and both in scale and number of projects Taiwan's investments in China are increasing. There are even investments in distant provinces like Qinghai. Finally, emphasis is generally already moving away from short-term processing industry to long-term projects like finance, real estate and energy.[32]

Although the interests of business and government diverge, the former may be restricted or encouraged by legislative guidelines. In spite of its ambivalence, Taiwan's government has been implementing measures conducive to business expansion on the mainland. Business motives are clear; the mainland market is huge, and even though living standards overall are low, the number of consumers with incomes above US$5,000 per year is growing. Moreover, China has a large land area, cheap labour and a policy of encouraging investment. Taiwan, in contrast, has limited space and labour power, is experiencing some social disorder, and there are calls for stricter anti-pollution legislation. Tacitly acknowledging the benefits which mainland investment brings, albeit with reservations, Taiwan's government has increased the number of sectors where capital input is permitted. In April 1994, for instance, the Industrial Development Bureau decided to allow indirect investment in formerly restricted textile items in China. The ban on 325 textile items, including wool, cotton yarn and cloth made of synthetic fibres, was to be lifted. Simultaneously, imports of most garments were to be permitted. In addition, in January 1995 investment did not require approval for new ventures up to a value of US$10 million if the relevant companies already had investments on the mainland previously approved.[33]

In fact, recent statistics indicate that the scale of Taiwan's investments in China has been increasing; as of early 1994, for example, there were over a hundred Taiwan-funded enterprises each with an investment of over US$10 million in the coastal province of Jiangsu. Even in the hinterland of Sichuan the scale is growing; in the same year 39 per cent of Taiwan's ventures had investments of more than US$1 million and one had funding amounting to US$100 million. Furthermore another trend relates to size of investor; whereas formerly Taiwan's investors tended to be medium and small enterprises, by 1993 large enterprises and even consortia were being represented. Currently, Taiwan's investment in China ranges across manufacturing industries producing plastic, electric, electronic, base metal, food, beverage, textile and chemical products. In addition, it includes agriculture as well as tourism and property.[34]

In general, it could be said that Taiwan's investors are beginning to shift the focus of their investment from labour-intensive industries, like textiles, to capital- and technology-intensive ones like information services and computer software. Two examples, one at each end of this spectrum, will be used to indicate the opposite poles of Taiwan's investment on the mainland. The first is the Quanzhou Yunxing Knit Company, established in 1988 as a wholly owned Taiwanese company near Quanzhou City in Fujian Province. When the company was established, a fifty-year contract was concluded for land and buildings, the rights for the use of which were acquired for US$800,000. The company employs 420 workers to produce weft-knit goods like sweaters. Production is vertical from knitting to finishing, and work is not contracted out. Most sales are to a trading group including Japanese companies like Marubeni and Mitsubishi; Yunxing receives orders from Japan, produces samples, resources raw materials from Taiwan for processing and exports most of the products. This is typical of a number of Taiwan-invested export-processing operations, and the company is mainly reliant on the Japanese market.[35]

The second example relates to the computer industry. Significantly, in 1992 investments by Taiwan concerns in that sector were growing more rapidly in China than the ROC. Moreover, whereas in the 1980s such investors had preferred ASEAN countries like Malaysia and Thailand, in 1993 and 1994 Taiwan's information electronics industry was beginning to shift its focus to China. In fact, more and more stages of the production process are being moved to the mainland. In addition, not only have power supply devices, monitors and mainframes gradually become production staples but a computer software industry, generally unsuccessful to date in Taiwan itself, is now beginning to be developed on the mainland by Taiwan's information industry using factory-type quantity production methods. The danger is always that Taiwan may create in China a competitor. Even though currently the mainland still cannot compete with Taiwan in high-quality information electronic products as a whole – the ROC's entrepreneurs still claim that the island has a three- to five-year lead – the mainland's industry is progressing rapidly.

Information electronics is but one instance of economic complementarity and potential synergy. China's scientists who can launch artificial satellites are unfamiliar with large-scale micro-computer production and sales. China's Minister of Electronics Industry has stated that Taiwan's computer electronics industry is a model for emulation, even if technological change precludes complete imitation. Cooperation with Taiwan is crucial for future development.

Undoubtedly, relocation on the mainland has benefits for Taiwan's computer companies, the ability to employ a highly qualified workforce and a huge market being but two, as stated by the leaders of major companies like Acer, which is based in Beijing. There are nevertheless disadvantages. The production technology provided by Taiwan's firms is transforming the mainland's information electronics industries, and quite soon the island's differential advantage may be lost. Moreover, computer components suppliers have been following their customers to target mainland markets, to the ultimate benefit of the mainland. If at least some stages of the manufacturing process are not retained in Taiwan, there could be long-term adverse effects on its economy. Erosion of a manufacturing base may be less important in the case of sunset industries where Taiwan already lacks competitiveness but in high-tech sectors the effects could be far-reaching. While financial and service sectors may be the wave of the future, Taiwan cannot survive without some manufacturing industry, and at its current stage of development the ROC must retain control of its computer and information sectors. Without manufacturing, there can be no service industries. With the departure of too many of Taiwan's firms for the mainland, finance and banking are likely to contract. Some local banks in the ROC are finding it difficult to operate. Finally, with investment in China, not only is employment reduced in Taiwan but talent is trained on the mainland. Once local staff are competent to direct Taiwan's plants in China, managers from the ROC will be replaced. Then less talent will be trained in Taiwan. For economic survival the island needs a balance of high-tech manufacturing industries and service sectors.[36]

The ROC's overall investment in and trade with China will now be assessed within the parameters of sub-regional integration in East Asia. In early 1994 the ROC's Mainland Affairs Council stated that Taiwan's capital investment in the mainland had reached a cumulative total of between US$25 and 30 billion; the island is now the second largest investor in China in terms of both number of enterprises and amount of capital.[37] Moreover, China absorbed 66.52 per cent of Taiwan's total investment in 1993.[38] As of 1994 the bulk of investment was still targeted at coastal provinces like Jiangsu, Shandong, Fujian, Zhejiang and Guangdong. At the end of 1993 the island's investment then was prominent; in 1994 for example, Taiwan-funded projects accounted for 20 per cent of total foreign investment in Shanghai.[39]

The Chinese leaders have, of course, been attempting to encourage foreign investment in the hinterland, even though sub-regional integration in south China is official policy. Inland provinces were increasingly recipients of ROC capital, Taiwan's enterprises accounting for 15 per cent of total overseas investment in Sichuan contracted during the first half of 1994.[40] Taiwan's investment is now being reflected in world trade figures; in 1992 the value of China's exports surpassed that of Taiwan for the first time, 3 per cent of it deriving from Taiwan-invested firms on the mainland.[41] Significantly, according to the statistics of the ROC's Board of Foreign Trade, in 1993 Taiwan's exports to China were worth US\$12.8 billion, representing 14.88 per cent of the island's total export value, as opposed to an equivalent figure of 7.71 per cent in 1992.[42] At first sight Taiwan's trade would appear crucial to China; the two states are now each other's fourth largest trading partner. But 65.7 per cent of Taiwan's indirect exports to the mainland in the first nine months of 1993 were composed of humanmade fibres for yarns and clothes, machinery and equipment, electrical and electronic components, and plastic raw materials. In these sectors Taiwan faces competition from Japanese and Western exports. Moreover, Taiwan is but one market for China's lumber, textiles and aquatic products.[43] China has more choice than Taiwan.

The above figures and export and import categories suggest an increasing ROC dependence on the Chinese market, both in terms of investment and trade. Certainly, this reflects economic complementarity; Taiwan's firms' desire for higher productivity and markets coincides with the need of the Chinese to diversify their industrial base. But the advantages may well lie with China.

In summary, the foregoing discussion suggests undoubted complementarities and synergies between China, Japan, Hong Kong and Taiwan. But any exclusive sub-regional integration would not seem to be in the interests of their governments, given their various dependencies on economic relations worldwide. There is no doubt that the south China coastal region, especially, is becoming a major venue for East Asian economic cooperation. Complementarities are based on resource endowments and stages of development. Japan has moved into a pioneer mode and, with the appreciation of the yen, it makes economic sense to relocate some of its manufacturing in China. But exports from Japanese-invested enterprises there are fuelling Japan's trade deficits with China, and these may best be reversed by sales of high technology and industrial plant to China. This is one aspect of an East Asian division of labour.

Hong Kong, like Japan, has wide experience in manufacturing but high labour costs have forced moves into services. Thus the colony's companies are similarly investing in Guangdong, for instance, especially in rural enterprises, while retaining designing and marketing functions at the home base. Hong Kong, as a capital market, is also helping to finance the upgrading of China's inefficient state enterprises, now being turned into joint stock companies. The circle is completed by the Chinese economic stake in Hong Kong, in preparation for retrocession in 1997; this is speeding integration with Shenzhen and the rest of the south China sub-region.

The ROC in Taiwan represents an alternative government, and is wary of too close economic links with the mainland lest these lead to unification on Communist terms. But Taiwan's trade deficits with Japan and the difficulty of penetrating Japanese markets indicate the importance of China to Taiwan's economy. Some declining industries which are suffering rising costs are being relocated in China. As Taiwan enters the ranks of the developed countries, there is focus on high-tech and service sectors. But China itself has some strengths in technology, mainly derived from military uses, and these have civilian applications, suggesting synergies with expertise in Taiwan. Investment from Taiwan in information electronics and computer software in China could prove a mixed blessing; the island must retain high-tech manufacturing, without which its service sectors cannot thrive. Taiwan's survival demands a balance of manufacturing and services.

Taiwan's industrialists, like those elsewhere in East Asia, have a number of options. There is the southern strategy, favoured by ROC official circles. Taiwan's multinationals have their global interests. Nevertheless, present complementarities and synergies are making sub-regional integration in East Asia a reality in an economic, though not in a political, sense. After all it is investment in the southern Chinese provinces of Guangdong and Fujian that has helped Hong Kong and Taiwan to achieve a degree of economic restructuring.

The Northeast Asia economic sphere

In this chapter so far sub-regional integration, now rapidly becoming a reality, has been assessed in the context of China's coastal area from Guangdong in the south to Beijing in the north. China's economic strategy, however, has lately been shifting from a regional to an industrial focus. Changes in the demand structure now place emphasis on heavy industry which is mainly located around the Gulf of Bohai and northeast China. Also favouring a northern focus in the 1990s is the time-honoured CCP tradition of diversifying markets, sources of supply and trading partners. In addition, this region forms a part of Northeast Asia which is relatively undeveloped. It is here, too, that a number of Asian powers, China, Japan, Russia and the two Korean states, are in close proximity. Now that the cold war has passed, priority is being given to economic factors like market forces, and as international relationships are more fluid, there is potential for regional cooperation.

The Chinese, however, ostensibly in support of free trade, reject any exclusive economic arrangements for East Asia, and see the necessity for funding from Western countries and international organisations. In addition, perhaps suspicious lest there be any revival of Japan's pre-war Co-Prosperity Sphere, the Chinese urge consultation among all parties on an equal footing rather than decision making by a predominant partner.[44] Nevertheless the Chinese have been prime movers in proposing economic integration, given complementarities born of the strengths and weaknesses of the states concerned. China's northeast, for example, is rich in natural resources and has a flourishing agriculture; crops include grain, fruit, vegetables and dairy products. The area is also rich in oil and coal resources, and has a thriving textile industry. But the region's industries are deficient in capital, technology, advanced machinery and manufacturing expertise; growth will also depend on much improved infrastructure.

The Russian Far East is advantaged in such natural resources as forests, oil, gas and coal; it also produces heavy machinery and chemical products like fertilisers. It is in need, however, of agricultural and light industrial products; it also lacks capital and modern machinery.

Japanese strengths lie in capital, advanced technology, sophisticated machinery and equipment, high-quality products and managerial expertise. It is nevertheless deficient in natural resources like energy and farm products, and is short of certain kinds of labour.

North Korea possesses mineral resources, exports marine produce and produces simple processed goods; it also has an abundant labour force. But it is short of capital as well as advanced machinery and technology; it is also deficient in both farm and light industrial products.

South Korea's post-war success story is reflected in its capital, advanced technology and industrial products, but it lacks energy, raw materials and sufficient labour. Another possible participant in regional economic cooperation is Mongolia. Abundant in livestock, minerals and ores, it suffers from a lack of direct transport to other potential trade partners. It is also deficient in capital, technology, machinery and even certain farm and light industrial products.

This summary sets the scene for the bilateral and multinational forms of cooperation which are creating the momentum for regional integration.

Attention will first be focused on Russo-Japanese relations which since 1945 have generally been hostile, although in the 1970s the

Japanese agreed to provide capital and knowhow to help develop Siberia and the Soviet Far East in exchange for forestry and gas resources. A major impediment in the past, however, has been the dispute over the northern islands which precludes a peace treaty, although at times the Soviet Union, and latterly the Russians, have adopted more flexible tactics to obtain Japanese funds and technology. For the Russians, the benefit of cooperation with Japan or multilateral cooperation in Northeast Asia as a whole could be considerable; the Asia-Pacific is the world's fastest-growing economic region with many markets, and logistically it is more convenient to bring capital and plant for development from the east than from Europe. Funds and technology from Japan would complement China's labour force and Russian natural resources.[45]

In purely bilateral terms, however, economic cooperation with Russia seems less attractive to the Japanese than it was during the oil crisis of the 1970s, now that, with economic restructuring, Japan's energy-consuming industries have moved offshore. Nevertheless, the Japanese fear protectionism in Europe and the United States; and, if the Russian Far East is developed, its market potential, in the wake of economic reform, could prove irresistible in the early years of the twenty-first century. But it seems unlikely that China or the other interested powers would allow Japan to lead a Northeast Asian community.

But, with reservations on both sides, limited forms of Russo-Japanese cooperation, particularly in infrastructural development, are in progress to create what the Japanese call the Japan Sea Rim Economic Sphere. Basic principles are similar to earlier Soviet proposals; Russia will provide resources; Japan and South Korea, funds and technology; and China and North Korea, a labour force. As the realisation of such a plan is long term, discussion is now focused on the tentative steps taken to lay the physical foundations for bilateral and multinational cooperation among Japan and Sea Rim countries.

Much initiative has come from regional authorities on the Japan Sea Coast which have been laying the groundwork for future trade and other exchanges with Japan Sea countries by instituting sealanes and air routes. In 1993, for instance, the first conference between governors of Japan's regions and the Russian Far East was held in Toyama Prefecture, Japan. There have been numerous economic missions like that from China's Jilin Province to Tottori and Niigata in Japan and that from Akita Prefecture to Khabarovsk.

Sistership ties have included a friendship agreement between Yamagata Prefecture and China's Heilongjiang Province. In addition, the authorities of Niigata Prefecture have pioneered a feasibility study of port development in Russia's Sakhalin. In recognition of the importance of such links, a Japan Sea Rim Economic Institute has been established jointly by the public and private sectors in Japan.

Tangible results of such lobbying have included the opening up of sealanes; for instance, the so-called Eastern Maritime Silk Road from Sakata Port in Yamagata Prefecture to Harbin via the Amur River was opened in 1992, cutting the time for travel from China's Heilongjiang Province to Japan in half and the cost to a third compared to the conventional route through Dalian. In addition, in 1993 regular container service was increased between Kitakyushu and Dalian and a passenger ship route was opened connecting Vladivostok with Toyama and Niigata. Furthermore, air routes between Toyama and Seoul and between Niigata and Vladivostok were established in 1993. Finally, to increase trade between Japan and Northeast Asia, a number of free access zones, that is import promotion regions with special customs regulations, have been established, Nagasaki being one example.[46]

There are also complementarities in China's relations with Russia and its other land neighbours in Northeast Asia. After the worsening of the Sino-Soviet dispute in 1960, trade between the two countries became minimal but since the dismemberment of the Soviet Union in 1991 economic contracts have increased. China's cross-border trade with land neighbours (excluding Hong Kong and Macao) accounted for only 10 per cent of its total trade with Asia and less than 1 per cent of its global trade in 1993. Nevertheless, cross-border trade is important in the economic development of China's border regions. Most of China's cross-border trade, 73 per cent, is generated by the northeast provinces of Heilongjiang, Jilin and Liaoning, and Inner Mongolia. In 1993 China exported US\$3.3 billion worth of goods to North Korea, Mongolia and Russia, and imported US\$5.3 billion. Russia is by far the largest trading partner, and cross-border trade with China has showed significant annual increases in the 1990s, 50 per cent in 1992 and 30 per cent in 1993, even though the total fell in 1994 when Russia placed new restrictions on private traders, moving the bulk of commerce back into the hands of state trading companies.

In 1992 Heilongjiang's border trade totalled US\$1.5 billion, about two-thirds of China's total trade with Russia. Heilongjiang exports grains, fruit, vegetables, sugar, textiles and other consumer goods, in exchange for timber, industrial chemicals, chemical fertilisers, steel products and machinery from neighbouring countries. Jilin Province's exports to and imports from both Russia and North Korea follow a pattern similar to that of Heilongjiang. Liaoning Province, through its port of Dandong, exports grain, vegetables, textiles, consumer goods, machinery and electrical products to North Korea, in exchange for seafood and rice.

In view of growing trade and the possibility of further economic development, investors from Japan, South Korea, Taiwan and Hong Kong have been particularly active in China's northeast, as have the provincial authorities. To facilitate further interaction with global markets, Liaoning Province has invested over US$3.6 billion in infrastructure to improve roads, harbours, railways, communications, power plants and water supply systems. Facilities for transporting natural gas and coal supplies have been improved. For example, a new US$500 million four-lane highway linking Shenyang and Dalian opened in September 1990, reducing travel time between the two cities to four hours. The Heilongjiang provincial authorities are constructing port facilities and a new airport. China and Russia are cooperating in the building of a railway from Tumen to link China's northeast with Russia's Far East. It is intended that this line will eventually connect with Asian trunk lines, allowing freight trains to travel from the Pacific coast through North Korea and Russia into China, thence to Mongolia and Europe.[47]

It is against this background of economic and political change in Northeast Asia that schemes for the development of the Tumen River Area, which faces the Sea of Japan and straddles the borders of China, North Korea and Russia, have been mooted. The Tumen Delta is seen as a future transportation and export-processing centre in Northeast Asia. Powers in the region hold differing views on the possible nature and scope of such a zone, one suggestion calling for separate special economic zones to be established by China, North Korea and Russia, and another for a single international zone to be jointly established by the three countries. It is the latter approach, coinciding largely with Chinese views, which is the focus of this section.

In fact, much impetus has come from the Chinese side and the original concept was proposed at a symposium on economic and technical development in Northeast Asia held at Changchun City, Jilin, in July 1990. There was strong interest in the proposal from the participants, researchers and entrepreneurs from China, the old Soviet Union, the two Korean states and Japan. In July 1991 a conference sponsored by the United Nations Development Programme (UNDP) was held in Mongolia to discuss development in the region; Mongolia, China and the two Korean states were already recipients of aid from the UNDP which sponsored a further meeting in Ulan Bator the next year. Meanwhile, in the wake of a second symposium held in August 1991, again in Changchun, the Chinese stated a number of objectives and made specific proposals. The originator of some of the Chinese thinking, Ding Shisui, Chairman of the Jilin Provincial Science and Technology Commission, spoke of a long-term development project, lasting thirty to fifty years and requiring US$35 billion in funds from the Chinese side alone. The objective was to facilitate the economic growth of the Chinese, North Korean and Soviet border areas which would serve as centres to expedite the development of the Chinese northeast, the Soviet Far East and North Korea. In addition, the land bridge passing through Tumen, Changchun in Jilin and Ulan Bator in Mongolia would considerably shorten the distance to European Russia and Western Europe compared with the Trans-Siberian railway. To achieve these objectives, the Chinese were proposing in 1991 a number of options for the region as a whole. The first suggested that China, Russia and North Korea each establish one or more economic zones in their own territories, the second that the countries set up an economic zone extending over their common border, and the third called for a single zone to extend over their territories. The Chinese preference was for the third option, for which the only suitable region was said to be the downstream area of the Tumen River. Products, people and capital would be able to move freely in such an economic zone which would be managed by an international organisation set up for coordinating the various national interests.

The developmental interests of the parties were, of course, in a number of respects divergent, Russian reservations concerning Chinese preferences being a case in point. The Nakhodka Free Economic Zone is the first of its kind designated by Russia. Planned to attract foreign capital and increase exports, industries envisaged include the processing of local raw materials like fish, lumber and minerals, the manufacture of machinery and equipment for these processing plants, and farm production, ship repair, construction and tourism. Given the importance of such a programme to Russia, its representative to the Second Changchun Conference in 1991 objected that large-scale development of North Korean ports and a short railway route through China to connect with the Trans-Siberian railway would isolate the coastal regions of the Russian Far East and reduce investment in the port of Nakhodka.

Mongolian leaders, however, are supportive of the Chinese view. In the midst of a transition to a market economy they have been strengthening their ties with China and, as a landlocked country, Mongolia needs routes to the sea and currently has to rely on the Chinese port of Tianjin. Accordingly, the Mongolians have expressed strong interest in new international shipping links through the development of the Tumen

River area, the idea of a land bridge connecting the Tumen Zone and Europe through their eastern territory being particularly attractive.

The UNDP sponsors' position was also close to that of the Chinese. After the July 1991 conference, a team of experts from the UNDP carried out surveys and had discussions with specialists from China, the two Korean states and Mongolia. Findings were presented to a UNDP-hosted conference in Pyongyang, North Korea, in October 1991 when governments of these countries together with that of Russia were represented. The Japanese were observers. The UNDP's study concluded that the trade potential was considerable, given the region's strategic location, adjacent to the markets of Jilin and Heilongjiang provinces, and to the labour forces and natural resources of Russia, North Korea and Mongolia; and there was access to Japan, South Korea and Europe. Resources and complementarities within the region also suggested that it could become a transportation link like Hong Kong or Singapore. Before the regional concept could be turned into reality, however, differences of opinion among China, North Korea and Russia had to be resolved. Coordination was crucial to secure the support of international investors, to avoid overlapping of facilities and to eliminate unprofitable competition. The conference concluded that further studies were required and in the mean time small-scale regional cooperation should be initiated.

In October 1992, however, possibly in response to conflict on certain issues between the respective countries, a sub-committee, earlier established by the UNDP, reported on the possibility of joint international development by China, North Korea and Russia of a considerably larger zone, an idea earlier broached by the authorities of China's Jilin Province. While the proposed zone could be increased with the progress of economic development, it would initially include the Chinese city of Hunchun, Russia's Hasan region, and North Korea's Sonbong region. This special international economic zone would involve an economic union among the three countries in that area; they would nevertheless retain sovereignty over their own territories. The purpose was to create a free trade zone, the extent of which would be about 1,000 square kilometres (compared to Hong Kong's 1,061 and Singapore's 618). Tariffs would be waived and the zone bonded, so that relay trade would also be tariff-free, with export and import procedures eliminated. Foreign currency would freely circulate.

Above has been discussed the growth of trade and investment as well as the development of infrastructure which make future economic integration a possible proposition. The realisation of plans to create a Tumen Zone, however, will depend on a number of prerequisites.

Firstly, direct private investment from countries outside the region must be attracted; indispensable here is a favourable environment for foreign investors. Before an adequate infrastructure has been built up, investors must be attracted by such incentives as low wage rates and tax concessions. To encourage foreign companies, initial priority should be given to labour-intensive assembly and processing industries and to the tourist trade, these being foreign currency earners. Secondly, given the scale of the zone, coordination among China, North Korea and Russia is crucial. Thirdly, funds must be procured domestically among the three countries and also from Japan and South Korea as well as from international financial institutions like the Asian Development Bank and the World Bank. A fourth prerequisite is continuing market reform in China, North Korea and Russia. China's northeast, for instance, is in this respect way behind the southern coast. North Korea's market reforms are only just beginning, while Russia's institutions must be put on a sounder footing. Fifthly, there are political issues. The territorial dispute would seem to preclude yen loans from Japan's Export-Import Bank to Russia. Investment by South Korean companies in North Korea awaits improvement in government-to-government relations.[48] In conclusion, the economic complementarities present in Northeast Asia suggest that a Tumen International Zone along the lines proposed has enormous potential, providing that infrastructural and funding problems can be overcome.

Summary

In summary, this chapter has examined the progress of sub-regional integration in East Asia. Trends in this direction have been driven both from within the region and by the protectionist tendencies of blocs like the European Union and NAFTA. In addition, there is a global movement towards regional development. But there is an awareness that states and territories in East Asia cannot rely exclusively on intra-regional trade and investment; the Chinese, ostensibly supportive of free trade, are anxious to diversify markets and sources of supply. Nevertheless, the region undoubtedly has economic complementarities, and it is on these that cooperation is based.

The initial focus of this chapter has been China's coastal region, itself divided into a number of sub-regions. One of these, the southern coastal area, is the site of the Special Economic Zones, initiated during the early years of the open door policy. This in turn is divided into the sub-region around Guangdong, where Hong Kong interests are strongly in evidence, and Fujian, in which Taiwan's enterprises have been active.

Growing in importance is China's largest city, Shanghai, where the Pudong Zone has been established by the central government; it receives substantial state assistance and is seen as a counterweight to the growing economic power of the southern provincial authorities. Shanghai is also a natural base for the development of the Yangtze region. In addition, since the early 1990s another development zone has been forming in northeast China, adjacent to the Bohai Gulf and the Liaodong Peninsula, and including Beijing and Tianjin. This is the locus of heavy industry which is of growing importance at China's current stage of development. A major centre is Dalian, now receiving major Japanese investment. In the above sub-regions integration is fast becoming a reality. The Tumen Development Zone in northeast China is not yet officially in existence but again economic complementarity, this time among China, Russia, the Korean states and Japan, suggests another focus of East Asian regional development in the twenty-first century.

Integration in China's southern sub-regions is informed by the motives of the key players, Japan, Hong Kong and Taiwan. The appreciation of the yen has often compelled Japanese companies to move production offshore, to China for example, to avail themselves of cheaper abundant labour and a growing local consumer market. In fact, their products are now of sufficient quality for the discerning Japanese consumer. Moreover, whereas in the past key components had to be obtained from Japan, integrated production from upstream to downstream is becoming the mode, with design and development functions also being located in China. Thus there is now not only a division of labour among the countries of the region like China and Japan but growing interdependence. This diverges from the model of the 1980s when states followed in the footsteps of their predecessors.

Similarly, economic complementarity has spurred Hong Kong's investment in China. While the colony has latterly moved into service industries, it retains manufacturing skills, invaluable, for instance, to the burgeoning rural industries of Guangdong. Thus Hong Kong industrialists benefit from lower labour costs; the colony's marketing expertise helps the Chinese to target international markets. Hong Kong is also a conduit for overseas Chinese who wish to invest in enterprises in China. Increasingly, also, Hong Kong's capital is helping to fund China's state enterprises, now becoming joint stock companies, through listings on the Hong Kong Stock Exchange. Infrastructural development in China is also being aided by Hong Kong interests.

If Hong Kong's stake in Guangdong and particularly the Special Economic Zone of Shenzhen is considerable, China, through official bodies like CITIC, is already playing a key role in the colony's economic life, with investments in airlines, telecommunications and housing as well as services, in preparation for retrocession in 1997.

The ROC in Taiwan presents a government alternative to the CCP. Economically successful, the island has limited space and resources but abundant capital and expertise. Investment in China, notably in Fujian Province, immediately across the straits, is a natural choice. Taiwan's trade surpluses with China compensate for the island's deficits with Japan, even though the ROC remains dependent on the latter's investment in order to target high-tech industries. The ROC authorities are nevertheless ambivalent about economic relations with China; too much reliance on investment in the mainland could lead to reunification on Communist terms. Accordingly, a southern strategy, investment in ASEAN countries, has been officially encouraged, although since the early 1990s the ROC government has eased restrictions on trade with and investment in China, which have hitherto been indirect via Hong Kong. Taiwan business is increasingly enthusiastic for mainland links. There are, however, additional threats and opportunities presented by Taiwan's investment in China. Advantages lie in division of labour and technological synergies, and the mainland's technical experts are now officially welcome in Taiwan. But if, for example, too many information electronics and computer software concerns invest in China, it may soon prove a competitor as its own technological levels rise, and consequently the island's economy could suffer a hollowing out, with detrimental effects on both manufacturing industry and services. Taiwan needs Japanese and other high-tech investment to retain employment and markets. On the other side the benefits of ROC investment for China are clear, and Taiwan's successful economic model is being given close attention in China's official academic journals.

In short, complementarity in East Asia has favoured division of labour and aided economic restructuring, especially in Japan, Hong Kong and Taiwan.

The Chinese leaders' economic strategy is now moving from a regional to an industrial focus. But they wish to correct imbalances in wealth and power among the sub-regions. Heavy industry, an emphasis in current economic strategy, is located in China's north, which in turn is adjacent to the northeast, including the Tumen River delta, where a number of powers, China, Japan, Russia and the Korean states, are in close proximity. With the dismemberment of the Soviet Union and the end of the cold war, Sino-Russian trade is increasing, as are Russo-Japanese economic contacts. This has resulted in improvement of infrastructure in China's northeast provinces and across the border in

Russia. New sea and air links between Japan and Russia are being established.

Momentum is gathering for the creation of a Tumen International Zone, proposals for which were originally mooted by China's Jilin provincial authorities in 1990, and since then regional conferences sponsored by the UNDP have sought to coordinate the views of the partners. Again, there are complementarities: China's northeast has labour and natural resources, Russia's Far East possesses raw materials, Japan and South Korea have capital and technology, and North Korea is endowed with minerals and an abundant workforce. However, a number of divergent interests must be reconciled. The Chinese, for example, are suspicious of too great a Japanese role. Consequently, they favour a larger zone than the Tumen River Area envisaged earlier. The most recent concept is an international zone, with sovereignty resting with the national partners in the various sectors. The ultimate objective is to operate a free trade zone, an industrial, trading and transportation hub for the Asia-Pacific region. There are, however, formidable barriers to its creation. Funding needed for infrastructure alone is phenomenal, and this will have to come from private investors and international organisations. Further market reforms must be instituted in China's backward northeastern provinces, the Russian Far East and North Korea. Finally, there are political barriers, like the Russo-Japanese territorial dispute and contention between the two Korean states, to be overcome.

The twenty-first century could nevertheless see sub-regional integration not only on China's southern coast but on its northeastern borders.

6 Conclusions: the future of Sino-Japanese relations

The open door economic policy: trends and prospects

Preceding chapters have presented an optimistic appraisal of Japan's economic relations with China and their future trends. But the open door policy of which these features are a part is itself dependent on a number of favourable international factors and the power configuration within China itself. These two sets interact and this conclusion will bring together, and draw implications from, the themes discussed earlier in the book. Ostensibly, China's open door policy has been very successful and the resulting opportunities for foreign partners in trade and investment would appear manifold. To take just a few economic indicators: from 1979 to 1993 the average income of China's urban population increased by 6.3 per cent annually and that of the rural population by 8.5 per cent after price adjustment, even though the gap between the cities and the countryside would seem to be widening in the 1990s. This growth is creating great discretionary income, particularly in the coastal cities, and the consultants McKinsey suggested in a survey in early 1995 that China's wealthier consumers, calculated to include only those with annual incomes exceeding the equivalent of US$1,000, will number more than 270 million by the year 2000, thus producing a market larger than the current United States population. Such features are gradually being reflected in the pattern of China's two-way world trade which rose from US$29.4 billion in 1979 to US$195.8 billion in 1993, a leap from thirty-second to eleventh in the international league. This impressive record has to be seen within the framework of the three-stage strategy of modernisation propounded by China's elder statesman Deng Xiaoping. Chinese official sources claim that the objective for the first stage, to double GNP on the basis of the 1980 figure, has already been achieved ahead of schedule. The aim of the second, a redoubling of GNP and a relatively high standard of living by the end of this century, is gradually being realised, although again with growing urban–rural differentials. It is projected that between now and the turn of the century China's national economy will grow at an annual rate of 8 per cent to 9 per cent. On that reckoning the goal of the second stage will also be achieved ahead of time. During the third stage, scheduled to last from the beginning to the middle of the twenty-first century, per capita GNP is targeted to rise to the level of the average of developed countries and modernisation as currently understood will have been achieved.[1]

These projections, however, beg a number of political and economic questions. One prerequisite is political stability. The open door policy, initiated by Deng Xiaoping, was based on a number of conclusions drawn from China's post-1949 experience. Deng's policies had also been foreshadowed in Zhou Enlai's launching of the 'Four Modern-isations' programme in the early 1970s. Trade and investment with the Soviet Union, China's international Communist partner, effectively ended in 1960, with the suspicion of Mao Zedong and some other CCP leaders that assistance from Moscow had ulterior political motives which threatened their national independence. In the half century or so prior to the Communist accession in 1949, China's intellectuals, including Mao Zedong and his cohorts, had sought a political doctrine to replace the discredited Confucian ethic. In the wake of the Sino-Soviet dispute the chosen doctrine, Marxism-Leninism, had to be adjusted, with greater emphasis placed on Mao Zedong thought and his claimed contribution to the Chinese revolution in the realm of everyday economic and political action.

With Soviet assistance eliminated and relative isolation from the advanced countries of the West, China was thrown back, virtually by necessity, on to a policy of self-reliance, if not self-sufficiency; foreign trade, with Japan becoming the country's major trading partner in 1965, was seen merely as an adjunct to domestic economic activity. By the late 1970s, however, with a leadership more orientated to economic rationality than mass mobilisation through ideological in-centives, it was concluded that there were limits to the generation of capital for growth, for example from the fruits of the primary sector, without the benefit of foreign trade and investment. But if exports were to be competitive, then market forces would have to be given freer rein in China itself. In retrospect, at least on the surface, there would appear to have been a fair degree of consensus among the country's leaders and population concerning the free market and associated prac-tices. Certainly, many have profited. But in 1978 it was only in the teeth of opposition from some government leaders like the veteran economist and recently deceased Chen Yun that the full range of reform policies was adopted.

Admittedly, though, the major disagreements concerned the actual extent of economic liberalisation rather than reform *per se*. Such arguments are still current and have implications for the continuation of the open door policy in its present form and, indeed, further liberalisation. In essence, this is a debate which has been proceeding in China ever since the first military impact of the West in the mid-nineteenth century. Chinese official reformers of the early 1860s, for instance, called for the use of Western technology for practical matters, while retaining the essence, that is traditional political thought, institutions and society, all of which were infused by the Confucian ethic. Unfortunately for the reformers of that time and later, institutions do affect values and no society can remain unaffected by foreign economic institutions, investment and technology transfer. The dangers are that if the institutions and values are not smoothly absorbed, the position of any incumbent establishment will be threatened. The current Chinese leaders have so far sanctioned economic reform but not political liberalisation, and have staked their own legitimacy on steadily rising living standards among China's populace. In the process they have sought to maintain the levers of economic power. But precisely as a result of the officially directed transition from command to market, more and more initiative has been slipping from the grasp of the central government. As a result, there are structural problems like inflation, also suffered by the Japanese in the 1950s and 1960s simultaneously with fast productivity. Power maintenance at the centre now depends on the development of sophisticated indirect macroeconomic controls in areas like taxation and pricing. But increasing personal wealth differentials and growing regional disparities are in turn bringing fundamental changes which are eroding, some believe, traditional social values, infused by the Maoist egalitarian ethic, and themselves influenced, however indirectly, by the Confucian ethic. In a broader sense, too, Western-style consumerism brings its own cultural features.

In response, privately acknowledging that a despotism is at its weakest when it initiates reform, the CCP has periodically attacked 'spiritual pollution', and the current ongoing corruption drive among Beijing CCP members is a reflection of anxiety over such social trends.[2] A classic CCP approach to problems of this kind is 'rectification', or Party housecleaning. At present, this means the re-education of grass-roots members in CCP directives and objectives. This also strengthens regional organisation, which is then in a position to direct the population in accordance with national goals. An integral part of this campaign is also economic; in Liaoning Province, for example, universities, research institutes and rich villages have been instructed to support poorer rural communities by upgrading agricultural production and facilities. In addition, much of the campaign has focused on the retraining of CCP branch secretaries, for instance, in areas as far afield as Guangdong, Zhejiang and distant Ningxia. Furthermore, the services of another ideology are being utilised in order to maintain social cohesion in the midst of rapid economic change and the resulting personal and regional wealth disparities. The CCP leaders have been ambivalent in their views of Confucianism but many of the Party's ideas concerning social control derive from the Confucian tradition. One feature is the group ethic as opposed to the individualism of the West. Even in its commitment to market forces the CCP is still attempting a form of social engineering based on group solidarity; the goal is national prosperity for China rather than the personal betterment of the individual *per se*. The interests of the nation are placed above those of the individual.

Not surprisingly, Confucianism is seen as a way of checking the moral degeneration allegedly deriving from contact with certain Western individualist values. Thus, moral degeneration is not caused by the market economy as such but by the abandonment of education in traditional culture, an integral part of which is community interest. China's modernisation means cultural borrowing but this in turn should be selectively integrated with tradition; Confucian loyalties are thus seen as a counterweight to uncritical Westernisation. CCP rectification owes much to the social pressures enforced by Confucianism.[3] In short, the CCP leadership has sought to maintain its power through cohesion in the Party via rectification campaigns, at the same time using legal sanctions to punish the perpetrators of corruption, even if they have connections with the establishment in Beijing. Similarly, the Confucian tradition is being enlisted to curb self-seeking among the population at large.

Economic dissonance, however, is less responsive to CCP dictates. Measures to attract foreign investment have often meant fostering local initiative, bringing to the fore the old delicate balance between the centre and the provinces in China. The effective implementation of the macroeconomic measures cited above is one means of enforcing central control, albeit indirect, and reforms accomplished to date suggest the need not for retreat but for further change, especially to meet the demands of trade and investment, both at home and abroad. In May 1995 China's Foreign Trade Minister, Wu Yi, reasserted the country's free trade stance; a better legal framework would be created, there would be improved access for foreign products even though domestic infant industries would be protected according to international rules, and foreign investment would be open to more sectors, particularly services. Among other priority sectors for utilising foreign investment are agriculture, energy, transportation, raw material industries and projects in basic industries with advanced technology. Aspiring to join the new World Trade Organisation, the Chinese will adjust their trade regime; in addition, the country seeks to strengthen its role in non-exclusive bodies like APEC. Thus legislation for central economic control at home is closely linked with adherence to international trade and investment norms.[4]

Even with these measures successfully in place, there is no guarantee that the current leadership's political authority will remain unquestioned. Even if wealth differentials, both regional and personal, are kept within reasonable bounds, and greater rewards for the successful are seen as fully merited, the fact remains that the open door is creating new centres of power and influence based on greater specialisation and division of labour. Industrial management, as has been shown, is being separated from state ownership, and forms of privatisation instituted. Economic reforms could eventually bring in their wake demands for political liberalisation. The ambitious modernisation programme still, however, calls for central discipline and direction, and any limited political liberties will not necessarily lead to a Western-style representative government. There are various ways of achieving a general political consensus; the Japanese example is instructive as it combines Anglo-American political institutions with a process derived from traditional social values and patterns, the latter also informing the factional group loyalties within competing political parties. More likely, however, is the evolution of the CCP itself, a possible model being the ROC where the dominant political party, the Guomindang, has since the 1980s permitted rival organisations to compete in a limited way at both local and national levels. There is a proposal to elect the ROC's President by popular vote for the first time in 1996. Similar developments could materialise on the mainland, if the National People's Congress, China's parliament, still primarily a rubberstamp body dominated by CCP decision making, is allowed to air divergent views, as it did concerning recent political appointments. The parameters of political dissent, however, will necessarily be ill-defined, and opposition, as a number of dissidents have already found, may in some instances still be regarded as treason in a country without a tradition of rival political parties. Increasingly, too, with private and foreign enterprises accounting for a growing proportion of industrial output, business interests, divided among themselves, will lobby government and represent independent forces. This will spur the creation of pluralism but real political democracy, as understood in the West, seems decades away. Finally, even those who would organise in the name of representative government nevertheless seem still to think in terms of freedom for the nation rather than the individual.

Meanwhile, the question of succession to the ageing leadership of Deng Xiaoping casts a shadow over political and economic stability. In totalitarian political systems like China's, mechanisms for effecting a smooth political succession are unsatisfactory. Moreover, China is a nation ruled by personalities rather than institutions and this itself makes prediction unreliable, as access to knowledge of the exact nature of relationships among protagonists for the succession is difficult to obtain. By virtue of official position Jiang Zemin, President of China and CCP General Secretary, and Qiao Shi, Chairman of the Standing Committee of China's National People's Congress, would appear to be strong candidates. More importantly, Jiang also chairs the Central Military Commission, and the army is likely to be a powerful arbiter in any power struggle, which could prove protracted.[5] In fact, some observers see a struggle for the succession to Deng Xiaoping ending in regional warlordism, as happened after the end of the Qing Dynasty in the 1920s and 1930s. Such an eventuality was also predicted during the Cultural Revolution when Mao Zedong gave the military a prominent role in national administration. But warlordism did not result. It must be remembered that during the Communist rise to power and even for a time after its accession the army was indistinguishable from the Party in that senior army officers were also Party leaders. Even though the armed services are now becoming a professional corps as opposed to the old type of guerrilla organisation, the traditional legacy persists; in a succession crisis the army might form a faction or be divided, but in any case would need Party civilian allies, precluding military predominance either regionally or nationally. In brief, in any succession struggle, the military may well prove influential but are unlikely as a result to enjoy exclusive prerogatives of power.

Given current political and economic changes in China, a number of possible future scenarios may be drawn which have implications for foreign traders and investors. First of all, it seems inconceivable that the open door policy will be reversed, even in the wake of an indecisive succession struggle, although opposing factions might disagree as to the desirable extent of economic liberalisation and concessions offered to foreign interests. Secondly, there is the fragmentation scenario, where China could break up into a number of autonomous regions, loosely linked in a national federation, each pursuing its own economic policies with independent governmental and legal systems. These entities might compete for foreign markets and investment. Such a scenario, while not impossible, would appear precluded because, in spite of past delicate relations between the centre and the provinces, throughout history cultural commonality has produced tendencies towards political unity. The third possibility is a chauvinist Chinese leadership, backed by enormous economic and political power, aspiring to domination of Asia and supported by overseas Chinese influence elsewhere in the continent. Chinese emphases in this scenario would suggest that investment from within Asia be given priority, reducing drastically input from the West. While the Chinese leaders would not necessarily be inward-looking, their claims to leadership of Asia would imply a reduction of Western economic and financial influence on the country. It is nevertheless argued that, as the Chinese have always sought to diversify economic contacts, they will remain reluctant to depend on exclusive relationships even in as broad a context as Asia. In any case such a chauvinist policy would likely incur the enmity of Japan. As is asserted later, this could be undesirable from the point of view of China's long-term interests. A fourth scenario would appear to be the most realistic prediction. By the early or middle years of the twenty-first century China would have become an economic superpower fully integrated into the world community. Both imports and exports will grow in line with rising prosperity. Economic growth would underpin CCP political legitimacy, and limited popular participation in government at central and local level could be increasingly permitted. China would have surpassed Japan in industrial output, the two countries becoming economic partners and competitors.[6] In general, arguments below will come closest to the latter assumptions, those inherent in the fourth scenario.

China and Japan: military rivals in Asia?

The Chinese leaders have asserted that they need a peaceful international environment in order to pursue their modernisation programme, the priority being friendly relations with neighbours. Negotiations on border demarcation have recently been conducted with such countries as Russia and Myanmar. In fact, while in cold war days the old Soviet Union presented a danger, there is now said to be no ostensible immediate threat to China's security, and the Chinese are prepared to develop relations with all countries on the basis of the five principles of peaceful coexistence. Accordingly, Chinese spokesmen have been at pains to emphasise that their country's military posture is defensive and that it has adopted a positive stance over disarmament. In 1985 the Chinese armed forces were reduced by one million, although they do not explain, as discussed later in this chapter, that this reduction in manpower is an integral part not of disarmament but of military modernisation. In addition, in response to criticism of China's underground nuclear test in May 1995, Chinese leaders have stated that they will cease testing when the Comprehensive Test Ban Treaty comes into force. Furthermore, they call upon nuclear weapons states to respond positively to China's proposal for a treaty on the non-first use of nuclear weapons against each other. Moreover, they call for an agreement not to use or threaten to use nuclear weapons against non-nuclear weapons states and nuclear-free zones.[7]

The nuclear issue is a particularly sensitive one for Japan which, in extending Overseas Development Assistance, takes into account the recipient country's disarmament efforts. The Chinese, however, may well be prepared to risk Japanese public wrath, calculating that given the trade and investment interests of Japan's industrialists in China in a time of recession, the offer of yen loans in 1995 is unlikely to be rescinded.[8] In fact, while stressing that the continuation of Sino-Japanese relations will contribute to the peace and stability of the Asia-Pacific region in the twenty-first century, the Chinese have been airing various contentious issues in 1994 and 1995, including the visits of ROC representatives to Japan and the justification by Japanese leaders of war crimes committed by militarists during the occupation of China. These statements do not necessarily suggest that the Chinese leadership believes that the Japanese currently harbour hostility towards them but may be a means of exerting diplomatic leverage.[9]

Nevertheless every nation maintains defence capacity, whatever the perceived threat to national security. Thus while there is believed to be no immediate threat, since the 1980s China has been acquiring interests and a new international position which demand military strategic rethinking. A greater role in international commerce means, for instance, that Asian sealanes are increasingly important to China. Moreover, in spite of its abundant raw materials, China is suffering from increasing population pressure on dwindling land resources, and there is a growing need to look offshore for resources like energy. Mao Zedong, who came to power largely through peasant guerrilla forces, conceived of defence in terms of a land-based people's army; now strategy has shifted to a more offensive posture capable of fighting small but intense local wars against more than one enemy. In addition, reassessment of strategic priorities has resulted in victory for those officers supporting small but elite armed forces equipped with the latest technology and weaponry over those adhering to the old militia-type guerrilla ethic. In accordance with this thinking, in 1993 a professional advocate, Liu Huaqing, Vice-Chairman of the Central Military Commission and a naval specialist, stated China's defence needs in terms of the integrated use of air, land and sea forces. Liu stressed that China was unprepared for large-scale conflict because of low levels of military technology. Because economic development, itself a guarantee of defence, should receive priority, meaning that limited funds are available for the military, these should be used effectively, for example for training technologically competent officers and soldiers and procuring the latest electronics technology and weapons systems from abroad. Fighter aircraft, for instance, have recently been purchased from Russia.

In spite of poverty pleas and protestations of peaceful intentions, China's military spending has been growing. In 1992 and 1993 military budgets amounted to US$6.9 billion and US $7.7 billion respectively. These are official figures, and foreign defence analysts believe that they grossly underestimate real expenditures, China's establishment being more secretive than that of most countries.

What is not in doubt is the new role being accorded to the navy. Formerly a coastal force, the Chinese navy is now to be engaged in offshore defence, and to acquire a 'first strike' capacity. This new role has been posited on the following assumptions. The central theme of naval strategy is that no large-scale foreign invasion of China, especially from the sea, is likely in the foreseeable future. Preparation to resist such an invasion is thus but one of the navy's tasks; a more important one is developing a capability for long-distance combat well beyond China's coast, given intensifying competition in the Asian region for maritime resources. Thus strategists announced in 1985 the intention to build a navy capable of seizing and maintaining control of offshore areas, of effectively controlling sea channels and lanes adjacent to China's territorial waters, and of launching combat there. In brief, the navy had three main tasks: defending China against foreign invasion, securing its sovereignty at sea and protecting its maritime rights and interests.

It is within this context that Chinese policy towards disputed island chains in the South China Sea must be understood. The theoretical underpinning for such policy has been provided by the Law on Territorial Waters and Adjacent Areas, promulgated in 1992. The law affirmed previous Chinese sovereignty claims in the South China Sea and the country's right to use military force to prevent violations of its territorial waters and contiguous zones. The South China Sea and the

Pacific contain a number of archipelagos claimed by China and other Asian countries; attention here is focused on two, the Spratly Islands and the Diaoyutai Islands, the latter called the Senkaku by the Japanese. To the Chinese the territories concerned have always been part of China, though in the last century they were lost as a result of alleged colonial depredations. In fact, the Spratly and Diaoyutai islands are uninhabited but under both there are believed to be vast oil and gas reserves, and the South China Sea as a whole is estimated to contain resources equivalent to those of the entire Middle East. Not surprisingly, ownership of the Spratly Islands is disputed between China, Taiwan, Vietnam, the Philippines, Malaysia, Indonesia and Brunei, and they have been the scene of frequent armed skirmishes by the protagonists. China has occupied a number of islands and in 1992 deployed there twenty-four Su-27 interceptors purchased from Russia. The islands remained in dispute and while the Chinese are not yet in a position to gain control of the archipelago as a whole, it remains a possible regional flashpoint, in view of China's naval build-up. The second archipelago, the Diaoyutai, is located northeast of Taiwan; in their claims the Chinese seem prepared to risk the wrath of Japan, a major source of loans for economic development.

But, in spite of China's assertive stance, its leaders' military ambitions are as yet not matched by military capability. Certainly, China's destroyers, frigates and submarines outnumber those of its rivals for the Spratly Islands. But China does not yet have a fleet able to dominate the South China Sea because of its other strategic concerns, like the need to keep its naval forces in readiness against any potential threat to its coast from Russia, Japan, Taiwan or Korea. Furthermore, the range of China's fighter aircraft is still limited; the Chinese navy could also benefit from refuelling technology for such aircraft. Arguments for the acquisition of aircraft carriers now seem especially compelling to China's strategists.[10] In fact, the stage at which the Chinese can alter the balance of power in the region in their favour has not yet been reached, and it is to the military capacity of Japan, their economic partner but potential rival, that focus is now directed.

Japan as an economic giant would appear to have abundant potential to be a military power in Asia. Since 1945 Japan has shared security arrangements with the United States but under the terms of the American Occupation-imposed Constitution it is denied the right of belligerency, even though liberal interpretations of Article IX have been sufficient to permit the maintenance of Self Defence Forces. Any attempt to revise the Constitution could mean hostility from countries like China which suffered wartime Japanese aggression. Moreover, in spite of vocal right-wing minority opinion in Japan, its defence policy has been cautious. The country is resource-poor, it imports nearly all its energy, and to move from recession at home and to restructure its economy, Japan is being compelled to relocate industries offshore in, for example, China. Its trade is heavily, though not exclusively, dependent on Asian markets.

These factors condition Japan's defence thinking. In addition, since the end of the cold war, concern with the Soviet threat has given way to anxiety about the military motives of an unknown quantity, North Korea. Japan's 1994 White Paper indicated a shift of emphasis from apprehension concerning global war to fears concerning regional war. There is suspicion about probable weapons development by North Korea which is known to possess medium-range ballistic missiles. Furthermore, North Korea has made a number of successful test flights of the Nodong-1 missile, the range of which is sufficient to reach western Japan. If equipped with a nuclear warhead, it could inflict serious damage in Japan. The North Koreans are also said to be developing a more advanced missile, the Taepo Dong, with a range of approximately 3,000 kilometres.

Any direct threat to Japan from North Korea would, however, activate the United States-Japan Security Treaty, and diplomatic manoeuvres since the death of the North Korean leader, Kim Il Sung, suggest that a political crisis has, at least temporarily, been defused.

Acquisition of nuclear weapons by Japan would, of course, require revision of the 1946 Constitution. But Japan's defence capacity, as it stands, is impressive. On paper the defence budget is the largest in Asia. In addition, its F16 fighters, the airborne warning and control system (AWACS) and Aegis destroyers are supplied with the most modern weaponry. The military strength of Japan in a comparative Asian context is given in Table 6.1.

As the table shows, in comparative terms Japan's defence capacity is, on a number of counts, less impressive than it might first appear. If its armed personnel numbers, 240,000, are compared to neighbouring countries' military power, population, territorial size and defence spending in relation to GNP, the Japanese ratios are generally lower. Furthermore, a high proportion of defence spending is devoted to personnel salaries, reflecting the problems of recruitment to a volunteer army. In coming years, Japan may need to compensate for personnel shortages by introducing high levels of technology.

Moreover the end of the cold war has prompted a reassessment of Japan's security needs. In 1994 the Council on Defence Affairs submitted a report to Japanese Premier Murayama suggesting that

Table 6.1 Japan and its neighbours: military strength

Country	(a) Population (thousands)	(b) Size (thousand sq. km)	(c) Personnel (thousands)	(d) Reserve forces (thousands)	c/a	c/b	d/c	Defence expenditure as % of GDP
Japan	124,593	378	240	48	2.0	0.6	0.2	1.0
South Korea	44,908	99	633	4,550	14.1	6.4	7.1	3.8
North Korea	23,760	121	1,132	540	47.6	9.4	0.5	26.7
China	1,148,593	9,561	3,300	1,200+	2.9	0.3	0.4	3.2
Taiwan	21,265	36	360	1,653	16.9	10.0	4.6	5.4
US	251,843	9,373	1,914	1,784	7.6	0.2	0.9	5.1
Russia	148,041	17,750	2,720	3,000	18.4	0.2	1.1	N.A.

Source: Tomohisa Sakanaka, 'Political Upheavals Sharpen Japan's Security Debate', Insight Japan, 1995, vol. 3, no. 4, p. 6. Reproduced by kind permission Insight Japan.

Notes: c/a = personnel per 1,000 population; c/b = personnel per 1,000 sq. km of territory; d/c = reserve members per active soldier; N.A. = not available the armed forces be reorganised and, if necessary, reduced in size, to become an elite force to play a role in international peacekeeping efforts, the International Peace Cooperation Law, enacted in 1992, having provided a statutory framework for sending the Self Defence Forces abroad, though not for combat. In that year, they were dispatched to the Persian Gulf. While the report may not be fully implemented, it nevertheless indicates a long overdue reappraisal of defence policy, and reflects also the Japanese desire to gain a seat on the United Nations Security Council.

In view of these policies, it seems unlikely that the Japanese would embark on any hostile military action in the region, whatever the suspicions of their motives on the part of the Chinese, for instance. But, given the geographical concentration of industry in Japan and the country's vulnerability to economic blockade, there are conceivable circumstances which could activate demands for the dispatch of Japanese forces abroad on combat duties, entailing revision of the Constitution. Interdiction of shipping lanes by China or any other power could provoke an armed response from Japan. Nevertheless, it must be remembered that the Japan–United States relationship is likely to remain as an important security framework for the region into the twenty-first century. Equally essential, of course, is a dialogue involving the countries of the region together with the United States on the comprehensive peace and security of Asia, the forums mentioned earlier being possible contexts for such deliberation. In short, United States participation in Asian security as well as economic affairs would seem indispensable. Finally, in the most optimistic scenario, China and Japan could emerge not as military rivals but as both economic partners and competitors for influence in East Asia.[11] This possibility is highlighted in the following section.

Sino-Japanese relations in the twenty-first century: cooperation and competition

Growing economic interdependence and trends towards greater integration could lessen the likelihood of military confrontation in the region. In one scenario, rejected as unlikely in earlier discussion in this chapter, the accession to power of the military in China could lead to a policy of overseas expansion to gain space and resources for China's growing population. Such regional ambitions, however, would require a high level of military preparedness, in turn dependent on modernisation of the armed forces, itself currently possible only with technology developed elsewhere. China's developmental priorities, shared by both the civilian and military establishment, would then appear to preclude a policy of armed conflict abroad. Japan, too, may be constrained from military adventures; its economic health depends on not only unimpeded shipping lanes but trade with and investment in the region, notably China.

It has become a commonplace to suggest that economic competition is replacing military conflict among nations and here regional inter-dependence is playing a part. But there are still a number of obstacles to Asian regional integration. There is as yet no consensus on the form such economic integration should take, witness division over the Malaysian proposals for regional cooperation. While no such arrange-ment need be exclusive, it must be emphasised that both Japan and the region generally are still heavily dependent on the United States market. Intra-regional trade, by extension, is also still very reliant on commerce with America and other Western countries. There have been signs in the 1990s that the European Union and the United States are becoming more protectionist and this in itself offers both challenges and opportun-ities for Asian countries. One obvious palliative is to promote intra-regional trade. Statistics point in that direction. Asian states have been reducing dependence on the United States market during the 1990s. Taiwan's exports to the United States accounted for 48.1 per cent of its total in 1985 but only 28 per cent in 1991. Hong Kong's sales to the United States in 1984 accounted for 44 per cent of its total exports but by 1990 this had fallen to 29 per cent. In the early 1990s China's growing imports from the region helped to compensate for the decline in US markets. Moreover, 40 per cent of imports and 37 per cent of exports of Asia-Pacific countries collectively are intra-regional. As for China itself, 80 per cent of its foreign investment and 70 per cent of its foreign trade are accounted for by the region. The establishment of the Joint Committee on Economic, Trade, Scientific and Technological Co-operation between China and ASEAN will provide even greater oppor-tunities for partnership.[12]

Trade with China is playing a crucial role in Japan's economic restructuring and contribution to the development of the region as a whole. In the wake of complaints concerning Japan's trade surpluses with the West, successive Japanese governments have sought to stimulate domestic demand for goods from Europe and the United States; an alternative or additional measure, however, is to contribute to the balanced economic development of the Asian region, an essential feature of which is trade with and investment in China.

Because of the rapid appreciation of the yen in the early months of 1990 most Japanese companies, especially car manufacturers, have been exporting to the United States at a loss. In its search for alternative markets Mitsubishi is currently negotiating with the Chinese government to initiate joint-venture production of a car especially designed for Chinese buyers. Sales in China of such vehicles may in time exceed those in the United States, and China's own automobile industry will be further developed with Japanese assistance.[13]

A prerequisite for regional integration, however, is close cooperation within sub-regions; this is becoming a reality on China's coast and is projected for Northeast Asia. Articles in the Chinese media have described China's relations with Hong Kong as the engine of the Asia-Pacific's economic growth. About 3 million Chinese workers are employed by Hong Kong industrialists in the Guangdong area, assembling and manufacturing export products. The number employed in the manufacturing industry there now exceeds that of native Hong Kong workers and is equivalent to half the colony's population. By 1995, 90 per cent of Hong Kong's manufacturing industry had moved to south China. This area has become Hong Kong's manufacturing base and an interdependent relationship has emerged in which Hong Kong specialises in marketing, while south China engages in production. Consequently, with a population of over 100 million, south China's economy is growing at the phenomenal rate of 30 per cent per year. Hong Kong is the Asia-Pacific's major financial, trading and container shipping centre; China is the fastest-growing economy in the region. The Hong Kong-Guangdong sub-region could become the economic powerhouse of the Asia-Pacific.[14] This sub-region is but one along China's southern coastline; investment from Taiwan, for instance, is more prominent in Fujian Province and Japanese input is growing in Shanghai and predominant in Dalian. Finally, a similar division of labour and complementarity among China, Japan, the Korean states and Russia promises growth in the projected Tumen Development Zone.

Chinese officialdom, however, is reluctant to rely exclusively on Asia-Pacific markets, even if this were possible. The plan, therefore, is for a diversified structure, with Asia as China's economic centre of gravity, supported by peripheral markets including both the developed countries of the West and the developing nations of Africa and Latin America. Such relations are seen as furthering the creation of a just international economic and political order.[15] Inherent also is the argument that China's developmental experience is relevant to African and Latin American countries.[16] While welcoming foreign trade and investment, the Chinese leaders seek to reassert their country's position as the Middle Kingdom, the centre of the universe. These options do not, of course, preclude a role for China in Asian economic cooperation but assert the Chinese view that such integration need not be exclusive. The Japanese, too, have options outside the region. While they may face increasing barriers to trade with and investment in Western Europe and the United States, the countries of Eastern Europe provide an alternative, although they are unlikely to offer the same advantages as China, given its cultural affinity, economic complementarity and geographical proximity.

One obstacle, however, to economic cooperation between the two states has been the Japanese fear of creating in China a superpower rival. Certainly there is a sense in which the 'flying geese' theory is becoming outmoded; China is showing signs of passing through developmental stages more quickly than did its Japanese mentors. The Japanese may not retain their technological lead much longer. In view of China's own strengths, technological synergies may be possible, with the two countries' contributions to joint ventures more evenly balanced. In other respects, too, China may prove a competitor. Considered worthy of emulation are Japan's trading companies with their organisational and reconnaissance capabilities, linked as they are with the all-embracing keiretsu. A Chinese version is seen as similarly likely to facilitate the integration of foreign trade, commerce and industrial production. In turn, this will necessitate further reform in such sectors as banking, crucial for financing trading company operations. Furthermore, late-developing countries like China can learn from the experience of their predecessors. China's investment overseas is already worth US$3.4 billion, and official sources refer to multinationals as an effective means of combating trade protectionism.[17] Such attitudes follow Japanese practice.

In certain respects China's international economic relations could compete with Japanese interests. But there is a sense in which the idea of competition between nation states is becoming outdated and being replaced by rivalry between corporate entities. Thus Sino-Japanese joint ventures could be in mutual conflict for markets in China and globally. Additionally, Chinese multinationals may eventually match the strength of their Japanese counterparts. With the growing strength of China's private sector and the influence of Japanese management practices, corporations in both countries will share the same approaches to human resource management and the social discipline derived from the Confucian ethic, in China's case now freed from the trammels of the anti-entrepreneurial command economy.

But in spite of the growing influence of multinationals in international affairs, the nation state remains a potent focus of political and cultural loyalty. At a national level, barring a reversal of the open door policy, Sino-Japanese economic relations seem set to flourish in coming decades. Kawashina Yutaka, director general of the Asian Affairs Bureau of the Japanese Foreign Affairs Ministry, has predicted that bilateral trade, currently worth US$40 billion, will rise to $70 billion by 2000 and $190 billion by 2010. But bilateral state relations could show features of both cooperation and competition: Japanese indirect investment will contribute to China's economic transformation and, while for the foreseeable future Sino-Japanese military confrontation would seem unlikely, the two countries will vie for influence and resources in the Asian region as a whole in the years to come. Should, however, joint participation in a division of labour in China's southern coastal regions and the Tumen Zone extend to bilateral cooperation internationally by the two countries, the fusion of technological synergies and Confucian cultural values could make Sino-Japanese partnership a force to be reckoned with in Asia and the world during the twenty-first century.

Suggested further reading

Books

A. Amsden, *Asia's Next Giant*, Oxford, Oxford University Press, 1989.

W. G. Beasley, *The Modern History of Japan*, 2nd edn, London, Weidenfeld & Nicolson, 1973.

R. E. Bedeski, *The Fragile Entente: the 1978 Japan-China Peace Treaty in a Global Context*, Boulder, Colo. Westview Press, 1983.

P. Bowles and G. White, *The Political Economy of China's Financial Reforms: Finance in Late Development*, Boulder, Colo. Westview Press, 1993.

W. A. Byrd, *Chinese Industrial Firms under Reform*, Oxford, Oxford University Press for the World Bank, 1992.

N. Campbell and P. Adlington, *China Business Strategies: a Survey of Foreign Business Activity in the PRC*, Oxford, Pergamon, 1988.

J. Child, *Management in China during the Age of Reform*, Cambridge, Cambridge University Press, 1994.

R. P. Cronin, *Japan, the United States and Prospects for the Asia-Pacific Century: Three Scenarios for the Future*, New York, St Martin's Press, 1992.

F. R. Dong, *Industrialisation and China's Rural Modernisation*, Houndmills, Macmillan Press, 1992.

P. Francks, *Japanese Economic Development Theory and Practice*, London, Routledge, 1992.

S. G. Goodman and G. Segal (eds), *China Deconstructs: Politics, Trade and Regionalism*, London, Routledge, 1994.

J. J. Guo, *Price Reform in China, 1979–86*, London, Macmillan, 1992.

H. Harding, *China and North East Asia: Political Dimension*, Lanham, University Press of America, 1988.

P. Hartland-Thunberg, *China, Hong Kong, Taiwan and the World Trading System*, London, Macmillan in association with the Centre for Strategic and International Studies, 1990.

Y. P. Ho, *Trade, Industrial Restructuring and Development in Hong Kong*, London, Macmillan, 1992.

R. C. Hsu, *Economic Theories in China, 1979–1988*, Cambridge, Cambridge University Press, 1991.

A. Irie, *China and Japan in the Global Setting*, Cambridge, Mass., Harvard University Press, 1992.

K. Ishihara, *China's Conversion to a Market Economy*, Tokyo, Institute of Developing Economies, 1993.

H. K. Jacobsen and M. Oksenberg, *China's Participation in the IMF, the World Bank and GATT*, Ann Arbor, University of Michigan Press, 1990.

R. K. Jain, *China and Japan, 1949–1976*, London, Martin Robertson, 1977.

C. Johnson, *MITI and the Japanese Miracle: the Growth of Industrial Policy, 1925–1995*, Stanford, Stanford University Press, 1982.

P. Korhonen, *Japan and the Pacific Free Trade Area*, London, Routledge, 1994.

A. Kumar, *China: Internal Market Development and Regulation*, Washington, DC, World Bank, 1994.

O. Laaksonen, *Management in China*, Berlin, de Gruyter, 1988.

N. R. Lardy, *Foreign Trade and Economic Reform in China, 1978–1990*, Cambridge, Cambridge University Press, 1992.

N. R. Lardy, *China in the World Economy*, Washington, DC, Institute for International Economics, 1994.

P. N. S. Lee, *Industrial Management and Economic Reform in China, 1949–1984*, Oxford, Oxford University Press, 1987.

J. Y. Li, *Taxation in the People's Republic of China*, New York, Praeger, 1991.

C. K. Lo, *China's Policy Towards Territorial Disputes: the Case of the South China Sea Islands*, London, Routledge, 1989.

W. W. Lockwood (ed.), *The State and Economic Enterprise in Japan*, Princeton, NJ, Princeton University Press, 1965.

C. J. McMillan, *The Japanese Industrial System*, Berlin, de Gruyter, 1989.

T. Matsumae, *The Limits of Defence: Japan as an Unsinkable Aircraft Carrier*, Tokyo, Tokai University Press, 1988.

R. Minami, *The Economic Development of China: a Comparison with the Japanese Experience*, London, Macmillan, 1994.

R. T. Mondejar, *China-ASEAN Relations: Foundations for Stability in Southeast Asia*, Cambridge, Mass., Harvard University Press, 1987.

W. R. Nester, *Japan's Growing Power over East Asia and the World Economy: Ends and Means*, London, Macmillan, 1990.

M. Noland, *Pacific Basin Developing Countries*, Washington Institute of International Economics, 1990.

M. Oborne, *China's Special Zones*, Paris, OECD, 1986.

A. J. Ody, *Rural Enterprise Development in China, 1986–90*, Washington, DC, World Bank, 1992.

K. Ohkawa and H. Rosovsky, *Japanese Economic Growth*, Stanford, Stanford University Press, 1973.

D. I. Okimoto, *Between MITI and the Market: Japanese Industrial Policy for High Technology*, Stanford, Stanford University Press, 1989.

T. Ozawa, *Multinationalism Japanese Style: the Political Economy of Outward Dependency*, Princeton, NJ, Princeton University Press, 1979.

M. M. Pearson, *Joint Ventures in the People's Republic of China*, Princeton, NJ, Princeton University Press, 1991.

R. W. T. Pomfret, *Investing in China: Ten Years of the Open Door Policy*, London, Harvester Wheatsheaf, 1990.

K. W. Radtke, *China's Relations with Japan, 1945–83: the Role of Liao Chengzhi*, Manchester, Manchester University Press, 1989.

Research Institute for Peace and Security, Tokyo, *Asian Security, 1994–1995*, London, Brassey's, 1994.

C. Riskin, *China's Political Economy*, Oxford, Oxford University Press, 1987.

R. A. Scalapino (ed.), *The Foreign Policy of Modern Japan*, Berkeley and Los Angeles, University of California Press, 1977.

M. Selden, *The Political Economy of Chinese Development*, Armonk, NY, Sharpe, 1993.

D. J. Solinger, *Chinese Business under Socialism: the Politics of Domestic Commerce, 1949–1980*, Berkeley and Los Angeles, University of California Press, 1984.

D. J. Solinger, *China's Transition from Socialism: Statist Legacies and Market Reforms, 1980–1990*, Armonk, NY, Sharpe, 1992.

J. T. Thoburn, H. M. Leung, E. Chau and S. H. Tang, *Foreign Investment in China under the Open Door Policy*, Aldershot, Avebury, 1990.

S. Tokunaga (ed.), *Japan's Foreign Investment and Asian Economic Interdependence*, Tokyo, University of Tokyo, 1992.

G. Totten and S. L. Zhou (eds), *China's Economic Reforms: Administering the Introduction of the Market Mechanism*, Boulder, Colo., Westview Press, 1992.

W. C. Wedley (ed.), *Changes in the Iron Rice Bowl: the Reformation of Chinese Management*, London, JAI Press, 1992.

A. S. Whiting, *China Eyes Japan*, Berkeley and Los Angeles, University of California Press, 1989.

The World Bank, *The East Asian Miracle: Economy and Growth and Public Policy*, Oxford University Press, 1993.

Y. M. Yeung and X. W. Hu, *China's Coastal Cities: Catalysts for Modernisation*, Honolulu, University of Hawaii Press, 1992.

W. K. Zee (ed.), *Investing in China: B Shares*, London, Euromoney Books, 1992.

Q. S. Zhao, *Japanese Policymaking: the Politics behind Politics: Informal Mechanisms and the Making of China Policy*, Westport, Conn,, Praeger, 1993.

Journals (English language)

Asian Survey
Beijing Review (China)
China Business Review
China Daily (China)
China Newsletter (Japan External Trade Organisation)
China Quarterly
China Today (China)
The Economist
Far Eastern Economic Review
Foreign Affairs Journal (China)
Foreign Broadcasts Information Service (*FBIS*)
Free China Journal (Republic of China, Taiwan)
Fuji Economic Review
Insight Japan
Japan Outlook
Joint Publications Research Service (*JPRS*)

Journal of Far Eastern Business
Journal of the Royal Society for Asian Affairs
Journal of Strategic Studies
Kyodo News Service
Look Japan
Pacific Affairs
Summary of World Broadcasts (*SWB*)
Xinhua News Agency (China)

Chinese language journals and newspapers (China)

Guangming Ribao ('Enlightenment Daily')
Gongye Jingji ('The Industrial Economy')
Guoji Shangbao ('International Commerce')
Guoji Wenti Yanjiu ('International Studies')
Guomin Jingji Jihua Guanli ('The Management of National Economic Planning'), formerly *Guomin Jingji Guanli yu Jihua* ('Management and Planning of the National Economy')
Jingji Lilun yu Jingji Guanli ('Economic Theory and Economic Management')
Laodong Jingji yu Renshi ('Labour Economics and Human Resource Management')
Renmin Ribao ('People's Daily') (overseas edition)
Shangye Jingji Maoyi Jingji ('The Economics of Commerce, the Economics of Trade')
Shangye Jingji Shangye Jeye Guanli ('The Commercial Economy and Company Management')
Shangye Jingji Wuzi Jingji ('The Commercial Economy and Resource Economics')
Tequ yu Kaifa qu Jingji ('The Economy of the Special Zones and Development Zones')
Waimao Jingji Guoji Maoyi ('The Economics of Foreign Trade and International Trade')
Xiandai Guoji Guanxi ('Contemporary International Relations')

Notes

1 Introduction: China and Japan in Asia

1 Sadako Ogata, 'The Business Community and Japanese Foreign Policy: Normalisation of Relations with the People's Republic of China', in Robert A. Scalapino (ed.), *The Foreign Policy of Modern Japan*, Berkeley and Los Angeles, University of California Press, 1977, p. 178.

2 These issues are discussed at much greater length in Robert Taylor, *The Sino-Japanese Axis*, London, The Athlone Press, 1985.

3 In fact, the article in question, originally published in the Chinese journal *International Affairs*, of Foreign Ministry provenance, was quoted in a Kyodo News Agency broadcast on 14 April 1992. See *Foreign Broadcasts Information Service* (hereafter *FBIS*), 16 April 1992.

4 *Xinhua News Agency* broadcast from Beijing, 27 August 1994, as reproduced in *FBIS*, 29 August 1994.

5 On North–South relations, see Qian Qichen, 'Current International Situation and China's Relations with Western Europe', *Beijing Review*, 11–17 March 1991, pp. 10–11.
   Third World solidarity is discussed in a Beijing Central People's Radio report, as reproduced in *FBIS*, 2 January 1992.

6 These views were expressed in an article by Zhan Shiliang, 'The Asia-Pacific Situation and China's Good Neighbour Policy', *Guoji Wenti Yanjiu* ('International Studies'), 1993, no. 50, pp. 1–3, as reproduced in *Joint Publications Research Service* (hereafter *JPRS*), 16 February 1994.

7 *Kyodo News Service*, Tokyo, 2 June 1994.

8 Shi Ding, 'Outlook of Situation in Japan for 1994', *Xiandai Guoji Guanxi* ('Contemporary International Relations'), 1994, no. 52, pp. 6–10. This appears in *JPRS*, 24 May 1994.

9 Kyodo News Agency, Tokyo, 27 February 1992, as reported in *Summary of World Broadcasts* (*SWB*), 28 February 1992.

10 For China's sovereignty claim, see a *Xinhua News Agency* report, as recorded in *SWB*, 8 July 1994. Discussion of strategic issues appears in James Pringle, 'Peking Raises Tensions over Disputed Islands', *The Times*, 9 February 1995.

11 See Zhan Shiliang, *op. cit.*

12 *The Independent*, 11 June 1994.

13 A full discussion of Chinese perceptions of defence issues appears in an

article by Yan Xiangjun and Huang Tingwei, 'The Security Situation in the Asia-Pacific Region and the Relevant Parties' Ideas on a Security Mechanism', *Xiandai Guoji Guanxi* ('Contemporary International Relations'), 1995, no. 3, pp. 6–7.

14 See a report in *The Times*, 9 February 1995.

15 These references to the further development of the Chinese navy are based on an article published in the February 1993 edition of *Modern Ships*, a monthly journal of the China Navy Ships Research Academy.

16 As reported in *The Sunday Times*, 11 December 1994.

17 'Three Large Naval Bases Planned for East Coast', *Kyodo News Agency*, 11 January 1993.

18 T. Matsumae, *The Limits of Defence: Japan as an Unsinkable Aircraft Carrier*, Tokyo, Tokai University Press, 1988, pp. 200–1.

19 *Daily Telegraph*, 31 July 1993.

20 A major Chinese critique of the Pacific century notion is provided by Yang Guanqun, 'Will the Pacific Century Really Arrive?', *Guoji Wenti Yanjiu* ('International Studies'), 1993, no. 1, pp 34–8.

21 'Discussing China's Role in the Division of Labour in the Asia-Pacific Region', *Waimao Jingji Guoji Maoyi* ('The Economics of Foreign Trade and International Trade'), 1994, no. 6, pp. 72–80.

22 *Ibid.*

23 Li Xiao pursues this theme in his article 'New Characteristics in the Present Phase of Regionalisation in the World Economy', *Guoji Shangbao* ('International Commerce'), 27 March 1993.

24 As reported in *SWB*, 25 March 1992.

25 Wen Jie, 'More Work Needed Before Free Trade in APEC', China Radio International Broadcast, as reported in *FBIS*, 15 November 1994; for Chinese discussion of global interdependence, see a report in *Waimao Jingji Guoji Maoyi* ('The Economics of Foreign Trade and International Trade'), 1994, no. 3, pp. 27–30.

26 Zhang Dalin, 'Economic Regionalism, Protectionism Drive Japan's Move Back to Asia', *Guoji Wenti Yanjiu* ('International Studies'), 1994, no. 51, pp. 17–21, translated in *JPRS*, 12 May 1994.

27 References to United States investment are given by Yan Xiangjun in his article, 'Cursory Analysis of the Asia-Pacific Situation during the 1990s', *Xiandai Guoji Guanxi* ('Current International Relations'), 1992, no. 38, pp. 32–6, as reproduced in *JPRS*, 1 January 1993.

28 Figures are taken from State Statistical Bureau, *Tongji Ziliao Xinxi* ('China Statistical Digest'), Beijing, China Statistics Publishing House, 1992.

29 North Korea's economic reliance on China is discussed in a report in *The Independent*, 4 June 1994.

2 The Japanese model of development and China's economic strategy

1 See, for example, 'Confucius Symposium: Jiang Zemin and Li Ruihuan on Practical Value of Confucianism', *Xinhua News Agency*, 5 October 1994, in *SWB*, 10 October 1994. A fuller analysis appears in 'Confucianism: Answer to Conflict between Morals and Science', *Renmin Ribao* ('People's Daily'), 19 September 1994, in *SWB*, 23 September 1994.

2 Economic controls during these periods are discussed by E. S. Crawcour, 'The Tokugawa Heritage', in W. W. Lockwood, *The State and Economic Enterprise in Japan*, Princeton, Princeton University Press, 1965, pp. 42–4.

3 A number of Chinese sources have examined these stages of development. See, for example, 'Discussing China's Function in the International Division of Labour of the Asia-Pacific', *Waimao Jingji Guoji Maoyi* ('The Economics of Foreign Trade and International Trade'), 1994, no. 6, pp. 72–80. See also 'Five Issues in China's Economic Development', *Guomin Jingji Jihua Guanli* ('The Management of National Economic Planning'), 1994, no. 9, pp. 130–3. Economic takeoff in the countries concerned is covered in 'The Battleground of Economic Development in East Asia and on China's Coast', *Tequ yu Kaifa qu Jingji* ('The Economy of the Special Zones and Development Zones'), 1994, no. 4, pp. 78–80. An elaboration of the flying geese theory is provided by P. Korhonen, *Japan and the Pacific Free Trade Area*, London, Routledge, 1994.

4 For savings ratios, see *Financial Times*, 25–26 July 1992.

5 Export-orientated strategies in the Asian region are discussed by Sueo Kojima, 'Alternative Export-Orientated Development Strategies in Greater China', *JETRO China Newsletter*, 1994, no. 113, pp. 18–20; China's strategy is covered by Jian Wang, 'Some Issues of China's Long Term Economic Development', *China Newsletter*, 1994, no. 110, pp. 7–10.

6 For general comment on the evolving role of the banking system, see Edward Balls, 'Still a Long Way to Go', *Financial Times*, 18 November 1993. The direction of Chinese government policy is outlined in 'Zhu Rongji Urges Macroeconomic Control in Reform', *Xinhua Domestic Service*, 19 August 1994, as reported in *FBIS*, 22 August 1994.

7 Because of the constraints of space, it is not possible to give full details concerning the wide range of taxes recently introduced in China. These are, however, discussed at length in Ma Junlei and Luo Liqin, 'Important Reforms in China's Tax System', *China Newsletter*, 1994, no. 110, pp. 12–17. The issue of revenue sharing is covered in 'Market Economy Reaching Critical Mass', *China Newsletter*, 1994, no. 109, pp. 10–14. For the decline in total tax revenues, see *Financial Times*, 18 November 1993.

8 These measures to increase local accountability come into focus in a number of sources. For a discussion of China's taxation system against the general economic background, see Kazuhiko Mitsumori, 'China's Economy after the National People's Congress', *China Newsletter*, 1993, no. 105, pp. 7–10. Details of revenue sharing are examined by Zhang Shujing, 'Division of Authority', *Shijie Zhishi* ('World Affairs'), 1992, no. 15, p. 15, as reproduced in *JPRS*, 30 October 1992. Defaulting by local governments is reported by the *New China News Agency*, as reproduced in *SWB*, 12 August 1993.

9 Chen Dezun, 'Establishing and Improving Price Regulation and Control Systems in a Socialist Market Economy', *Renmin Ribao* ('People's Daily') 11 July 1994, as reported in *FBIS*, 10 August 1994.

10 For categories of direct and indirect price control in Japan, details concerning Japanese wholesale markets and Japanese laws against monopolies and profiteering, see Zhang Shutian and Hong Feng, *Shangye Jingji Shangye Jeye Guanli* ('The Commercial Economy and Company Management'), 1992, no. 5, pp. 135–44. See also an article entitled 'Japan's Price

Control Policies', *Shangye Jingji Shangye Jeye Guanli* ('The Commercial Economy and Company Management'), 1992, no. 12, pp. 126–7.

11 The development of wholesale markets in China is examined by Zhang Shutian and Hong Feng, *op. cit.*

12 Chinese measures deregulating prices are covered in Geng Yuxin, 'China Turns to Market Economy', *Beijing Review*, 9–15 November 1992, p. 4. See also *China Newsletter*, 1991, no. 104, p. 1.

13 *International Herald Tribune*, 27 June 1994.

14 Discussion of the importance of such macroeconomic controls appears in Robert Taylor, 'Chinese Macroeconomic Reform and the Japanese Model: Implications for Japanese Companies', *Japan in Extenso*, December 1994.

15 'The State Council's Outline for State Industrial Policy in the 1990s', *Xinhua News Agency*, 22 June 1994, as reported in *SWB*, 28 June 1994.

16 The extent of such losses is discussed at length by Minoru Nambu, 'Problems in China's Financial Reforms', *China Newsletter*, 1991, no. 92, pp. 2–10.

17 The management contract system has been elaborated in a number of articles. See, for example, Zhai Linyu, 'Current Situation and Problems of China's State Enterprises', *China Newsletter*, 1992, no. 98, pp. 8–12. Another source is Akira Fujimoto, 'Business Management in China', *China Newsletter*, 1991, no. 90, pp. 8–12.

18 Sources on this topic include 'Labour Ministry Official on Implementation of a New Social Security System', *Xinhua News Agency*, 17 January 1994, and 'Beijing Makes Unemployment Insurance Compulsory', *Xinhua News Agency*, 4 July 1994.

19 *Renmin Ribao* ('People's Daily'), 15 November 1994.

20 Jeanne L. Wilson, 'Labour Policy in China: Reform and Retrogression', *Problems of Communism*, September–October 1990, pp. 44–65.

21 *China Daily*, 2 March 1994, as reproduced in *FBIS*, 3 March 1994.

22 'Shanghai Reforms Labour Employment System', *Xinhua News Agency*, 7 March 1994, as reproduced in *FBIS*, 9 March 1994.

23 Hilary K. Josephs, 'Labour Reform in the Workers' State: the Chinese Experience', *Journal of Chinese Law* (Lincoln, NB), Fall 1988, pp. 212 and 255, as quoted in Wilson, *op. cit.*

24 Wilson, *op. cit.*

25 See *Xinhua News Agency*, 11 August 1993.

26 *Xinhua News Agency*, 14 September 1992, as reproduced in *SWB*, 23 September 1992.

27 For details of the reforms announced at the Fourteenth CCP Congress, see H. Lyman Miller, 'Holding the Deng Line', *The China Business Review*, January–February 1993, pp 22–31.

28 Katsuji Nakakane, 'Whither the Economy', *China Newsletter*, 1994, no. 110, pp. 3–6.

29 Robert Thomson, 'Pain in the Provinces', *Financial Times*, 18 November 1993.

30 *Ibid.*

31 Discussion of agricultural reforms appears in Kenji Furusawa, 'Rural Enterprises under Reevaluation', *China Newsletter*, 1990, no. 88, pp. 10–14. For employment statistics, see a statement by Vice-Premier Zou Jiahua in *Renmin Ribao* ('People's Daily'), 15 November 1994, and Edward

Balls, 'Migrant Labour Moves to Cities', *Financial Times*, 18 November 1993.

32 'Five Key Issues in China's Economic Development', *Guomin Jingji Jihua Guanli* ('The Management of National Economic Planning'), 1994, no. 9, pp. 130–3.

33 'Japan's Reform and Management of State Enterprises', *Gongye Jingji* ('The Industrial Economy'), 1994, no. 8, pp. 174–5.

34 *Shangye Jingji Maoji Jingji* ('The Economics of Commerce, the Economics of Trade'), 1994, no. 8, pp. 87–9.

35 Geoffrey Parkins, 'Beijing Ten Year Plan for Hi-Tech', *The Times Higher Education Supplement*, 4 June 1993.

36 See, for example, an article entitled 'The Special Features of Technological Developments in Japan's Medium Sized and Small Enterprises', *Gongye Jingji* ('The Industrial Economy'), 1994, no. 7, pp. 185–8.

37 Zhang Lin, 'University to Expand Enrolment This Year', *China Daily*, 2 March 1992.

38 Deficiencies of work organisation in state enterprises and the need for strategic thinking are examined in Akira Fujimoto, 'Business Management in China', *China Newsletter*, 1991, no. 90, pp. 8–12.

3 Japanese investment in China

1 See, for example, CCP General Secretary Jiang Zemin's statement on human rights, as reported by the *Kyodo News Service*, Tokyo, on 9 May 1992, and the Chinese Ambassador to Japan's address to a press conference, as outlined by the *Xinhua News Agency* on 21 February 1992.

2 A summary of Zhu Rongji's views appears in John Elliott, 'Peking Posts Given to Political Reformers', *Financial Times*, 9 April 1991.

3 Such issues are examined in William R. Nester, *'Japan's Growing Power Over East Asia and the World Economy'*: *Ends and Means*, London, Macmillan, 1990, pp. 101–7.

4 Lin Xiaoguang, 'Japan Seeks a Greater Role in the World', *Beijing Review*, 1992, nos 5–6, pp. 10–12.

5 *China Daily*, 12 June 1992.

6 'Investment Roundup 1992–93', *China Newsletter*, 1994, no. 109, pp. 15–18.

7 For Hong Kong's 60 per cent share, see a *Xinhua News Agency* broadcast, 27 March 1991; the ranking appears in 'Foreign Investment in the People's Republic of China, 1991–92', *China Newsletter*, 1993, no. 102, pp. 16–17.

8 Satoshi Imai, 'China's Foreign Debt', *China Newsletter*, 1991, no. 93, pp. 16–21.

9 'Japan Ties up the Asian Market', *The Economist*, 24 April 1993.

10 *Financial Times*, 18 November 1993.

11 Bill Clifford, 'Japan's Lending Program in China', *The China Business Review*, May–June 1992, pp. 30–5.

12 The visit by the Japanese Minister of International Trade and Industry was reported in a broadcast by the *Xinhua News Agency* on 26 September 1992 and by the *Kyodo News Service* on the same day.

13 Clifford, *op cit*. See also 'Loan Negotiations between China and Japan', *Renmin Ribao* ('People's Daily'), 14 January 1995.

14 'Japanese Official Discusses Yen Loans to China', *Xinhua News Agency*, 16 November 1994, as reported in *FBIS*, 16 November 1994.

15 *Ibid.*

16 'Japanese Bank Gives Two-Step Industrial Development Loan', *Kyodo New Service*, 18 January 1994, as reproduced in *SWB*, 2 February 1994.

17 'Japanese Major Commercial Banks to Participate in Long Term Loans to China', *Kyodo News Service*, 27 March 1994, reported in *SWB*, 6 April 1994.

18 'China Makes First Government Bond Issues on the Japanese Market', *Xinhua News Agency*, 7 July 1994, in *SWB*, 13 July 1994.

19 For a full examination of the complex issue of returns on investment in these sectors, see Alexa C. Lam, 'Infrastructure Investment Tips', *China Business Review*, September–October 1994, pp. 40–50.

20 Seiichi Nakajima, 'China's Energy Situation', *China Newsletter*, 1992, no. 100, pp. 17–24.

21 'Japanese Banks Fund South China Sea Oil Fields', *China Daily*, 27 September 1994. The report is carried by *FBIS*, 28 September 1994.

22 The development of China's oil resources is discussed at length by Robert Tansey, 'Black Gold Rush', *China Business Review*, July–August 1994, pp. 8–16.

23 'United States and Japanese Oil Groups to Explore Tarim Basin', *Xinhua News Agency* report, carried by *SWB*, 5 January 1994.

24 For Sino-Japanese regional environmental cooperation, see 'The Chinese and Japanese Governments Negotiate an Environmental Cooperation Agreement', *Renmin Ribao* ('People's Daily'), 21 March 1994.

25 An overview of Japanese environmental funding is provided by Peter Evans, 'Japan's Green Aid', *China Business Review*, July–August 1994, pp. 39–43.

26 Port facilities are discussed by Lam, *op. cit.*

27 For pressure on the railways, see *ibid*. The bullet train project was reported in 'Japanese Visitors Pledge Support for Bullet Train Project', *Kyodo News Service*, 14 September 1994, *FBIS*, 14 September 1994.

28 'The Telecommunications Market', *Financial Times*, 18 November 1994.

29 Clifford, *op. cit.*

30 *Financial Times*, 7 November 1994.

31 'Investment Roundup 1992–93', *China Newsletter*, March–April 1994, pp. 15–18. For GNP and per capita income growth rates, see a speech by CCP General Secretary Jiang Zemin delivered in Moscow in September 1994, reported in a *Xinhua News Agency* broadcast, 3 September 1994, as recorded in *FBIS*, 6 September 1994.

32 'Investment Roundup 1992–1993', *op. cit.*

33 The general development of Dalian is discussed in a report entitled 'Dalian Expands Ties with Japan', *Beijing Review*, 1–7 October 1990, pp. 29–30.

34 See 'Investment Roundup 1992–93', *op. cit.*

35 Emphasis on investment in the hinterland is discussed in 'Background to Growth in Sino-Japanese Trade', *Waimao Jingji Guoji Maoyi* ('The Economics of Foreign Trade and International Trade') 1994, no. 5, pp. 77–80.

36 Masahiro Hirano, 'Recent Trends in Investment and Operations of Foreign Affiliates', *China Newsletter*, 1993, no. 104, pp. 2–8.
37 This overview appears in Bai Chengyi, 'What are the Characteristics and Problems of Japanese Investment in China?', *Chengchi Taopao* ('Economic Reporter'), no. 14, 12 April 1993, pp. 26–7, as reproduced in *JPRS*, 3 June 1993.
38 This summary is analysed in Chen Tianan, 'Japanese Firms with Direct Investment in China and Their Local Management', in Shojiro Tokunaga (ed.), *Japan's Foreign Investment and Asian Economic Interdependence*, Tokyo, University of Tokyo, 1992, pp. 260–71.
39 See, for example, a report of the visit of Zhu Rongji to Japan, *Beijing Review*, 14–20 March 1994, p. 10.
40 As reported in *FBIS*, 22 November 1994.
41 This information was given in the *China Daily*, 17 November 1994, and carried in *FBIS*, 22 November 1994.
42 Nester, *op. cit.*, pp. 104–5.
43 For discussion of the foregoing, see 'Company Law of the Chinese People's Republic', *China Business Review*, May–June 1994, pp. 49–55.
44 Julia W. Sze, 'The Allure of B Shares', *China Business Review*, January–February 1993, pp. 42–8.
45 'Vice-Finance Minister Meets Japanese Group', *Kyodo News Service*, 22 November 1994, as reproduced in *FBIS*, 23 November 1994. A lengthy examination of these issues also appears in Joyce Peck, Peter Kung and Khoon Ming Ho, 'Enter the VAT', *China Business Review*, March–April 1994, pp. 40–5.
46 'New Income Tax Rates for China Employees', *China Business Review*, March–April 1994, p. 4.
47 Foreign exchange controls are outlined in 'Swap Centres Still Open for Business', *China Business Review*, May–June 1994, p. 4.
48 See, for example, Michael J. Dunne, 'The Race is On', *China Business Review*, March–April 1994, pp. 16–23; Kim Woodward and Wei Zhu, 'Revved and Ready', *China Business Review*, March–April 1994, pp. 24–30; Sueo Kojima, 'New Policies in Auto Industry', *China Newsletter*, 1994, no. 110, p. 1; and Katsuji Ishiro, 'China New Auto Industrial Policy', *China Newsletter*, 1994, no. 113, pp. 2–6, 22.
49 For the labour dispute at the Japanese concern, see 'Workers End Strike', as reproduced in *FBIS*, 18 January 1995. Strike statistics appear in 'Workers' Rights Modified', *China Newsletter*, 1994, no. 112, p. 1.
50 The foregoing issues are discussed at length in Ryusuke Ikegami, 'Reforms in China's Labour System and Their Impact on Foreign Ventures', *China Newsletter*, 1994, no. 111, pp. 19–23.
51 The company survey is analysed and the three models outlined in Shigeto Sonoda, 'Growth Process of Japanese Ventures in China', *China Newsletter*, 1994, no. 111, pp. 8–11.
52 Much of the foregoing is drawn from an investigation by a Mr Wang, an expert seconded to a Japanese company. His report, 'A Japanese Company's Search for Talent', appears in *Laodong Jingji yu Renshi* ('Labour Economics and Human Resource Management'), 1992, no. 11, pp. 86–8.
53 Details are provided in 'Bossing around in a Joint Venture', *Beijing Review*, 16–22 September 1991, pp. 17–18.

54 See an excellent discussion in Jill Ireland, 'Find the Right Management Approach', *The China Business Review*, 1991, no. 90, pp. 14–16.
55 Wang, *op. cit.*
56 Tsuneo Kobayashi, 'Kanebo's Joint Venture in China', *China Newsletter*, 1994, no. 109, pp. 2–10.
57 The case studies of Kunshan Cellutane, Canon Dalian and Huaguang Electronics appear in Mitsuhiro Seki, 'Japanese Ventures in China – a Status Report', *China Newsletter*, 1994, no. 111, pp. 2–7. The Cellutane case is also treated in Tatsuhiro Masuda, 'Pointers on Investment in the Chinese Market', *China Newsletter*, 1994, no. 111, pp. 12–18, as is that of Sumida.
58 See a report published by the Zhongguo Tongxun She (China Information Agency), Hong Kong, on 8 June 1994, as reproduced in *SWB*, 14 June 1994.
59 Discussion of disparities in wealth appears in Yoko Okumura, 'The Consumer Market and Consumer Trends in China', *China Newsletter*, 1993, no. 107, pp. 15–20; for food consumption figures, see 'Three Great Leaps in Chinese Consumer Activity', *China Today*, 1994, vol. XLIII, no. 5, pp. 10–11.
60 Figures are taken from Gu Haibing, 'Investigating Chinese Consumer Behaviour', *Jingji Lilun yu Jingji Guanli* ('Economic Theory and Economic Management'), 1993, no. 2, pp. 50–5.
61 Consumption in the cities is analysed by Gu Jirui, 'Changes in Consumption Patterns', *Shangye Jingji Shangye Jeye Guanli* ('The Commercial Economy and Company Management'), 1992, no. 1, pp. 107–8; Chen Jaihe and Chi Jianwei, 'Trends in Consumption Goods Ownership in China in the 1990s', *Shangye Jingji Shangye Jeye Guanli* ('The Commercial Economy and Company Management'), 1992, no. 9, pp. 86–8.
62 These details of consumption patterns are taken from an article entitled 'Adjustment in the Structure of Production as Seen from the Vantage Point of Changes in the Consumer Demand of Residents', *Guangming Ribao* ('Enlightenment Daily'), 18 February 1994.
63 A report concerning quality entitled 'Characteristics of the Consumer Goods Market' was carried by the *Shanghai Jingji Bao* ('Shanghai Economic Daily'). This is reproduced in *JPRS*, 6 April 1994. Such market behaviour is also analysed in Liu Qiusheng, 'Analyse China's Consumer Market Behaviour', *Guanli Shijie* ('Management World'), 1994, no. 3, pp. 24–31, as reproduced in *JPRS*, 19 August 1994, pp. 19–26.
64 Forecasts of such consumption trends appear in a report published by *Zhongguo Guoqing Guoli* ('China's National Conditions and Power Monthly'), 1994, no. 1, pp. 10–11, as translated in *JPRS*, 17 May 1994.
65 See 'Adjustment in the Structure of Production as Seen from the Vantage Point of Changes in the Consumer Demand of Residents', *op. cit.*
66 Urban–rural contrasts and consumption trends are discussed in Chen Jiahe and Chi Jianwei, 'Trends in Consumption Goods Ownership in China in the 1990s', *Shangye Jingji Shangye Jeye Guanli* ('The Commercial Economy and Company Management'), 1992, no. 9, pp. 82–8. Calls to increase peasants' purchasing power appear in Sun Shangqing, 'Several Issues in Consumer Policy', *Shangye Jingji Shangye Jeye Guanli* ('The Commercial Economy and Company Management'), 1991, no. 6, pp. 97–101. Consumption expenditure forecasts are drawn from Gu Jirui, 'Changes in Consumption Patterns', *Shangye Jingji Shangye Jeye Guanli* ('The

Commercial Economy and Company Management'), 1992, no. 1, pp. 107–8. Discussion of short-term and long-term consumption patterns appears in a report by Zuo Chunwen of the Economic Research Centre of the State Planning Commission of China, published in 1994.

67 See Li Peng's statement, as reported in *SWB*, 29 January 1994.

68 The reform of food distribution is discussed by Theresa McNeil and Kerstin Nilsson, 'The Food Chain', *The China Business Review*, November–December 1994, pp. 34–9.

69 An excellent commentary on Japanese participation in the Chinese retail sector is presented by Sadayuki Matsudaira, 'Trends in Consumption and Foreign Retailers', *China Newsletter*, 1994, no. 113, pp. 7–13.

4 Japan's role in China's world trade

1 See, for example, a statement by China's Minister for Foreign Trade on unreasonable sanctions by foreign countries, as reported in *SWB*, 8 February 1995.

2 Devaluation options and monetary policy, together with their effect on foreign trade, are discussed in Wang Wong, 'Foreign Trade Set for Moderate Growth', *China Daily* (Business Weekly), 5–11 March 1995, as reported in *FBIS*, 7 March 1995.

3 For the need to export technology-intensive and value-added goods, see 'Foreign Trade Takes up New Challenge', *Beijing Review*, 30 January – 5 February 1995, p. 7; imports and exports are mentioned in a *Xinhua News Agency* report, 'Minister in Press Conference on Foreign Trade Reform', 28 January 1994, as carried by *SWB*, 1 February 1994.

4 Details appear in *Beijing Review*, 24–30 January 1994, pp. 11–16.

5 See the above *Xinhua News Agency* report, in *SWB*, 1 February 1994.

6 Discussion appears in an article by Shi Zhaoyu, 'Study the Foreign Trade Law, Implement the Foreign Trade Law – Cursory Discussion of the Scope of the Foreign Trade Law', *Guoji Shangbao* ('International Commerce'), 17 September 1994, as published in *JPRS*, 8 November 1994.

7 For the number of trading companies, see Wang Wong, *op. cit.*; the responsibility of foreign trade enterprises for their profits and losses is discussed in 'Reform of the Foreign Trade System', *Beijing Review*, 10–16 January 1994, p. 12; the extension of foreign trading rights is examined in 'Ministers in Press Conference on Foreign Trade Reform', *op. cit.*; labour deployment, personnel contracts and remuneration are discussed in Wu Yi, 'On Developing Reform of Foreign Trade', as reported by the *Xinhua News Agency* in *SWB*, 7 February 1995.

8 For partnerships and enterprise groups, see Wu Yi's statement, *op. cit*. The Beijing model is discussed in Su Jinghua, 'Beijing Should Offer Good Experiences and Take a Good Lead in Developing Foreign Trade and Economic Cooperation and in Building Development Zones', *Beijing Ribao* ('Beijing News'), 15 February 1995, as reported in *FBIS*, 6 March 1995.

9 The Japanese model is praised in 'The Success and Organisation of Japanese Trading Companies', *Shangye Jingji Wuzi Jingji* ('The Commercial Economy and Resource Economics'), 1994, no. 8, pp. 87–9. The development of Chinese multinationals is the focus of an article in *Waimao Jingji*

Guoji Maoyi ('The Economics of Foreign Trade and International Trade'), 1994, no. 3, pp. 27–30.

10 For comments on the greater openness of China's trade system, see Edward Balls, 'Astonishing Record', *Financial Times*, 18 November 1993. The trade–GNP ratio is given in a report entitled 'China's Foreign Trade Volume Reaches US$236.7 billion in 1994', *Zhongguo Xinwen She* ('China News Agency'), as carried by *SWB*, 6 January 1995. China's ranking among major trading countries appears in Zheng Silin, 'China to Expand Foreign Trade in 1994', *Beijing Review*, 24–30 January 1994, p. 13.

11 Figures for the contribution of foreign enterprises in two-way trade to early 1991 appear in 'Foreign Funded Firms: More Imports, Exports', *Beijing Review*, 12–18 August 1991, p. 5. Figures for two-way trade in the more recent period are cited in 'Customs Statistics for 1994 Show 20.9 per cent Rise in Foreign Trade', *SWB*, 1 February 1995.

12 'China's Foreign Trade Volume Reaches US$236.7 Billion in 1994', *Zhongguo Xinwen She* ('China News Agency'), *SWB*, 16 January 1995.

13 'Customs Statistics for 1994 Show 20.9 per cent Rise in Foreign Trade', *op. cit.*

14 The structure of imports is examined in *ibid.* and in 'China's Foreign Trade Volume Reaches US$236.7 billion in 1994', *op. cit.* Changes in the commodity composition of China's exports and the pattern of China's international trade are also analysed in Nicholas R. Lardy, 'China's Foreign Trade', *China Quarterly*, no. 131 (September 1992), pp. 691–720.

15 Relevant statistics concerning China's commodity imports and exports and their geographical direction appear in 'China's Industrial Structure', *Beijing Review*, 2–8 January 1995, p. 28.

16 For the reorientation of China's trade see 'China to Seek New Trading Partners', *Beijing Review*, 30 January – 5 February 1995, p. 28. Discussion of China's top trading partners appears in 'Figures for 1994 Trade with Foreign Nations Reported', *SWB*, 25 January 1995.

Trade with the United States is discussed in 'Chinese Pirates Terrorise High Seas of Commerce', *The Sunday Times*, 8 January 1995.

Japan's position as China's number one trading partner is discussed in 'Sino-Japanese Trade: Background of Growth', *Waimao Jingji Guoji Maoyi* ('The Economics of Foreign Trade and International Trade'), 1994, no. 5, pp. 77–80.

17 These proportions are given in *China Newsletter*, 1994, no. 110, p. 20.

18 For Sino-Japanese trade in 1993, see *China Newsletter*, 1994, no. 109, p. 21. Figures for 1994 are given by a Japan External Trade Organisation (JETRO) source quoted in 'Sino-Japanese Trade in 1994 Exceeds US$45 Billion', *Xinhua News Agency*, 26 January 1995, as carried by *SWB*, 8 February 1995. Further analysis appears in 'Last Year Sino-Japanese Trade Exceeded US$46.24 Billion', *Renmin Ribao* ('People's Daily'), 27 January 1995.

As will be noted, there seem to be some discrepancies between figures given and percentage increases.

Chinese figures also differ slightly from Japanese sources; for example, Chinese customs statistics give US$39 billion for two-way trade in 1993.

19 'China Business: Trade with China Blossoming, Accompanied by a Rush

of Japanese Companies There', Yamaichi Research, *Japan Outlook*, July 1992, pp. 13–14.

20 Ongoing trends in two-way trade are analysed in 'Two Way Trade Hits Historical High of US$37.8 Billion', *China Newsletter*, 1994, no. 109, pp. 21–2.

21 Two-way trade figures and commodity composition for early 1994, and reference to the growing importance of Chinese food exports to Japan, appear in 'Trade for First Half Tops US $20 Billion', *China Newsletter*, 1994, no. 112, pp. 21–3.

22 'China to Buy Japanese Fertilizer Equipment', *Xinhua News Agency*, 18 November 1994, reported by *FBIS*, 22 November 1994.

23 Technology imports are discussed by Wang Dajun, 'Creating New Vistas for Sino-Japanese Cooperation', *Beijing Review*, 21–27 March 1994, p. 4.

24 John Burton, 'Close Partnership Could Develop', *Financial Times*, 13 July 1992.

25 See report, 'Firm Sues for Damages for Poor Quality', *SWB*, 12 February 1992.

26 *SWB*, 22 November 1994.

27 This Chinese approach to trade friction appears in 'Sino-Japanese Trade: Background to Growth', *Waimao Jingji Guoji Maoyi* ('The Economics of Foreign Trade and International Trade'), 1994, no. 5, pp. 77–80.

5 Greater China: sub-regional economic integration

1 Zhang Baoxiang, 'The Single Market is Expected to be Completed by the End of 1992', *Foreign Affairs Journal* (Beijing), September 1991, pp. 63–6.

2 Figures for the export ratio of the coastal region appear in 'The East Asian Economy and the Economic Development Battleground of China's Coastal Region', *Tequ yu Kaifa qu Jingji* ('The Economy of the Special Zones and Development Zones'), 1994, no. 4, pp. 78–80.

   For direct investment in Guangdong, see 'Economic Cooperation between China and the Asia-Pacific', *Waimao Jingji Guoji Maoyi* ('The Economics of Foreign Trade and International Trade'), 1994, no. 3, pp. 27–30. Cross-national comparisons are discussed in 'Four Little Tigers: the Secret of Their Success', *Beijing Review*, 30 September – 6 October 1991, p. 10.

3 For the Chinese official view of economic cooperation, see Fang Shang, 'Economic Cooperation between Mainland, Taiwan and Hong Kong', *Beijing Review*, 25 November – 1 December 1991, pp. 24–6; attitude to the contribution of overseas Chinese is carried in the report of an interview with China's trade minister, reproduced in *SWB*, 22 February 1992; the internal CCP source is discussed in *JPRS*, 10 March 1994.

4 *Renmin Ribao* ('People's Daily'), 19 August 1994, *FBIS*, 29 August 1994.

5 For the government in waiting, see *The Times*, 3 July 1993.

6 These views are given coverage in Fang Shang, *op. cit.*

7 *Ibid*. See also 'China and the Asia Pacific Economy in the Twenty-First Century', *Guomin Jingji Guanli yu Jihua* ('Management and Planning of the National Economy'), 1994, no. 2, pp. 163–7.

8 Relevant divisions are delineated in 'The East Asian Economy and the Economic Development Battleground of China's Coastal Region', *op. cit.*

Justification for the new regional policy is explained in Nobuo Maruyama, 'New Directions in East Asian Regional Economy', *China Newsletter*, 1995, no. 114, pp. 2–7 and 14–15.

9 This emerging division of labour is discussed in Maruyama, *op. cit.*

10 Investment statistics appear in 'The East Asian Economy and the Economic Development Battleground of China's Coastal Region', *op. cit.*

11 Industrial development in Guangdong is discussed in 'Economic Co-operation between China and the Asia-Pacific', *op cit*; the role of the Shenzhen-Japan Joint Committee is given full coverage in 'A Japanese Economic Specialist Evaluates the Development of Shenzhen', *Tequ qu Kaifa qu Jingji* ('The Economy of the Special Zones and Development Zones'), 1994, no. 3, pp. 61–3.

12 Much of the foregoing is drawn from an article by Kazuhiko Ueno, 'The Dynamism of Rural Enterprises in China', *China Newsletter*, 1994, no. 108, pp. 8–13.

13 Compensation trade normally involves a foreign partner in a venture supplying machinery, while the Chinese side provides the site and labour. At the conclusion of the venture, the Chinese retain the capital plant. The Chinese partner pays for equipment with the goods produced. Through compensation agreements, which are now going out of fashion, at least as far as the Chinese leaders are concerned, because of their low technology, Chinese enterprises have in the past obtained equipment and raw materials required without spending foreign currency.

14 The interview with Li Hao appears in 'Shenzhen to Become a Socialist Hong Kong', *Ming Pao* (Hong Kong), 23 February 1992, as reported in *SWB*, 28 February 1992.

15 Simon Holberton, 'China Envelops Hong Kong Economy', *Financial Times*, 6 March 1992.

16 Such developments are examined by David Whittall, 'Heavy Hitting H Shares', *China Business Review*, May–June 1994, pp. 44–7.

17 Holberton, *op. cit.*

18 Makoto Ebina, 'For Success in China, Go to the Experts', *Fuji Economic Review*, November–December 1994, pp. 1–3.

19 Laurence Tuckerman, 'A Surge of Power for Hainan', *International Herald Tribune*, 30 June 1992. See also 'Colony's Tycoons Turn Towards the Motherland', *Guardian*, 14 July 1992.

20 These trade figures have been taken from Sueo Kojima, 'Export Orientated Development Strategies in Greater China, *China Newsletter*, 1994, no. 113, p. 21.

21 Nick Rufford, 'Sons of Mao's Revolution Turn into Hong Kong Tycoons', *The Sunday Times*, 22 May 1994; and Huang Wei, 'China's Overseas Investment', *Beijing Review*, 21–27 March 1994, pp. 18–22.

22 An excellent overview appears in an article by Tsao Hsiao-heng, 'Taiwan's Deficit with Japan Hits Another Record High', in the Hong Kong journal *Ching-Chi Tao Pao* ('Economic Reporter'), no. 2355, 24 January 1994, pp. 33–4, as reproduced in *JPRS*, 15 April 1994.

23 A number of sources from Taiwan have discussed economic restructuring and sub-regional integration. See, for example, Deborah Shen, 'Taiwan Urged to Move Fast Toward Role as Asian Hub', *Free China Journal*, 27 May 1994, p 7; Allen Pun 'Greater China, Intriguing But Elusive', *Free*

China Journal, 1 July 1994, p. 7; and Deborah Shen, 'Japanese and United States Investors Fuel Increase in Investment', *Free China Journal*, 28 October 1994, which provides figures for foreign investment in Taiwan. Spending on infrastructure is discussed by Luisetta Mudie, 'Fleeing Investors Shake Taiwan', *Financial Times*, 28 August 1992.

24 Virginia Sheng, 'Taipei Calls for End to China Representation Argument', *Free China Journal*, 8 July 1994.

25 The background to the gradual changes in ROC government attitudes is chronicled by Liu Wen-fu, 'Politics on Taiwan: Democratisation and Relations with the Mainland', *China Newsletter*, 1992, no. 101, pp. 2–7.

26 The Chinese official view of these developments appears in 'China's State Council Taiwan Office Reaffirms its Welcome to Cross-Straits Visits', *Xinhua News Agency*, 29 January 1994, as reported in *SWB*, 2 February 1994.

27 See 'Privatisation of Taiwan's State Enterprises', *Guomin Jingji Guanli yu Jihua* ('Management and Planning of the National Economy'), 1994, no. 5, pp. 177–83. The technological issue is referred to in 'Taiwan Decides to Relax the Rules concerning Investment in the Mainland', *Renmin Ribao* ('People's Daily') (overseas edition), 23 January 1995.

28 'Taiwan Mainland Steel Industry Exchanges Urged', as reported in *FBIS*, 17 January 1995.

29 'Mainland-Taiwan Symposium Opens in Beijing', *Xinhua News Agency*, 12 January 1995, as reproduced in *SWB*, 13 January 1995.

30 Such issues are raised in an article in a Taiwan source, *Tien-Hsia* ('Commonwealth'), no. 12, 1 December 1993. This is reproduced in *JPRS*, 10 March 1994.

31 See the report 'Government's Southern Strategy to Promote Cooperation with Southeast Asia', *Central News Agency* (Taipei), 15 January 1994, as reported in *SWB*, 26 January 1994.

32 Assessment of current ROC government policy appears in 'Cross Strait Trade Policies Analyzed', *Ching Pao* ('The Mirror'), a Hong Kong Journal, no. 2, 5 February 1994, pp. 80–1, carried by *JPRS*, 6 April 1994.

33 'Taipei Lifts Ban on Textile Investment in PRC', *Ching-chi Jih Pao* ('Economics Daily'), Taipei, 16 March 1994, as reported in *JPRS*, 9 April 1994; for liberalisation of the investment approval system, see 'Taiwan Decides to Relax the Rules Concerning Investment in the Mainland', *Renmin Ribao* ('People's Daily') (overseas edition), 23 January 1995.

34 Figures for Jiangsu were given by the *Xinhua News Agency* on 13 January 1994 and reported in *SWB*, 26 January 1994. For overall trends in Jiangsu, see also *Renmin Ribao* ('People's Daily'), 26 January 1995. The same agency gave the statistics for Sichuan on 4 August 1994, as reproduced in *SWB*, 17 August 1994. Size of investors is discussed in *Renmin Ribao* ('People's Daily'), 21 January 1994, reproduced in *SWB*, 2 February 1994.

35 Kazuhiko Ueno, *op. cit*.

36 The advantages for the respective parties of investment on the mainland by Taiwan's computer companies is discussed in 'New Triangular Relationship: Deterioration of Taiwan Firms' Two Sides of the Strait Advantage', *Tien-Hsia* ('Commonwealth'), December 1993, no. 12, pp. 21–31, as reproduced in *JPRS*, 10 March 1994.

37 Taiwan's investment total appears in a report from Taiwan in *SWB*, 9 February 1994; its ranking is given in 'Chief Planner Says Economy Steadily Growing', *FBIS*, 26 September 1994.

38 China's share in Taiwan's total foreign investment is provided in a report from the Central News Agency, Taipei, carried in *SWB*, 9 March 1994.

39 For the distribution of Taiwan's investment in China, see 'Mainland People's Daily Assesses Cross-Straits Investment, Trade and Visitors', *SWB*, 2 February 1994; the ROC's input in Jiangsu Province is from the *Xinhua News Agency*, 13 January 1994, and reproduced in *SWB*, 26 January 1994; Taiwan-financed projects in Shanghai are discussed in a *Xinhua News Agency* report, 9 August 1994, carried by *FBIS*, 10 August 1994.

40 'Sichuan Increases Investment from Taiwan', *Xinhua News Agency*, 4 August 1994, as reproduced in *SWB*, 17 August 1994.

41 'Taiwan Firms Shape a New Mainland; Increasing Joys and Temptations', *Tien-Hsia* ('Commonwealth'), 1993, no. 12, pp. 37–51, as carried by *JPRS*, 10 March 1994.

42 See a summary in *JPRS*, 9 April 1994.

43 'Taiwan: Indirect Cross-Strait Trade Rising Steadily', *Xinhua News Agency*, 2 December 1993, as reported in *SWB*, 5 January 1994.

44 Wan Guang, 'Northeast Asia in Asia-Pacific Context: Changes versus Challenges', *Foreign Affairs Journal* (Beijing), 1991, no. 21, pp. 49–51.

45 Zhou Jihua and Yang Jiarong, 'Soviet-Japanese Relations during a Transitional Period', *Foreign Affairs Journal* (Beijing), 1991, no. 19, pp. 56–64.

46 See 'Maritime Silk Road', *China Newsletter*, 1993, no. 102, p. 1, and 'Trends in Japan Sea Rim Trade in 1993', *China Newsletter*, 1994, no. 110, pp. 18–20.

47 Cross-border trade is analysed in Frederick Crook, 'Trade on the Edges', *The China Business Review*, January–February 1995, pp. 26–30. Foreign investment in infrastructural development in Liaoning is treated in Stephen C. Thomas, 'Catching Up', *The China Business Review*, November–December 1990, pp. 6–11.

48 A detailed assessment of the zone's potential appears in Satoshi Imai, 'The Tumen River Area Special International Economic Zone', *China Newsletter*, 1993, no. 104, pp. 14–22.

6 Conclusions: the future of Sino-Japanese relations

1 The above statistics for income and the GNP growth programme appear in a speech by Jiang Zemin in Paris in September 1994 and are quoted in a news release from the Consulate-General of the People's Republic of China, Manchester. Predictions for income levels in the year 2000 are provided by the *China Business Review*, January–February 1995, p. 5.

2 For details of recent corruption cases in Beijing, see Louise Evans, 'Peking Power Struggle Closes around Deng', *The Sunday Times*, 14 May 1995.

3 On 4 April 1995 the CCP newspaper *Renmin Ribao* reported that a total of 450,000 government workers had been sent to rural areas to strengthen organisation building at grassroots levels. See *SWB*, 15 May 1995. The role of Confucianism in combating moral decline was evaluated in an article appearing in the *Renmin Ribao* (overseas edition), also carried by *SWB*.

4 These statements by Wu Yi are contained in a *Xinhua News Agency* report, as produced in *SWB*.

5 The personalities of key players in a succession struggle are evaluated by Tony Walker, 'The Long Wait for Heaven's Mandate', *Financial Times*, 7 November 1994.

6 A number of commentators have attempted to draw up possible scenarios for China in the early twenty-first century. The views expressed in the text draw on a number of sources. See, for example, Doug Randall and Piero Telesio, 'China in 2010', *The China Business Review*, January–February, 1995, pp. 16–17.

7 China's need for a peaceful international environment is emphasised in Ge Yang, 'China's Rise: Threat or Not', *Beijing Review*, 30 January – 5 February 1995, pp. 23–5. For Chinese justification of the underground nuclear test, see a *Xinhua News Agency* report, as carried in *SWB*, 16 May 1995.

8 Japanese reaction to China's nuclear test was reported by the *Kyodo News Agency*, as carried in *SWB*, 17 May 1995.

9 These issues are discussed by Tian Zengpei, '1994: a Victorious Year for China's Foreign Relations', *Beijing Review*, 2–8 January 1995, pp. 9–13.

10 Figures for China's military budgets are given in *Asian Security 1994–1995*, Tokyo, Research Institute for Peace and Security, and London, Brassey's, 1994, p. 94. This source also discusses Liu Huaqing's ideas concerning the integrated use of air, land and sea forces and the Chinese purchase of Su-27 fighters from Russia. An excellent survey of China's naval strategy appears in Jun Zhan, 'China Goes to the Blue Waters: the Navy, Seapower Mentality and the South China Sea', *The Journal of Strategic Studies*, 1994, vol. 17, no. 3, pp. 180–208. A recent account of power rivalry in the South China Sea appears in Nick Rufford, 'China Leads Predators Circling Oil Paradise', *The Sunday Times*, 14 May 1995.

11 The North Korean threat and Japan's modern weaponry are discussed in *Asian Security 1994–1995*, pp. 14 and 131; the evolution of Japanese defence policy is evaluated, for example, in Tomohisa Sakanaka, 'Political Upheavals Sharpen Japan's Security Debate', *Insight Japan*, 1995, vol. 3, no. 4, pp. 4–7.

12 For exports from Taiwan and Hong Kong to the United States, see 'China and the Asia-Pacific Economy in the Twenty-First Century', *Guomin Jingji Guanli yu Jihua* ('Management and Planning of the National Economy'), 1994, no. 2, pp. 163–7. The same source carries details of the region's stake in China's trade and investment.

Intra-regional trade details appear in 'Discussing China's Role in the International Division of Labour in the Asia-Pacific Region', *Waimao Jingji Guoji Maoyi* ('The Economics of Foreign Trade and International Trade'), 1994, no. 6, pp. 72 and 80. For Sino-ASEAN cooperation, see Tian Zengpei, *op. cit.*

13 Japan's automobile sales in the United States are discussed by Garth Alexander, 'Car Sanctions Shunt Japan into Reverse', *The Sunday Times*, 21 May 1995; for Japanese investment in China's car industry, see 'Japanese Automaker to Provide Service Network', *Xinhua New Agency*, 14 April 1995, as carried by *FBIS*, 17 April 1995.

14 Gao Shangquan, 'China's Economy Vital for Asia-Pacific', *Beijing Review*, 16–22 January 1995, pp. 17–19.
15 *Ibid*. See also Tian Zengpei, *op. cit*.
16 Zhong Yanwen, 'CPC Expands Foreign Relations', *Beijing Review*, 9–15 January 1995, pp. 19–21.
17 The value of the trading company is assessed in 'The Success and Organisation of the Japanese Trading Company', *Shangye Jingji Wuzi Jingji* ('The Commercial Economy and Resource Economics'), 1994, no. 8, pp. 87–9.

The figure for China's investment overseas appears in 'Economic Co-operation Between China and the Asia-Pacific Region', *Waimao Jingji Guoji Maoyi* ('The Economics of Foreign Trade and International Trade'), 1994, no. 3, pp. 27–30. Another article in the same issue gives coverage to China's need to establish multinationals: 'Discussing China's Role in the International Division of Labour in the Asia Pacific Region'.

Index